Food and Beverage Operation

Prentice-Hall Series in Foodservice Management

Coltman, *Food and Beverage Cost Control*
Danenburg, Moncrief, and Taylor, *Introduction to Wholesale Distribution*
Kahrl, *Advanced Modern Food and Beverage Service*
Kahrl, *Introduction to Modern Food and Beverage Service*
Keister, *Food and Beverage Control*
Levinson, *Food and Beverage Operation: Cost Control and Systems Management*

Food and Beverage Operation

Cost Control and Systems Management

CHARLES LEVINSON
Hotel College
University of Nevada
Las Vegas, Nevada

Prentice-Hall, Inc. / Englewood Cliffs, N.J.

Library of Congress Cataloging in Publication Data

Levinson Charles (date)
  Food and beverage operation.

  (Prentice-Hall series in foodservice management)
  Bibliography; p.
  1. Food service management. I. Title.
  TX943.L48   658' .91'6425   75-33104
  ISBN 0-13-322958-0

Printed in the United States of America

10   9   8   7   6

Prentice-Hall International, Inc., *London*
Prentice-Hall of Australia Pty. Limited, *Sydney*
Prentice-Hall of Canada, Ltd., *Toronto*
Prentice-Hall of India Private Limited, *New Delhi*
Prentice-Hall of Japan, Inc., *Tokyo*
Prentice-Hall of Southeast Asia Pte. Ltd., *Singapore*

This book is dedicated,
with much love,
to my mother

Mrs. Blanche Brandon

who whetted my appetite for knowledge
and, with keen insight, directed my interest
to foods and the hospitality industry.

Contents

PREFACE   xiii

1 COST CONTROL   1

2 THE FUNCTION AREAS   7

Primary Function Areas, 11

Purchasing. Receiving. Storage and Inventory Control. Issuing. Menu Planning. Prepreparation and Preparation. Checking. Service. Cash Receipts.

Supporting or Ancillary Function Areas, 19

Accounting and Internal Auditing. External Auditing. Personnel. Sales. Sanitation. Maintenance.

3 LIQUOR PURCHASING AND INVENTORY CONTROL   23

Liquor Purchasing, 23

Methods of Purchasing, 26

Beers. Distilled Beverages. Wines. Other Items—Mixers, Fruits, and Supplies.

Forms, 29

Purchase Requisitions. Purchase Orders. Invoices. Credit Memos. Alternatives to Purchase Order and Purchase Requisition.

Receiving, Storing, and Issuing Beverages, 39

Receiving. Storage. Methods of Inventory Control.

Alternative Methods for Receiving, Storage, Inventory Control, and Issuing, 48

Physical Facilities, 52

Bottle Stamping, 54

Case Studies, 55

4 BEVERAGE SERVICE   59

Automated Systems, 59

Ounce or Drink Controls, 67

Par Stock—Bottle Control, 68

Necessary Controls for All Systems—Portion Control, 70

Standard Cost or Potential Sales, 72

Bottle Sales, 74

Fraud and Special Problems, 76
Short Pouring. Substitutions. Dilution of Merchandise. Theft of Merchandise. Complimentary Drinks. Returns of Merchandise Issued to Private Parties. Methods of Payment and Types of Service for Private Parties.

Beer and Wine, 81

Bar Checking Systems, 82

Summary, 84

5 CASH RECEIPTS   86

Types of Fraud and Areas of Loss with Cash Collection, 87
Customers. Waiter or Waitress Theft. Waiter or Waitress Errors. Bartender Fraud or Errors. Cashier Theft or Error. Previous Balance Fraud. Methods of Cash Collection.

Basic Principles for Cash Control, 106
General Rules.

Case Problems, 108

6 FOOD PURCHASING PRINCIPLES   111

General Purchasing Policies, 111

Purchasing Practices, 114
Rebates. Discounts. Kickbacks. Date of Purchase. Specifications. Sources of Specifications.

Methods of Buying, 118
Quotations. Contract Buying.

Quotation Sheets, 128

Factors Influencing Amounts and Frequency of Orders, 130

Other Forms and Controls, 131

7   **SIMPLIFIED MATHEMATICS FOR FOOD
    COST CONTROL   133**

The Basic Formulas, 133
Terminology. Food Cost Control Problems.

Why a Simplified System Is Needed, 137

How the Simplified System Works, 138
Portion Factor. Portion Divider. Amount to Buy. Portion Costs. The Best Buy.

Establishing a Simplified Program, 143

8   **YIELDS   147**

Meats, 148
Basic Formula for Determining Yields for Price Comparisons. Trim Tests.
Aging. Boning Yields. Yield by Carcass Weight. Steaks. Chopped Meat. Price
Comparisons. Cooking Yields. Serving Yields. Summary of Yield Formulas.

Poultry, 160

*Summary of Purchasing Meats, Yield Tests,
Calculation of Comparable Prices, 162*

Fish and Seafood, 166

Produce, 166

Canned Vegetables, 166

Frozen Products, 166

9   **RECEIVING, STORAGE, AND INVENTORY CONTROL
    OF FOODS   170**

Priority Ratings, Dollar Values, and Inventory Turnover, 171
In-Process Inventories. Batch Inventories.

Inventory Control Methods, 173
Open Storerooms. Bin Cards. Dual Bin. Perpetual Inventories.

ABC Analysis, 174

Receiving, 176

Food Storage and Inventory Control, 180

Perishable Merchandise, 181

Issues to Determine Amounts to Order, 182

Re-issuing of Merchandise, 182

General Problems in Inventory Control, 183

Spoilage of Merchandise While in Storage. Estimating Value of Merchandise.
Goods in Process.

High-Value Merchandise, 185

Cost of Goods Sold = Purchases = Dollar Value of Inventory, 185

10 FOOD CHECKING AND SERVICE   188

Dupes, Prechecking, and Food Checker, 188

Low Average Check Operations, 192

High Average Check Operations, 195

11 MENU PLANNING   196

Classification of Markets, 196

Captive Versus Free Market, 196

Factors Affecting Market, 196

Age. Sex. Economic Status. Ethnic or Regional Preferences.
Occupational Status. Meal Served. Day of Week.

Non-Cost-Related Factors, 199

Types of Service. Method of Pricing.

Cost-Related Factors, 205

Classification of Menus. Fixed Menus. Changing Menus. Cyclical Menus.
Combination Menus.

Internal Factors Influencing Menu Planning, 211

Physical Equipment. Personnel Loads. Number of People Served.
Hours of Service. Skill Level of Employees.

Summary, 212

12 MENU PRICING   215

Food Cost Percentages, 216

Weighted Sales Values and Food Cost Percentages, 218

Establishing Prices, 219

Competition. Service. Atmosphere. Waste. Clientele. Quality. Taste. Portion
Size. Location. Wage Rates. Other Costs. High-Low Items. Type of Cash
Collection.

Determining Portion Sizes—Formulation of Menu Prices, 225

13 LABOR COST CONTROL   230

Factors Influencing Labor Costs, 231

Permanent Factors. Temporary Factors. Employee Turnover.
Minimum Staffing.

14 LABOR COST ANALYSIS   239

Approach to Labor Analysis, 239

Productivity Per Man-Hour. Labor Cost Percentage. Sales Per Employee.
Productivity Analysis.

Productivity Scheduling, 243

Assignment of Tasks, 244

Labor Contract or Laws, 244

Overtime, 246

Training, Motivation, Incentives, 246

GLOSSARY   248

BIBLIOGRAPHY   251

Preface

After teaching courses at three separate schools of higher learning (a two-year college and two four-year institutions), it is apparent to me that faculty members, as well as leaders in the industry, recognize the need for more sophisticated cost-control systems in food and beverage operations. It is also apparent that colleagues and industry leaders alike agree with me that there is a dearth of material relating to cost-control areas and that only recently have sophisticated computer systems been adapted for use in the hospitality field.

This book, then, is the outgrowth of my frustrations in attempting to teach cost-control methods while being unable to direct students to specific sources. It is a recognition, too, that techniques being applied today have not kept pace with rapidly changing systems for food service and preparation.

It is not the intent of this book to present answers to specific problems, but rather to alert the reader to the range of solutions that may be adopted. For each food and beverage operation, there are many control problems. For these problems, there is no one definitive answer. Problems are interrelated and difficult; indeed, some may be insoluable. This book explores alternatives and seeks to guide the reader to the available solutions and methods, both new and old.

May I express my thanks to the Hotel College of the University of Nevada, Las Vegas, particularly to its staff members Charlene Baca and Joan Reynolds, for their many hours typing preliminary drafts. Special thanks are extended to my former student Robert Lapp, and to my colleague James Abbey, both of whom read the original text and offered innumerable clarifying suggestions.

Finally, I owe a special note of love and appreciation to my wife for lonely hours spent while the text was being written and for contributions of additional hours proofing the manuscript.

CHARLES LEVINSON

Food and Beverage Operation

1

Cost Control

Control means to exercise authority over, to restrain, to regulate or verify, to check. As a noun, it indicates a method, device, or system that accomplishes one or more of these functions.

"In the food service industry the term cost control has come to mean control over all items of income and expense concerned with the function of the food service unit."*

Every operation, regardless of its size or method of service, must have some system of cost control. Systems may be formal or informal in that written records may or may not be maintained. All, however, attempt to achieve the same objective—informing management of exactly what expenses are being incurred, what incomes are being received, and to what extent these expenses and revenues fall within the guidelines laid down by management.

In the early days of food service the types of controls needed and the records maintained were relatively simple. Old-time operators speak with delight of the days when the sole figure in the income account was the sales figure. The cash went into the owner's pocket, and daily expenses were taken care of by a transfer of cash to the employee or to the purveyor. Envelopes may have been used for monthly expenses—so much for rent, electricity, water, etc. At the end of the week or month, whatever was left over was the profit. The owner felt relatively comfortable in spending that amount since no additional expenses might be incurred.

Today, however, with the advent of taxation, business and license fees, accruals, credit cards, accounts receivable, withholding taxes, pension plans, vacation plans, social security, and innumerable other items, the individual entrepreneur, as well as corporations and chain organizations, requires more detailed information. Complex approaches and sophisticated systems must

* Bessie Brooks West, Levelle Wood, and Virginia F. Harger, *Food Service in Institutions,* 4th ed. John Wiley and Sons, Inc., (New York: 1966), p. 397.

be used. Often, businesses are run by absentee management or perhaps are services to the community (hospitals and schools). Additional controls and reports therefore may be necessary. Although for schools and some hospitals a profit may not be an objective, losses must be avoided, and other information must be available so that various governmental agencies and the public may be kept informed.

Regardless of whether there is a profit or a loss, federal, state, and local governments require monthly, quarterly, or yearly reports concerning the progress of the business. At the same time businesses have become agents of the government—collecting taxes on sales, withholding payments from employees, and eventually paying these sums to the government.

In less complicated times the decision to purchase equipment or to build might have been based exclusively on the needs of the organization, e.g., would the labor savings be sufficient to pay for the cost of the machine. Today, however, this decision may be colored by the investment credit obtainable, the depreciation rate allowed by the government, and the chances of acceptance by the union, as well as by the obsolescence of the equipment or building.

Working and ownership arrangements have changed markedly. A proprietor may own one or more establishments and can no longer personally supervise day-to-day operations. Authority must be delegated to many persons. In turn, systems must be devised to determine who bears the responsibility should deviations from expected norms occur.

Management uses control systems to help pinpoint responsibility for inefficiencies, errors, or fraud. The employees should be concerned that any control system protects them and/or rewards them for good performance. If an employee is doing an outstanding job, management should be able to detect this and reward or promote the employee. If thefts occur, innocent employees have a substantial interest in the system. The knowledge that they are not under suspicion is important for employee morale. Employers and employees thus have a vital interest in insuring that control systems are adequate and effective.

"The scope and size of the business entity has increased to the point where its structural organization has become complex and widespread."*

The size and dollar volume of food and beverage operations may now run into millions of dollars in any given unit. This means that the number of employees has increased in each unit. In turn, these employees must be controlled by some type of system that will assure management that all income is being received and all materials are being sold or properly utilized.

The primary responsibility for safeguarding the assets of concerns and preventing and detecting errors and fraud rests on management. Controls for the food service industry are thus designed for two primary purposes:

* *Management Series on Internal Control,* American Institute of Certified Public Accountants (New York), p. 5.

1. To determine the efficiency of the operation.
2. To prevent fraud or theft by employees or guests. (Unlike the retail industry, however, practically all thefts in food service organizations are performed by the employees—not the customers.)

Regardless of the type of food served, the particular function of the unit, the method of service, or the type of ownership or organizational structure, the cost control system should cover every facet of food service. The primary objective of a controller may differ in various types of operations. For the restaurant operator, the first concern will be to increase profits; for the school food supervisor, it may be to lower operating costs. Each must approach the task with different systems, and each system must be tailored to the needs of the organization. For the restaurant operator an increase in profits may be obtained by changing portion sizes, by changing the menu, or perhaps by increasing menu prices. The school food service supervisor may not be able to utilize these strategies but instead may devise more efficient production systems to lower operating costs. The net results may in effect be the same (that is greater profits), but the approaches used may have to be different.

Other factors may have higher priorities and will force the administrator to forgo cost reductions in order to achieve more important objectives. For example, the hospital dietician may be able to reduce costs by cutting services or perhaps lowering the quality of the food. Her primary objective, though, is to provide for the dietary needs of patients and to insure that these services assist in the patient's recovery. Any reduction in costs that will detract from these objectives must be avoided.

A school lunch room supervisor may be able to save a school district money by reducing the labor involved in preparing attractively presented foods. But if this makes the food unappealing to the children and they leave more of it uneaten on their plates, then in fact he or she has done a disservice to the community.

The restaurant operator who in cutting costs actually reduces sales has erred by not viewing the entire operation and the net effect of this cost reduction. At times, increasing some types of costs may result in greater profits, because of increased sales and better utilization of staff and facilities.

The types of systems used in food and beverage operations will differ. What may be effective in one organization will be utterly useless in another. The types of services provided, the number of employees, the organizational structure, and the size of the operation will basically determine the type of control system that must be adopted. Even the skill levels and personal habits of employees may necessitate a change of the types of controls that must be instituted.

For example, the food and beverage controller may determine that bakery costs are too high because personnel in the pantry department are not properly rotating stock, despite training and periodic spot-checking by supervisors. Thus, instead of the weekly inventory that would normally be performed by the chef, a daily inventory should be taken to help alleviate the situation. This corrective measure now becomes an integral part of the control system and in turn affects other parts of the total control system.

Even though two organizations may be of the same size, the systems used may differ. The knowledgeable food and beverage controller must be aware of all the idiosyncrasies of his own organization as well as being familiar with all types of controls. In a small organization the person in charge of control may, in fact, be the owner. Even if no other employees are involved, certain records must be kept. Simple tools such as portion control, inventory and stock rotation, and a system to determine which goods to purchase must be established. A sales record must be maintained.

As the establishment adds employees, areas of responsibility must be delineated and fixed. If overlapping areas exist, it becomes impossible for management to determine who should be charged for errors or mismanagement, nor can any one individual be blamed should there actually be theft or fraud. Clearcut lines must be drawn, and accurate records maintained for each area. Although the size of the organization may determine the number of records that must be maintained, the basic functions areas in all food and beverage service remain the same.

Control systems must be designed to provide needed information to the responsible individuals of any area as well as to oversee the individuals responsible for that area. Various kinds of data and statistics may be required at different levels or be utilized by several different area supervisors.

A system may provide, for example, forecasting data that predicts a low volume of sales for a given period. This enables the purchasing agent to determine how much to buy for that period of time. The same information may also be used by the sales department to plan a campaign to promote sales for that period, as well as by a production department head to reduce the scheduling of his employees. In this case the data may be identical. In another case, however, data utilized by the storeroom clerk may indicate that certain merchandise must be ordered. The controller interpreting the same data, and with other conflicting information, may determine that there has been the theft of merchandise by someone with access to the storeroom.

The type of system adopted by a food service organization may finally be determined by the cost of the operation of the system itself and the related savings that may be accomplished or effected. Unlike many other types of businesses, the number of transactions that occur in a food service is extremely high in relationship to the dollar value of sales.

A food organization may sell a hamburger and a soft drink for less than one dollar, yet the sale must be recorded, the original raw products must be purchased, and the product must be processed. In the processing it may be necessary for one or more bookkeeping entries to be made. A total of three or four entries or records is necessary, each involving time on the part of the worker and a bookkeeper or accountant, and all of these costs must be absorbed in the sales price of one dollar. Compare the number of entries required for this transaction, the ratio of the bookkeeping costs to sales, with those involved in the sale of a car or large appliance. Obviously, should the cost of the accounting become prohibitive, another control system must be adopted.

In establishing a new system that will cost less, certain types of recordkeeping will probably be eliminated. Each time a control is eliminated the system as a whole becomes less effective. It is the function of the food and beverage controller to determine at what point the system no longer functions, at what point the cost is prohibitive in relationship to the dollar savings that are effected, and which type of system is best suited for the establishment.

Fortunately, with the improved computer technology developed in the past few years, the food service operator has been able to increase the controls available while at the same time reducing the ratio of accounting costs to sales.

The determination of the type of system used and the overseeing of the system itself is basically the function of the food and beverage controller. In various operations he may be the manager, the food and beverage manager, the purchasing agent, or the head dietician. Regardless of the title, the functions of the individual remain the same.

The cost control principles that are required for food service apply equally as well to beverage operations, although the terminology may be somewhat different. In beverage (liquor) operations, preparation is performed by a bartender, whereas in food establishments this task is performed by the cook or chef. In some cases beverage operations may do some prepreparation (premixing of cocktails), in others this task may be omitted. Thus, although there may be some minor differences in the terminology or in the actual operations of food and beverage services, the principles are somewhat the same. There are, however, major differences in the application of these principles, since the handling of the merchandise and the areas for fraud and/or theft differ considerably.

Chapter 2 will discuss the function areas for food service operations. By merely substituting "beverage" for "food service" the system and function areas may be adapted to bar operations.

Chapter I
1. What types of expenses should management be concerned with in food and beverage operations?
2. List and categorize various types of food and beverage operations that require different types of control systems.
3. What are the purposes of control systems?

4. What interest do employees have in insuring that there are adequate control systems?

5. Why has there been a need for more sophisticated control systems?

6. Discuss factors influencing the types of control systems that may be adopted by a food or beverage establishment.

7. Why is it necessary to fix responsibility in control systems?

8. What types of information would be available with control systems?

9. What is the function of the food and beverage controller?

2

The Function Areas

In almost every food or beverage operation there may be ten to twelve primary function areas, each area being necessary for the operation as a whole. In some cases function areas may be combined or even eliminated by management. In large organizations the separation of these areas is normally more clearly delineated. As a result of this and the greater number of personnel involved, the interchange of merchandise from area to area (employee to employee) must be accounted for and recorded. In all organizations, controls should be established even when the merchandise is not transferred from one employee to another. When more than one employee is involved, controls are mandatory.

Figure 2-1 shows the actual function areas and points out some of the interrelationships of these areas. Just as in our solar system, should one of the "planets" be moved or modified the entire system would be out of balance. Each type of food or beverage operation or establishment must balance its own solar system. All functions (planets) are interrelated with each other. The heart of the system and the final control rest with the food and beverage controller.

In all organizations every function area must in some way be controlled. Since all areas are interrelated, should any part of the system fail to be controlled, the net effect is an imbalance and thus no control at all. It is the function of the controller to determine the necessary controls for each area and to monitor the system to insure that all controls are in operation.

As stated before, regardless of the type of food served, or the method of service, cost control should encompass every facet of food and beverage service. In turn, the food and beverage controller must be familiar with the idiosyncracies of his own unit and monitor all phases of the operation. To limit the authority of the controller to certain areas would negate his function as well as impose an impossible task for the controller, since without full control his job cannot be performed effectively.

FIGURE 2-1 *The Solar System of Food and Beverage Service*

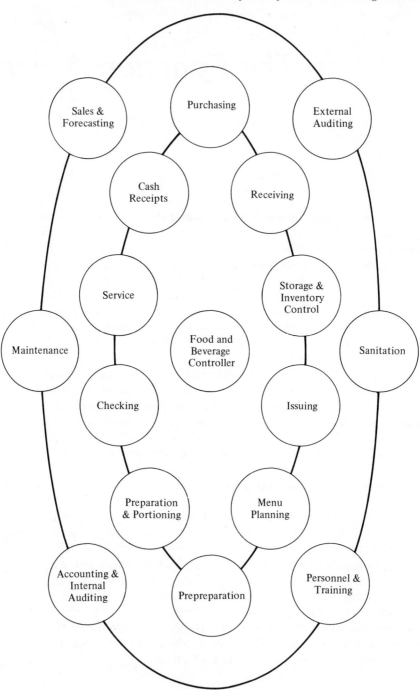

For example, a sales department may, in order to book a large convention, negotiate a special lunch price that is far below the established sales price for that particular menu. Under normal accounting procedures the cost of producing that luncheon may far exceed the food cost percentages desired by management. This practice may be permissible for short periods of time or under special conditions. Should the sales department continue to operate in this fashion, however, the entire food service facilities in the establishment may be jeopardized. By giving the necessary authority to the controller, he may insist on having the sales department change its procedures and pricing policies.

Another case in which the controller may exercise authority over the sales department is by requiring data and information on future sales to be furnished by the sales department. Without such data, the entire food service operation may be impaired, since information regarding the amounts of goods to purchase and the staffing requirements are absolutely essential to an efficient operation.

In Figure 2-1, each function area has been defined, but many of the areas may overlap and separate controls may not be used. This is particularly true of the areas of prepreparation and portioning. The term *checking* is used to denote the function area or transfer area in which food is moved from the area of jurisdiction of the kitchen personnel to personnel in the dining room. However, in many food service operations (or bars) such as diners, fast food operations or cafeterias this function is not performed. In these, food is transferred directly from the control of the kitchen staff and/or serving line personnel to the customer without a waiter or waitress intermediary.

Thus, one can readily see that even the types of service will affect the types of controls that are introduced into a food service operation. For larger hotels offering varying types of food services, specific controls must be introduced that are tailored for each of the types of services offered.

In some cases the personnel available (scheduled according to the volume of business) may change the systems of control even within one type of service. This is especially true when a limited number of service personnel are utilized during slack periods.

Often the manager of an operation will schedule a hostess for busy periods, and one of her functions may be to record the number of people that each waitress is assigned. During the slower periods, however, a hostess may no longer be used, and the manager may neglect to institute another control. At these times no exact record of how many people were served is kept and the manager is no longer able to verify that he has, in fact, been paid for all the customers who were served. An owner or manager may make an assumption that, because he is on premises and working during all the hours that an establishment serves food and beverage, no detailed systems of controls need to be installed. This hasty and false assumption leads quickly to bankruptcy, since theft can occur at any time. While he is performing tasks in the back of the restaurant, customers in the front may be walking out without paying or employees in the back of the house may steal food while he is busy counting cash in the front.

Many operators never carry large sums of money to a bank at the same time each day, so that they reduce the possibility of a hold-up from persons who may determine from a regular schedule the best time to rob them. Unfortunately, they may within their own operation establish a fixed and regular routine so that at any given moment their whereabouts are known and the employee who wishes to steal is quickly able to determine the best time to do it.

In any establishment, controls for each function area must be operative as soon as the department has personnel working in it or when personnel from other departments have access to the function area. A bank would never consider leaving cash around during the evening hours when maintenance employees may be cleaning. Yet food service operators will leave food and beverages unlocked under the same conditions, either because of the difficulty in locking up all the merchandise or because they rely upon their employees' honesty. In these cases the manager is either naive or else he considers the value of the merchandise negligible in relationship to the bother that it creates.

This type of philosophy unfortunately creates an atmosphere in which the employees gradually come to feel that all merchandise is of negligible value. Inevitably the number of thefts and the net value of the losses increase. Management's initial approach should be that no portion of an operation is unimportant and that every item should be accounted for.

Figure 2-1 indicates the function areas as well as the normal operating departments for large organizations. In smaller organizations many of these departments may be combined but none can be omitted. Those departments in the outer circle are supporting, or ancillary, or may be considered staff function areas, but without their services, the operation as a whole would quickly fail.

Often the operators of smaller organizations believe that because there is no formal department, the function ceases to exist, but this is not the case. Even in fast food operations such as McDonald's, the function of service is not eliminated—the customer serves himself. A very small bar or restaurant may not have a sales department to sell or to predict the number of guests that will be served. The owner still will have calculated some expected sales figures and perhaps at times will buy a round of drinks to promote sales. He thus accomplishes the same purposes as a fullblown sales department. In the hospital food service organization, bed counts are furnished, menu cards distributed to accurately determine sales of each item, and often the dietician will visit patients to insure that service and quality are satisfactory. School lunch rooms normally have a "popularity" record to determine and predict total sales. Some even promote sales of items with buttons, menu boards, and attractive posters.

A control system must be tailored to each operation so that should several departments be combined, personnel eliminated, or several functions be performed by the same personnel, the system will allow for these changes in organizational structure. Controls then may be added or eliminated. The effects of these changes for specific cases will be studied in later chapters.

Due to the operating differences between marketing channels involved with foods and those involved with alcoholic beverages, the specific types of controls required in the purchasing departments for these groups of products differ. These differences will also be noted as the products are utilized and routed through an establishment. The general function of these departments will be discussed in this chapter. Detailed analysis of the methods for the control of food and beverages will be the subject of later chapters.

PRIMARY FUNCTION AREAS

Purchasing

For ease of discussion it will be assumed that the starting point of controls and the system itself will be in the purchasing department. In actual practice this may not be the case, since the amounts to purchase are determined by sales volume and other related factors.

It is the duty of the purchasing department to purchase all products that will be used in the establishment. In purchasing the items it is necessary to follow the maxim "the best possible product for a specific purpose at the lowest possible price." Which item is really the best and which is really the most economical may seem simple questions. In actual practice, however, there may be a choice of hundreds of products. There may be alternates available that are equally suitable. One price quotation may appear to be lower than others, but the true value obtained may, in fact, be far less than for one that seemed to be more expensive. To compound the difficulty in making decisions, the market for purchasing most of the items is constantly fluctuating. Thus a decision that is reasonable and valid one day may be invalid the next.

The second primary function of the purchasing department is to insure that all merchandise that may be needed is on hand. Delays in obtaining merchandise become expensive and cannot be tolerated. Obviously, the simple solution would be to buy every item that may be used during a period of time and keep it in stock. This type of practice for any industry is unwise, since as a result an excess of merchandise will be on hand and funds used to purchase this merchandise will be tied up for undue periods of time. More importantly, however, in the food service industry, merchandise is highly perishable. If it is kept in stock for undue periods of time, either it would spoil or excessive shrinkage would occur. The rate of spoilage will vary depending upon the type of food. The food buyer who blithely assumes that he is well stocked, since he purchased the required amount of merchandise at the beginning of the period, may be rudely awakened one day to find that a sufficient amount is not on hand because of spoilage or excessive shrinkage.

In order to accomplish the function of purchasing, the purchasing agent (buyer, chef, dietician, or food service manager) must coordinate his department with the sales department to determine the predicted number of meals that will be sold or served during a given period of time and the exact types or kinds of merchandise required. Additional information must be obtained from the preparation areas to determine exactly when the merchandise is required, since in some cases preparation may begin some time prior to actual service. Finally, inventory information must be obtained so that if merchandise is already on hand, excess supplies will not be purchased.

In order to accomplish all of these functions and obtain the necessary information, different controls will be required in various types of organizations. The choice of controls depends on the number of personnel that must be contacted by the purchasing agent and also on the number of other departments that will be affected by the decisions made within the purchasing department.

Receiving

The function of the receiving department is to insure and verify that all the merchandise that has been ordered is received.

Controls must be set up to insure that the quality is the same that has been ordered and that there have not been any substitutions, changes, or deterioration in the products. Products must be weighed, counted, and inspected and a determination made as to whether they meet the standards as laid down by the purchasing department. If there are shortages, deterioration, or damaged merchandise, it must be determined whether the products will be accepted and, if so, what allowances or credits requested.

Once agreement is reached on this, the items that have been accepted are the responsibility of the receiving department. Items are then transferred either directly to preparation areas or to storage areas.

In some operations it is also the receiving department that is responsible for the return of merchandise. This action may occur when there has been a change in the requirements of the establishment, when it has taken temporary custody of merchandise for the convenience of the shipper, or when merchandise is simply returned for credit, as in the case of bottles that are returned for deposit. Another instance might be the bones and fat that are picked up for rendering. Often this area of income is neglected by management. In well-run establishments, however, this type of allowance should be controlled by the receiving department and appropriate credits forwarded to the accounting department.

Merchandise of great monetary value is constantly being shipped in and out of an establishment, and adequate security measures should be instituted at the receiving dock to protect this sensitive area. If a truck is already at the establishment, large quantities of merchandise could be removed and easily transported away without any undue alarming of personnel, since the trucker is supposed to be there anyway.

Adequate space, equipment, and personnel must be available for a receiving department to function effectively. In too many operations, this important function is delegated to the lowest employee (dishwasher, porter, etc.), who has had no training and is primarily used to tote the items to the next function area. As a result, inspections are not performed correctly and undesirable merchandise may be accepted.

Storage and Inventory Control

Every piece of merchandise must be placed somewhere and kept for a period of time. The orderly placement of merchandise is essential, so that it can be easily found, retrieved, and issued. In some cases the storage period may only be for a matter of hours. In other cases it may be for months. The period of time and the conditions for the storage of the product are governed by the characteristics of the product itself. Obviously, it would be impossible (at least with present-day technology) to store lettuce for several months or to store it without refrigeration. Even when storing it under ideal conditions for short periods of time there are changes in the product and some of it may be "lost."

It is the function of the storage department, therefore, to hold all products under optimum conditions for as short a period of time as possible while at the same time informing management so that enough is on hand to meet the normal needs of the operation. Since in many cases the value of the products is reduced due to natural shrinkage, it also becomes the duty of the storage department to rotate stock and to record inventories to account for these losses.

Few, if any, food control systems allow for the fact that in storage there is some natural shrinkage, as well as merchandise that is stolen. Financial statements and work sheets do not allocate space for this, nor does the Uniform System of Accounts set up separate control accounts in which these losses are accounted for. Inevitably, at the end of an accounting period the actual differences between real inventory and book inventory are simply written off or fudged in some way so that a true determination of the efficiency of the storage department cannot be determined. No norms are established, and management tends to look at the entire amount that is written off as stolen merchandise. In fact, some portion of it may simply be attributable to normal operating practices, or even to poor ones that could have been rectified.

Fresh produce and meats are highly susceptible to spoilage. If 10 cases of lettuce have been received, each containing 24 heads, and only 200 heads of lettuce issued out (none remaining), there is a shortage of 40 heads. Few, if any, food and beverage controllers are equipped with efficient enough systems to account for the differences and to determine the cause of this high loss. Butcher shops may receive 1000 pounds of meat but issue only 600 pounds. Few, if any, have sophisticated control systems that will account for the differences, let alone determine whether, in fact, this is the correct amount that should have been issued.

The inventory department records the amount of merchandise that is on hand, properly cares for this merchandise, and allocates the goods to the various departments that request supplies. This dual function of physically caring for the merchandise and of maintaining records necessitates that the person or persons responsible for this function not only be physically capable of handling products but also be trained in simple bookkeeping.

In actual practice, for many food service establishments the functions of receiving, storage, and inventory control are the responsibility of one department. Liquor normally should be stored in a separate area and controlled by other personnel with a separate accounting system.

Issuing

Just as in the case of the transfer of control from the purveyor to the receiving department, the transfer of goods from the inventory department to the department responsible for the further preparation or use of the product must be recorded. In some cases the goods are to be used in the kitchen, in others the dining room, and in still others the bar. When cases of this nature arise (and we will see the recurrence of this type of situation further on in the processing as well) some record of the transfer of responsibility must be kept.

Usually, when products are taken from inventories, the term *issue* is used. Issuing is a joint function shared by the storage department and the next department that is to use the product. In the cases where the product is to be used by the kitchen, the chef or steward will sign a requisition form that is given to the inventory department. When the dining room needs the product, the maitre d', headwaiter, or an authorized representative may sign the form. In the case where the bar requires the product, it may be the bar manager. Once the responsibility for the product has been transferred, the new department may further process the goods.

Although there is no physical act performed on the merchandise itself except to transport it to the appropriate area, the function of issuing is an extremely important one in all food service establishments. This is particularly true in larger establishments in which several outlets for food and beverages are in operation and in which a determination of true costs must be made for each outlet. Without adequate issuing controls, no determination of costs can be made. Management cannot effectively insure that any degree of efficiency has been achieved, nor even if theft has occurred.

In all the function areas, but particularly in the area of issuing, only authorized personnel should be allowed to have access to the goods, to sign for merchandise, or to transport this merchandise from one area to another. Extra precautions must be taken with high value merchandise that has a tendency to "lose something in the transportation."

The function of issuing may be further complicated in some operations, since a redistribution of goods may be made after some processing has been performed. In large operations, food may be issued to a main kitchen, prepared, and then reissued to different dining rooms or to different private parties.

Even more intricate is the case in which a product may be left over in one area, and then reissued to either another dining room or perhaps to an employees' dining room.

The accounting and control incurred in crediting and charging each area may prove costly, and a system designed to account for all these variances may be too cumbersome to operate. Yet, obviously, without complete information as to the disposition of the products, no control system is accurate. Unfortunately, too many operations have no provisions in their control systems to account for any of these situations.

Menu Planning

The types of services and menus (see Chapter 11) are determined by the market catered to by any establishment. With each type of market an operator, manager, or supervisor must determine the best type of menu suitable for the needs of the market. In designing a given menu he must consider not only information on the market itself (ages, sex, economic status, frequency of eating, etc.) but also the skill levels of the personnel, the availability of products, and innumerable other factors that will affect the overall saleability and profitability of the menu.

Basic formats (the type of menu and the basic price structure) are usually determined by management. However, with menus that are changing frequently, the function of menu planning is most often the duty of the chef or dietician.

Menu planning is too often neglected by management. This neglect is due not to lack of interest but rather to a misunderstanding or ignorance on the part of those involved with menu planning. Menu planning is probably one of the most complex tasks of food service. This complexity is caused by the large number of variables, which directly affect the cost of food (and beverages), and the difficulty in assigning a value to each variable.

Although in this study only one chapter will be used to further outline these factors, a whole book would be required to fully explore menu planning. Further research is needed in this area not only by the industry as a whole but certainly by every operator to determine whether, in fact, the menu utilized is the most profitable, suitable, and feasible for his operation.

Continued surveillance and monitoring of menus should be performed even after menus have been decided upon—changing customer markets as well as supply markets may call for a change in menus.

Sequentially, menu planning is the first step in the proper design and organization of any restaurant. As a matter of convenience this function has been inserted at this point in the solar chart rather than at an earlier stage. For current publications that direct themselves solely to this function area, the reader may wish to consult Lendal H. Kotschevar's *Management by Menu* or Lothar A. Kreck's *Menus: Analysis and Planning.* (See Bibliography for additional information.)

Preparation and Preparation

Various mechanical and other measuring devices or controls may be used to insure that the restaurant or bar is, in fact, processing the products in the most efficient manner. For example, the bartender should be required to measure when mixing drinks. The temperature at which meats are cooked dramatically affects the amount of the finished product as well as the taste. Ovens in kitchens should have thermostatic controls. In addition, management may require that a thermometer be inserted in meats to insure that the final cooked temperature does not exceed the optimum desired.

In examining Figure 2-1, note that preparation and prepreparation are listed separately, since in operations that are very large or in those in which there are many independent units (such as a chain with a commissary) a transfer record may be required.

For example, one school district may purchase totally prepared, preportioned salads. Another school district may prepare all the salad greens, tomatoes, radishes at a central commissary (which in effect is prepreparation) and then issue to each individual school the amounts ordered for that day or that week. The final preparation or dishing up into the salad plates may be completed at the school itself. Another school district, however, may just issue the crates of lettuce, tomatoes, radishes to each school, or each school may order directly from a local purveyor. The end products may be exactly the same but it is obvious that different types of records must be kept since the preparation systems as a whole are different.

Correct recipes must be used and the proper amounts prepared for the predicted number of persons. Excessive leftovers may indicate either improper preparation procedures or inadequacies in the forecasting by the sales department.

The preparation department is also faced with the challenge of feeding personnel and the proper utilization of leftovers. Fully utilizing all products is a necessity for well-run food operations.

Finally, all food must be carefully handled to avoid waste, while at the same time presenting it to the guest in the most attractive manner possible. Overportioning may result in a great deal of plate waste, but it is difficult to distinguish between the plate waste caused by overportioning and that caused by poorly prepared or sloppily presented food that makes the student, patient, or guest lose his appetite. Drinks that must be remade due to the negligence of the bartender create the same type of problem. Customer dissatisfaction and the eventual loss of business caused by this carelessness seldom are noticed until it is too late.

In every operation the size of the portion must be determined, standardized recipes established, method of preparation studied, and preparation systems analyzed to evaluate efficiency and to determine what is best for the given establishment.

For example, practically every food service establishment serves a hamburger of some type. How to prepare it, what size portion should be used, and what other accompanying items may be served with it must be established by management. Even within one establishment several alternatives may be used, such as a regular hamburger or a giant hamburger. Some are served with pickle, some without, some are grilled, and others charcoal broiled.

Once the standard has been established, it is the function of the chef (food manager, cook, etc.) to continue to verify that these standards are practiced at all times.

Checking

The transfer of the control of the cooked or ready-to-be-served product from the kitchen (or bar) to the customer, patient, or guest must now be considered. In many cases the food or beverages go directly from the control of the kitchen to the customer, as in the cases of a fast food operation such as McDonald's, or in those cases where the guest is sitting at a bar and orders directly from the bartender. In other cases, another intermediate step must be taken as the food or drink is transferred to the control of the waitress or waiter. If a waiter or waitress is employed, the product must be transferred both to and from his control. The process of giving the food to the waiter and receiving his check or "dupe" may be termed *checking*. In fact, there really is no common term for this function—*dupes, prechecking, postchecking,* and *validation* are all used. The process of transferring the goods to the customer is then recorded on a check.

This vital function, and the auditing of it, is perhaps one of the most difficult to control in all types of operations. The systems used depend to a great degree on the volume of the operation, the dollar value of each sale, the type of service, and the system used to obtain the food or beverage. In food operations, in particular, it is perhaps the most sensitive area, since it is at this juncture that the food that is issued can be readily turned into actual cash. Unless the amount of food issued to a waiter or waitress is accurately recorded, it is impossible to determine what the true cash receipts should be.

Service

The primary function of service is to insure that the guest, patient, or student is served as rapidly as required in as pleasant a manner as possible. A secondary function often overlooked by management, yet which falls in the domain of service, is the recordkeeping process that service personnel must perform. The recording of all sales on a check of some type is just as essential a function of waiters and waitresses as the actual service of the food or beverages.

In the hectic rush to serve as fast as possible (which may not be the wishes of the customer) and because the control of the food or beverage items may already be under the control of the service personnel, it may not be feasible to account or use checking for all merchandise. Waitresses may have access to coffee, juices, salads, desserts, and other items and merely help themselves whenever a guest orders one of the items. Obviously, stopping to record each item may be an unwarranted delay, and utilizing a checker may slow down service to the point where it becomes undesirable. On the other hand, having an open-door, help-yourself policy may lead to unnecessary losses. Should a large percentage of the total business be involved with these low-value items, then losses may become unmanageable.

The food and beverage manager must design a system for service and checking that serves both functions; accounting for merchandise while also insuring that the guest is served in the most efficient method possible for the specific type of service.

Cash Receipts

Insuring that all sales that have been recorded on the check are actually collected from the customer is the function of cash receipts. This area is of extreme importance in the system as a whole. Unless adequate controls are established, large amounts of income may be lost. The system established must also allow for the type of service in the operation. Excessive controls may result in delays in service, lowering the overall quality of the food or beverage operation.

The type of service may also govern the method or system used. A cafeteria may use a cashier at the end of the service line, but this system obviously will not work in a table service restaurant in which there is no line. Nor will the system used for a gourmet restaurant be effective in a coffee shop.

Cash collection may be either directly from the customer to a cashier or payment may be made by the guest to a waiter or waitress who in turn pays the cashier. Other methods are also available. Various mechanical systems are used and controls established that are designed to suit the particular needs of the establishment. Even within one establishment, several different types of systems may be used, depending on the type of service and even on the particular meal being served. Credit cards may require one system of collection, lunch hour may require a different method from breakfast, and banquet service still another.

Although the term *cash collection* is used, many persons charge merchandise. Protective devices must be established to insure that any charge sales to hotel guests are immediately posted to the appropriate guest account. Credit card sales must be recorded and also verified to establish that the credit card holder is using a valid card. Since the dollar amount eventually received from credit card companies is less than the actual sales, adjustments in pricing policies may be necessary in operations that have a large volume of this type of sale.

Within the scope of cash receipts, there are amounts that must be paid out to service personnel and other payouts that often are paid from the cash register, such as small COD shipments.

If several personnel are involved, as in the case of the waiter who collects from the guest and in turn pays the cashier, then the system must be designed so that the ultimate responsibility for the actual cash can be fixed upon one person.

Earlier, it was stated that the primary thefts in food and beverage establishments were performed by employees. The one area in which guests are involved is in the area of cash receipts; that is, a guest simply walks out without paying. Thus control systems must be designed and physical plant layout so constructed as to minimize the danger of theft by guests in this function area.

SUPPORTING OR ANCILLARY FUNCTION AREAS

Accounting and Internal Auditing

The major portion of the recordkeeping, and the tabulation of the records presented by the various other departments, is the duty of the accounting department. Without adequate checking and verification of the information furnished by these departments the entire system would be useless. Often, due to the pressure of daily service crises or to the apparent success of an established system, inadequate accounting controls are performed. This can result in unnecessary losses and eventually a complete breakdown of the entire system.

Although listed as a separate function, the accounting department may perform many of its services within other departments or act as the verifier as to the efficiency of these departments. In effect, the accounting department's jurisdiction overlaps all other departments. But accounting is primarily a staff function, and personnel within this department may or may not fall under the jurisdiction of the food and beverage controller, since they, in turn, must verify the controller's efficiency.

Although normally a food preparation area would not have anyone from the accounting office involved in its operation, the accounting department may be able to assist the chef by doing bookwork, verifying yields, and, as a major portion of its overall accounting function, tabulating the number of portions that the kitchen issues.

In the bar preparation area the accounting office may establish tolerable or acceptable limits for spillage, and verify the drinks poured by checking mechanical counters or comparing the number of drinks served to that actually recorded on checks.

Since this is a separate function, personnel within the accounting department must be under separate jurisdiction and not under the control of the departments whose actions they are evaluating.

External Auditing

Auditing and accounting are usually handled by the same department, but in addition, auditing by an outside company must be performed. Since the accounting department also normally receives and dispenses cash, obviously their actions must be verified as to accuracy and honesty.

Personnel

In addition to the above-mentioned areas, various other departments also may be involved in the complete cost control system, although they may not be directly concerned with the day-to-day operations. Without adequate training and staffing, no department personnel can properly perform the task to which they may be assigned. Thus, the personnel department may assume a direct responsibility to insure that the performance standards established by management are carried out. Time and motion studies may be performed so that improved methods of operation may be designed and implemented, in order to lower payroll costs or to improve quality and service.

Certainly, without adequate recruiting practices and generally modern methods of personnel management, department heads would soon find themselves without skilled personnel and thus unable to perform their functions. Standards for performance and service would be impossible to meet, resulting in eventual deterioration of the entire operation.

In many cases no formal personnel department is maintained but rather each department services itself, performs its own training, sets its own standards, and even creates it own personnel policies. This type of approach has certain advantages and disadvantages, which cannot be discussed at this time. The eventual goals of formal and informal personnel departments remain the same no matter which techniques are applied.

Sales

Sales encompasses any task or function whose purpose is to increase the volume of sales or to predict the volume of sales. Advertising, promotion, merchandising, menu planning, and even the training of personnel (to promote sales) may be included in this category. Although normally not considered a part of the function of the food and beverage controller, it is obvious that the effects of the sales department will be felt throughout the food and beverage operation. Since a discussion of sales would encompass a book (or several) by itself, only those areas that directly affect day-to-day control will be discussed in later chapters. A device such as a free dinner, or perhaps a special sales price that changes operating percentages, must be examined by the controller to determine whether or not these methods are effective for the operation. The overall effects of these methods will be studied and may be placed under the jurisdiction of the food and beverage controller.

The design of a menu may enhance the sales of a particular item. Certainly, personnel trained in suggestive selling can improve the entire profit structure of an organization. In some restaurants, waiters and waitresses are given a percentage of wine sales should they sell more than a specified minimum. One establishment really makes an all-out effort by having their personnel ask, "Would you like one doughnut or two with your coffee?" giving the customer little opportunity to refuse and thus augmenting sales. On the other hand, devices such as two-for-one dinners radically change food costs and must be closely examined in order to determine whether they achieve the desired results.

In larger companies, the sales department must inform all other departments as to the predicted volume of business and particularly as to any special arrangements that may have been made. Adequate notice must be given so that specific items that are not normally served may be purchased in time and so that enough staff are available.

In the cases where a slow period is predicted (these forecasts may also come from the accounting department) each operating department must be notified so that immediate steps may be taken to reduce staff and lower inventories. This important cost reduction function is often neglected as a major function of the sales department. Unnecessary costs may thus be incurred because the functions of the sales department have not been adequately defined.

Sanitation

Sanitation is listed as an ancillary department, since normally most of its primary functions are not directly concerned with the actual control or processing of either food or beverages. Certainly, however, no establishment can function, and indeed costs may even be increased, without an adequate housekeeping department. Food or beverages rejected by customers due to dirty glasses or plates may be thrown out—thus increasing food costs. Each time a cook or waiter rejects a plate or utensil because it is dirty, this causes an increased labor cost due to the time involved. The dirty plates, glassware, etc., must be rewashed, increasing sanitation costs. Finally, the costs of breakage or losses of silverware, plates, etc., due to inefficient sanitation departments can become prohibitively expensive.

Maintenance

A well-functioning maintenance department is capable of saving any establishment hundreds, if not thousands, of dollars. Equipment life will be extended if preventative service is performed regularly, rather than waiting for breakdowns. Equipment should also be examined to insure that adequate safety precautions are practiced and devices are furnished, since injuries can be disastrously expensive as well as demoralizing to the staff. Certainly, thermostats should be maintained at proper temperatures—or overcooked food may result, or should the thermostat be faulty in a refrigeration area, spoilage may occur.

New equipment is costly and becoming increasingly so. On the other hand, restaurant equipment (if purchased with adequate thought and with adequate specifications) normally will last for long periods of time and will stand up to very heavy usage and wear. It is the duty of the maintenance department to assist in obtaining the maximum possible usage for every piece of equipment.

Chapter 2

1. What is a function area?
2. List and discuss the primary function areas.
3. List the auxillary or supporting function areas.
4. Discuss the effects of the efficiency or effectiveness of supporting function areas upon the primary function areas.
5. Give examples of various types of food service in which function areas may be combined or eliminated.
6. Discuss the major objectives for each primary function area.
7. Discuss the differences between preparation and prepreparation.
8. What types of circumstances complicate checking procedures?
9. When are controls in a function area operative? Why?
10. What is the importance of portion control?

3

Liquor Purchasing
and
Inventory Control

LIQUOR PURCHASING

The function of the liquor department like that of the food, is to purchase the best quality at the lowest price for a specific purpose. Unlike foods, however, liquors are purchased primarily by brand names, with the exception of the variety of brands of lower quality or repute that may be purchased for "well" stock. This is the liquor that is used by the bartender whenever a customer does not specify a call liquor or brand name.

In many states the wholesale selling price of alcoholic beverages is controlled, or liquor must be purchased through state-owned stores. If it is not controlled, a common regulation is to have the purveyors (vendors-sellers) list the prices for each brand in a monthly magazine. Quotations, therefore, become unnecessary since the prices are public knowledge, and little deviation occurs from month to month. When variations do occur it is generally due to the fact that a particular brand is listed as a "special" for that period of time, and certain discounts become available should the purchasing agent wish to buy that product. As an example, J & B Scotch may normally be sold for $96.00 per case, but if purchased in 5-case lots a 1% discount is available and if purchased in 10-case lots a 3% discount may be allowed. The alert purchasing agent may therefore be able, by judiciously purchasing specials, to lower costs simply by taking advantage of these sales.

Most brands are assigned to only a few distributors. In some areas of the country only one distributor may carry a particular brand or line. Thus it becomes impossible for the purchasing agent to shop around to get the lowest possible price if only one distributor carries the line, and even if more than one wholesaler distributes the merchandise the price is very often fixed by the distiller or importer.

Obviously then, since mostly brand names are purchased, there is no major task involved in obtaining quality, since all liquor of a particular brand will be of the same quality. There is normally no deterioration of quality while in transit or storage. In turn, it is no longer a major function for management to verify the honesty of the purchasing agent in regard to obtaining the lowest price and best quality on name brands, since they are normally purchased at a published price. Therefore, the primary controls regarding the purchasing agent would be to insure that he is taking advantage of specials, purchasing at the most opportune time, and specifically, that in the purchase of well liquor, he is obtaining the best quality and lowest price.

Thus the function of the purchasing agent in the buying of alcoholic beverages, and other supplies for the beverage department, is basically to insure that adequate but not excessive supplies of all required products are on hand at all times. Adequate, of course, means that in essence you do not run out of any particular brand or item, so that all types of drinks can be served to your guests at all times. It does not mean that all brands should be stocked, and on occasion, supplies of some items may be exhausted. There are, however, a number of basic ingredients or brands that you must always have on hand. Excessive supplies, while they are nice to have, mean that undue amounts of inventory are kept, tying up money that could have been utilized in more productive projects. This creates unwarranted expenses for the operator. Once in a while, however, if a sharp price rise is forecast, it may be advisable to purchase a large amount.

Determining how large an inventory to stock and how large a selection of brands to carry are primary responsibilities of management. Decisions are based on the types of guests and the type of establishment, as well as the volume of the operation. For example, a small bar that has a volume of $1000 per week would certainly not be able to stock as many brands as one that does $10,000 per week, nor, in fact, would the clientele expect the variety. The large bar would, however, certainly be expected to stock all the major brands and perhaps have a larger selection of wines, beers, and liquors.

Management must decide what brands should be carried. This decision will to a large part be influenced by the requests and tastes of guests. A club that caters to a small number of members certainly should stock the brands that they prefer, bearing in mind how often a particular brand is requested. It would be unwise to stock a specific brand requested by only one member who patronizes the club once a month and then has only one drink. At that rate it would take two years to get rid of one bottle. If this were a beverage, such as wine, that spoils, it would be foolish. The selection of the particular stock that is to be carried will be influenced by the time of year (more of the lighter spirits being consumed during the summer months), any special events being scheduled (such as a fish dinner that may call for a white wine), customer preferences, and of course space limitations.

It is unwise (as well as illegal) to substitute one brand for another when a specific request has been made by a customer. However, it would be permissible to use one rye or one scotch in place of another should you run out of one, providing the guest has not called for that brand.

In many states the method of payment made by the establishment to the purveyor is governed by state law. These payments must be made within a specified period of time, and penalties are imposed should an establishment fail to pay within the time period. Usually, the wholesaler is then required by the state to have the establishment pay for all future purchases at the time of delivery. In some states all deliveries are on a COD basis.

Since prices are posted or listed monthly, no salesman may cut prices, although other inducements are sometimes offered. In most cases the salesman's functions are to convince the operator to use his well brand liquors, to suggest specials, and to take the order.

Misuse of power on the part of the purchasing agent and the salesman occurs now and then, particularly if a salesman is interested in the establishment purchasing his brand of liquor for the well stock. If a substantial portion of liquor sales is from well stock, then it may be desirable for management to establish two or three brands that should be used for this purpose. This limits the possibility of fraud on the part of both the purchasing agent and the salesman. At the same time it allows enough leeway so that some savings can be effected by switching from one brand to another (presuming that the qualities are the same) to take advantage of specials.

Another law that sometimes must be considered is the one that prohibits bars from purchasing their liquor any place other than from authorized wholesale dealers. Heavy penalties may be imposed should inspectors find an establishment with a brand of merchandise that the operator is unable to prove was purchased from a wholesaler. It may also be illegal to borrow from another bar or liquor store (competitor) should the operator run out of a brand.

Normally, alcoholic beverages are classified into three major categories. Wholesalers usually deal in one or two of the categories but seldom all three, so that even a bar stocking only a few items will require at least two dealers.

Distilled spirits consist of those alcoholic beverages made by a distillation process and usually contain at least 20% of alcohol by volume. Liquors such as ryes, whiskey, gin, rum, brandy, cordials, and liqueurs are included in this category.

Malt beverages are produced from malted barley, corn, sugar, hops, and other ingredients. Beer, ale, porter, stout, and bock fall under this category.

Wine is the pure, naturally fermented juice of fresh ripe grapes.*

* Wine Advisory Board, *Wine Series Handbook No. 2* (San Francisco, California, 1955), p. 1.

Wine, malt beverages, and distilled spirits are all fermented beverages. In most states malt beverages are sold by distributors who are not licensed to sell wines or whiskies. Whiskey dealers may or may not carry wines and wine dealers may or may not carry whiskies, depending upon the laws of a particular state, and also upon the product lines of the wholesaler.

METHODS OF PURCHASING

Beers

Beers (using this term for all malt beverages) can be purchased either in large containers such as kegs or barrels or in cans or bottles, depending upon the method of serving within an establishment. Before a bar is opened, management must decide which system is to be used. Sometimes both draft beer (kegs) and bottle sales may be used. Each system has inherent advantages and disadvantages:

Bottles—advantages	*Bottles—disadvantages*
exact count	handle and dispose of each bottle
larger unit sale	poorer taste
several brands stocked	breakage
cleaner	easily stolen
less work to maintain	careful rotation of stock required

Kegs—advantages	*Kegs—disadvantages*
good taste	limited in number of brands stocked
good merchandising	must be cleaned and maintained
higher profit %	heavy kegs hard to handle
less handling	proper pressure must be maintained
	no exact count
	may waste and go flat
	must always be refrigerated

Whether purchasing kegs or bottles, it is imperative to order and maintain a fresh stock. Beer will spoil if it is old or has not been kept at proper temperatures. Bottles are normally sold in 7-, 12-, and 16-ounce containers. The most common one used in the industry would be the 12-ounce bottle. Many patrons object to canned beer, and it is normally little used in bars.

Distilled Beverages

Every bar must keep in stock certain popular brand names as well as a number of various types of liqueurs. The purchasing agent's responsibilities must include the stocking of this merchandise as well as insuring that the proper sizes, brands, and other items, such as olives, onions, lemons, are on hand. Most ryes, gins, scotches, and other "hard liquors" are purchased in quarts. Some large bars with automated systems, however, are now purchasing these items in half gallons or even gallons, depending upon the system's capacity and state laws. Liqueurs and some unusual items (such as cordials and wines) may be purchased in fifths or in odd-sized bottles such as 23 ounces for Benedictine, Galliano, etc.

Wines

Most American wines are sold in fifths. Foreign wines may come in odd-sized bottles that may be as much as four ounces less than a fifth, although the container may appear to be the same size. Purchasing agents should be aware that a case of foreign wine that appears to be the same price as an American wine may, in fact, be more expensive, particularly if the wine is to be sold by the glass. A fifth must contain 25.6 ounces, whereas the foreign wines may have a little as 21 ounces.

Purchasing agents must also consider buying a variety of wines for cooking as well as those for serving. Larger size bottles (gallons) of wines may be used in cooking or for decanting for sale either by the glass or in carafes. It would not be wise to purchase cooking wine of very poor quality, since wine used in cooking should impart a distinctive flavor and improve the taste. Poor wines may not have this capacity and could do the opposite. It is not, however, necessary to use a "vintage" for cooked foods.

Since wine tends to "evaporate" in kitchens (consumed by the staff), it is suggested that the chef "salt" the wine. This merely necessitates that less salt be used in a recipe than is normally required. There are, however, certain kinds of dishes that require wine but in which salt would impair the flavor. Certainly a dessert item such as strawberries in white wine should not have salt added. The wine used for this must be separated from the normal stock.

The amount of wines kept in inventory and the extent of a wine list will vary considerably in food service establishments. Very fine restaurants may have thousands of dollars tied up in inventories. A smaller establishment may decide to limit the wines to one or two types in each category, and thus not only save money but also space.

In the gourmet room of a very fine hotel, one of the finest in the area, wine is included in the price of the meal. Management is able to limit its stock to one red, one white, and one champagne, each served with the appropriate course. Each guest is allowed to drink all the wine he wants, at no extra charge. This not only fits in with the style and intent of the restaurant but also has become one of its merchandising features. In the same area, another hotel stocks thousands of dollars worth of wine for its gourmet room and often buys a year's supply at a time. This bulk purchase not only creates a discount for the hotel but insures that adequate supplies will be on hand (since some of the items may become scarce). It also has protected the hotel from severe price increases that have occurred over the past few years.

The philosophy of management for each restaurant is correct, despite being diametrically opposite. It is possible to emulate either of these positions or to compromise somewhere in between. The purchasing controls for the operation having only three types of wines remain relatively simple, since the buyer is limited in the selection of items and must merely replace stock. Tighter controls must be imposed on the buyer who has the option to purchase vast quantities of wine. It is possible to purchase wines that will not sell, or inferior wines. The prices of wines may not be fixed. The actual prices paid are subject to negotiation, particularly if a year's supply is purchased at one time.

It may be necessary for the food and beverage controller to limit the kinds of wines offered, or to actually participate in the negotiations for larger quantities. He may limit the dollar amounts of any one order or place ceilings on the inventories that may be carried. Should the buyer be aware of special circumstances that warrant the placing of larger orders, the controller should be called in to approve or disapprove the order.

Other Items—Mixers, Fruits, and Supplies

In addition to supplying the alcoholic beverage, every bar must have on hand all the ingredients necessary to make the various drinks. The items used depend upon the system used by the establishment.

For example, sodas, such as ginger ale and colas, are used to mix with rye or other items. Management has the choice of using bottles, premix, or postmix bulk systems. A postmix is one in which the mixer flavor comes in large syrup containers, and the syrup is then mixed in a carbonator with water to produce a carbonated beverage. Management may decide to purchase bottles or tanks of premixed soda even though the cost is greater, since space limitations or style of service may be of greater importance.

In purchasing premixed bottles the decision must be made whether to use large quart bottles or small splits (7-ounce) and further whether to purchase deposit bottles or throwaways. The decisions may be partly made upon the cost of the ingredients. The style and the volume of service may dictate that only splits (7-ounce) be used. In large volume operations it may be impossible to conveniently use bottles, and a bulk system is therefore mandatory. Besides deciding upon which system, the beverage controller must decide upon what quality is to be purchased. There are marked differences in the qualities of carbonated sodas.

Since the cost of the mixers is usually low as compared to the cost of the alcoholic beverage, operators should attempt to use only high-quality mixers. A comparison may be made with the chef who is unable to make good sauces but still utilizes the finest quality meat—the end product still tastes poor.

Juices may be purchased in #5 cylinder (46-ounce) cans, in #3 cans, or in 5 1/2-ounce individual servings. The larger cans are less expensive but may be more difficult to handle. In some cases juices will spoil within a short period of time.

Bar juices and fruits may be purchased either by the bar department or by the food department and then issued to the bar. Issues may be in bulk or as needed, depending upon the procedure of the establishment, the storage space for beverage inventories, and the type of accounting controls utilized.

Some establishments, particularly smaller ones not selling food items, may deal with a vendor specializing in non-alcoholic bar supplies. Others may buy fruit from a produce wholesaler, prepared products such as cherries and olives from a wholesale grocer, and soft drinks from a local bottling company. Each establishment will base its decisions upon its particular needs, volume of sales, and its internal control methods.

FORMS

A number of departments or individuals are concerned with the purchase of all beverages. It is necessary that they be informed as to what beverages are being purchased, when they are to be delivered, what quantities are in stock or have been ordered, what brands or substitutes are to be used, what size bottles are needed, and the cost of the items.

Not all establishments will require every form listed. The size and volume of the operation dictate the extent to which formalized controls are needed, but the information on the forms must be furnished by some method or combination of controls.

Purchase Requisitions

A purchase requisition is a request forwarded to the purchasing agent that indicates that the supplies of a particular item are not sufficient to handle expected demand. Depending upon the size of an organization it may be initiated by the bar manager, the bartender, the storeroom clerk, or the buyer. All those who may be involved with the ordering or the storage of liquor should receive a copy of the purchase requisition. Thus a copy of the requisition would go to the purchasing agent, bar manager, and storeroom clerk.

In small organizations no written record may even be kept. An oral communication to the person authorized to purchase products may be sufficient. In larger companies a special form may be required. The intent and purpose in all cases are the same, and the information provided needs to be exact. Simply requesting scotch is not sufficient, since the brand name, the quantity desired, and the size of the bottle must be specified. In some liquors the desired proof must be included.

Figure 3-1 illustrates one type of purchase requisition.

FIGURE 3-1 *Purchase Requisition*

BEVERAGE PURCHASE REQUEST

Date _____3/15/76_____   Requested by _Bar Manager's Name_

Bottle Code #	Brand	Size	Quantity C	Quantity B	Last Price	Value
012278	J & B	Qt.	36C		95.00/C	3420.00
012280	Dewars	Qt.	16C		95.00/C	1520.00
013370	Beams – 6 yr.	Qt.	10C		86.00/C	860.00
013371	Beams – 6 yr.	F	2C		74.00/C	148.00
023379	Almaden Chablis	F		6B	4.00/B	24.00
004444	Benedictine	F		2B	10.00/B	20.00

Ordered by ___(P. A. Name)___ Date Ordered __3/17__ Total Value__$ 5992.00__

The Bottle Code Number will usually be the code used by the purveyor. At times, however, two codes must be used, the second being the code used by the establishment to identify its own stock. The name brand must be included. Unit size may vary depending upon how a particular unit is normally ordered and/or priced. Only one unit size should be used if possible. Organizations having a large volume of bottle sales in room, banquet, or table service may find it desirable to use fifths for bottle sales and quarts for bar use. Rather than list by cases and by prices per case, it would be preferable to use the smallest unit normally purchased.

Since most purveyors will furnish any type of liquor by the bottle, prices and units should be listed by the bottles, to avoid confusion and possible misunderstandings between departments or individuals. A simple abbreviation may be used, however, if the establishment purchases in varying units—"B" may be used for bottles and "C" for case lots, or two columns may be used. Initials are preferable, since a clerical error can easily be made by placing the quantity in the wrong column. Both are used in Figure 3-1.

Purchase Orders

Amounts of liquor to be ordered are determined from issues, purchase requisitions, and minimum inventories or reorder points as determined from the inventory sheet. Purchase orders normally are only used in large organizations.

An example of a purchase order is given in Figure 3-2.

Prices may be obtained either from quotation sheets or from official monthly publications. Should a special price be in force, a notation should be made on the purchase order in a discount allowance column or in special instructions placed in the extended column.

Additional information that is sometimes listed on purchase orders includes:

Terms	Requisition Number
Delivery Date	Shipper
Special instructions	Freight Charges

Copies of the purchase order are usually forwarded to:

A. The purveyor (2 copies)

B. The receiving department

C. The accounting department

D. The bar manager

The copy forwarded to the receiving department may have the last two columns, which list the unit and extended prices, blacked out or eliminated from the form.

FIGURE 3-2 *Beverage Purchase Order*

Purchase Authorization: W.W.W. Restaurant
South Street
New York, New York

Registration # _____(License)_____ PO # ___X1000___

Order From: A.B.C.L. Corporation
Lave Way
Valley, New York

Terms: _____ Freight: _____ Del. Date ___12/20/76___

Special Instructions: ___Discount $2.00 per case on Widmer's___

Code #	Item	Size	Quantity	Price	Total
012278	J & B Scotch	Qt.	6B	8.25	49.50
023370	Widmer's Rose Wine	F	2 cs	22.00	44.00
	Discount for Dec. Special				- 4.00

ORDER TOTAL		800.00

Distribution:

Purveyor — 2 white
Bar Mgr. — green
Accting. — yellow
Receiving — pink
Purch. Agt. — blue

Authorized by: ___W.W.___
(PA)

Date: ___12/2/76___

FIGURE 3-3 *System of Routing Purchase Requisitions and Purchase Orders*

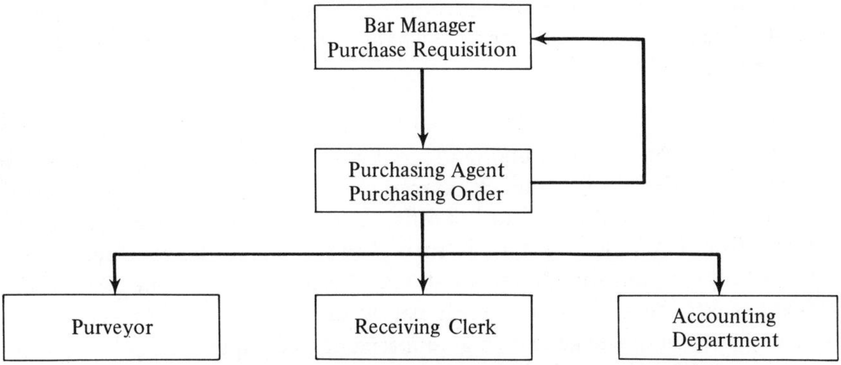

Note that a purchase requisition may also be initiated by the storeroom manager.

The distribution of the purchase order form indicates that this form is normally used in a large establishment in which many individuals are involved with each of the operating departments. (See Figure 3-3.) This distribution is done so that each of the persons involved understands exactly how much merchandise has been ordered, when it is to be delivered, and the other arrangements that may have been made.

The use of the purchase order simplifies the mode of communication and insures a clear understanding by all parties. The purveyor knows exactly what to ship. The receiving clerk can prepare for the arrival of this merchandise. The bar manager is informed that his request for items has been filled and will not be worried that there will be a stock-out (running out of an item). Finally, when the bill must be paid, the accounting office will be aware of any discounts and the exact amount that should be paid by the organization, in case of error by the purveyor. Without a purchase order, the purchasing agent would have to have had some kind of communication with each of these individuals, but more probably the information would not be relayed to the responsible parties and the chance for error or fraud would have been vastly increased.

These possible areas of confusion or fraud are avoided by the use of purchase orders with purveyors. A company insures itself that no unauthorized merchandise has been delivered to the establishment (or elsewhere). It prevents the purveyor from changing prices or quantities without prior notification. It enables the receiving clerk to compare deliveries with actual amounts ordered so that shortages may be immediately noted. It enables the accounting department to double check all methods and controls within the system and insures that no payments will be made to purveyors without authorized purchase orders. It allows the bar manager to be aware of expected delivery dates for merchandise so that he may plan future orders as well as allow for shortages in present stock should merchandise be delayed or omitted in the order. Thus all personnel concerned with the purchase and receipt of merchandise can compare what actually arrives with what should have arrived.

Invoices

Invoices are furnished and made up by the purveyor. Normally, at least three copies of the invoices must be signed by the receiving clerk. One copy is forwarded directly to the accounting office, and the other two are returned to the purveyor. The purveyor may, in turn, forward one of the returned copies directly to the accounting department with the statement for the accounting period (weekly, monthly, or whatever period of time has been agreed upon). It is the function of the accounting department to compare the prices on the monthly quotation sheets with those on the purchase order and invoice to insure that no changes have been made. Total amounts received and total amounts billed must also be compared. (See Figure 3-4.)

The purveyor, the accounting department, and the receiving clerk are the only persons that must have copies of the invoices. *In smaller establish-*

FIGURE 3-4 *Alternate Methods or Routings for Adjustment of Incorrect Invoices*

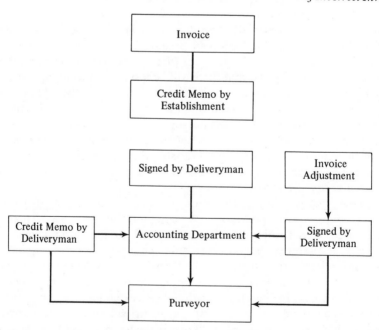

ments where a purchase order is not utilized, the invoice is normally returned to the purchasing agent (bar manager or other person charged with the responsibility of ordering) so that he may sign the invoice, indicating that he was aware of the purchase and approves payment of it.

The receiving clerk must sign all copies of the invoices. Purveyors should be instructed that no invoices will be paid unless they have copies *signed by authorized personnel.* This, in turn, means that should items that were on the original purchase order and/or on the invoice fail to be delivered, a credit memo must be made out by the deliveryman or a short slip should be initiated by the receiving clerk. An immediate notification (by phone) to the purchasing agent should be made at this time by the receiving clerk.

Credit Memos

Credits are also issued by the purveyor for unacceptable items, broken items, or return of bottles, kegs, cases, or tanks. The same procedure that is used for the processing of invoices must be used with credit memos, except that it is also necessary for the deliveryman to sign the credit memo. (See Figure 3-5.) Having the receiving clerk as well as the deliveryman counting returns provides an essential double check. Without this it would be possible for the deliveryman not to give full credit for empties.

A special procedure should be set up so that all empties are physically returned prior to taking delivery. This protects the house from a dishonest

FIGURE 3-5

WINDSOR PURVEYING CO.
CREDIT MEMO

NUMBER_____ INVOICE NO. _____ DATE _____

Quantity and Item: _____

Amount of Credit: _____

Reason: _____

Receiving Clerk: _____ Purveyor: _____

deliveryman who substitutes empties for full cases and then takes them right back out. One simple method of protection against this type of fraud is to have the receiving man weigh in all cases. Shortages, broken bottles, and empty cases may be easily detected by a protective device such as this. A better method is to store empties in a separate area. In actual practice, however, this may be difficult to do. Also, the deliveryman normally is much more efficient if he delivers full cases and picks up empties in one trip. Continued vigilance, spot checking of returns, the counting of empty cases prior to delivery, and verifying the fact that no empty cases are left after deliveries will protect the firm from this type of theft.

Various methods are used by different purveyors to indicate credits when items are shorted, broken in transit, or refused by the establishment. In some cases a note is added to the invoice indicating the shortage or the amount of the credit. In other cases a separate credit memo is issued by the purveyor. In still other cases a pick-up slip signed and issued by the deliveryman is used, as well as a separate notation on the invoice. Credit slips may be lost (intentionally or otherwise). If just a notation is placed on the invoice, it is often overlooked by the accounting department, or it may have been carelessly written so that no one knows exactly what the credit should be. If the purveyor does not have a credit memo system, the deliveryman may sign a form used by the operator. Naturally, copies of the credit memo must accompany the invoice and refer to its number.

It may be necessary for a copy of this credit memo to be forwarded to the purchasing agent immediately.

In some operations merchandise that is returned must pass through a security area to insure that no person is taking merchandise out without proper authorization. It may be necessary to have an extra copy of the credit memo to be left with the security guard. For example, a keg of beer may not have been of high enough quality to be served. The beer was originally in the custody of the inventory clerk and must be transported from the storage area to the delivery truck. The extra copy of the credit memo is turned in at the security desk when the merchandise is returned.

Reasons for credits for beverages
1. Wrong goods shipped—brands, sizes, vintage.
2. Wrong amounts shipped.
3. Broken or damaged merchandise.
4. Not in stock (back ordered).
5. Short on truck.
6. Normally, surplus merchandise (that is, alcoholic beverages) is not returned once it is in stock; overages on sodas, beer, etc., are excluded from this rule, particularly in resort areas in which excess stock at the end of the season may be returned for full credit.

Alcoholic beverages by law normally must be carried over to the next season.

7. Empties.

8. Special credits due to math errors, wrong billing, wrong pricing (initiated by accounting department).

9. Merchandise not of acceptable quality (e.g., flat beer).

Alternatives to Purchase Order and Purchase Requisition

In smaller organizations in which the same person is performing the duties of inventory control clerk, buyer, receiving clerk, and issuing clerk, it may not be advisable to use either the purchase order or the purchase requisition. Since the purchase order is in part made up from a purchase requisition, the reason for the requisition is to have a written record of communication so that all items requested may be ordered. Obviously, if the same person is initiating both forms, there is no need to communicate. Again, if the purchasing agent does the receiving as well as the ordering, the only concern is for the purveyor to have a written record of the exact items that have been ordered and for the buyer to have some form of notation so that he will not double order any items.

In actual practice, a buyer who is involved with the purchase of hundreds of items must keep some record as to which orders have already been placed, which are going to be placed, and often which items have been delayed in transit and must be reordered. For the purveyor or salesman a written record may be required so that there can be no question as to exactly what merchandise was ordered and at what price. Many salesmen, therefore, write up the order given to them by the purchasing agent and return a copy to the buyer for his records. (See Figure 3-6.) This simple procedure is very effective for smaller organizations in which there are a limited number of

FIGURE 3-6 *Alternate and Normal Routing of Invoice*

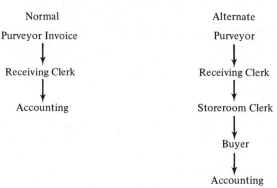

Normal	Alternate
Purveyor Invoice	Purveyor
↓	↓
Receiving Clerk	Receiving Clerk
↓	↓
Accounting	Storeroom Clerk
	↓
	Buyer
	↓
	Accounting

personnel involved with these function areas, that is, purchasing, receiving, storing, and inventory control.

The purchase order was partially designed to prevent the payment of bills for merchandise that either was not or should not have been received by the establishment. This may occur in larger organizations, where the receiving clerk could sign for merchandise without the knowledge of the purchasing agent, particularly since the normal routing of invoices does not require that the signed invoice go back to the purchasing agent for approval.

The purchase order is also used to insure that all merchandise that was ordered is actually received. In the larger organizations, without a purchase order in the hands of the receiving clerk, the clerk would not know if items were shorted or if the wrong items were shipped. In the smaller organization this verification becomes automatic since the buyer would immediately discover the wrong items by comparing them with his copy of the order from the salesman. He would also notice if the wrong item was shipped by visually checking the shipment (this often happens when the wrong code number is punched into a computer).

Finally, the purchase order is used by the accounting department to compare the prices with those on the invoices. If the purchasing agent is assuming the responsibilities of the receiving clerk, then he should be signing the invoices upon delivery. He can compare the prices on the invoice with the ones originally quoted. Note that although in this case he assumes one of the normal duties of the accounting department (verifying prices) the verifying function itself is still performed.

With the elimination of the purchase order, the storeroom clerk or the bar manager may not be informed by written memo of what merchandise is expected and has been ordered. However, normally the lines of communication are not as complex in a smaller organization. Verbal communication may be permissible, particularly in view of the fact that much paperwork can be eliminated and yet an adequate degree of control can be maintained. Should mere verbal communication prove unsatisfactory, the purchase requisition may continue to be used by the bar manager. This written communication now pinpoints the responsibility should there be a stock out. If the bar manager can prove he requested the item by referring back to the requisition, then the onus is upon the purchasing agent. On the other hand, if no request has been forwarded then it is the responsibility of the bar manager.

Due to the way in which the liquor market operates, management is not overly concerned with the need to verify the honesty and integrity of the liquor purchasing agent (if the suggestions for purchasing "well" liquors and wines have been followed). Rather, the system of controls at this stage is primarily designed to insure the smooth flow of goods, to prevent the receipt of payment for unauthorized merchandise, and to prevent merchandise from disappearing once received.

RECEIVING, STORING, AND ISSUING BEVERAGES

Receiving

With the exception of very large organizations, it may not be feasible or economical to employ one person just to do receiving. Yet to ignore this vitally important function would be intolerable. For this reason in some establishments the duties of the receiving clerk are combined with those of the inventory storeroom manager so that one person may be employed to perform both functions. This is particularly true in beverage receiving, as normally only a few deliveries per week are made. In combining the two functions, however, it is important that deliveries are made at scheduled times so that responsible personnel are available to sign for and receive the merchandise. In some cases, temporary custody of the liquor must be assumed by another individual (chef, etc.), but when merchandise is finally delivered to the storeroom, another count of the amount received and delivered to the storeroom should be made.

With few exceptions, very little quality inspection must be performed for the receiving of merchandise for the beverage department. A case of J & B scotch is J & B; there are no quality differences nor other variables. Proof differences and vintages in wines must be carefully examined, however.

Therefore, the items that must be inspected are those in which there are variables in proof or vintage, or there is a possibility that improper handling has caused some form of deterioration. Breakage also may be considered at this time. Beers that are dated or coded must be inspected to insure that fresh beer is received at all times. Frozen items such as juices that are used in the mixing of drinks must be examined to insure that they have not been allowed to thaw while in transit.

For the most part, however, controls are established to insure that the proper amounts, sizes, proofs, vintages, and brands are received and properly transported to the storage areas. It is amazing how rapidly sealed bottles of liquor "evaporate" if not properly secured.

Alcoholic beverages may be ordered either by the case or by the bottle. Normal procedures must allow for the fact that any case that is not sealed must be opened and inspected prior to the signing of the receipt and invoice. Full cases may be weighed to detect hidden breakage (dry breakers). An area in which there may be confusion or possibility of error is in the receiving of wines where a specific vintage has been ordered.

A simple procedure for insuring that they have been inspected is to require your receiving clerk to initial any special items. Thus should they be merely inspected for quantity by the receiving clerk his initial would not be noted, and the accounting control clerk should then spot the omission on the invoice. Should he initial them without inspecting the merchandise he would then be spotted as the "culprit" if the wrong item was received. If the purveyor shipped the wrong merchandise it would of course be noted by the receiving clerk when he inspected the merchandise.

Once the merchandise has been received it must never be left unattended but must be immediately placed in a high-security area (locked storeroom). In small operations the receiving clerk may also be responsible for the storeroom (as in the case of those operations where the only person authorized to receive merchandise is the bar manager or the beverage inventory control clerk). In other operations the merchandise must be turned over to a storeroom man.

Most systems fail to incorporate a control device when the merchandise is transferred from the receiving clerk to the storeroom. This occurs in larger operations where merchandise must be transported for some distance. Often "something is lost in the transportation." Without a control at this point the inventory clerk may receive fewer goods than actually were received and billed to the house. The simplest control is merely to have an extra copy of the invoice and receiving slip and to route these forms through the inventory control clerk. These are then signed by the inventory clerk, so that the responsibility for the merchandise now rests with him. In some establishments a copy of the receiving sheet (see Receiving, Storage, and Inventory Control of Foods, Chapter 9) may be used, and this form is initialed by the storeroom clerk.

Blind receiving is sometimes used (either for beverages or foods) by an establishment to force the receiving clerk to check all merchandise. Merchandise from the vendor is shipped with an invoice but the amounts shipped are omitted. Neither the receiving clerk nor the deliveryman is aware of the quantities (weights or numbers of cases, bottles, etc.). Each item must be verified and checked upon receipt. In some cases a copy of the purchase order (again with quantities omitted) may be left with the receiving clerk to insure that all items that were ordered are delivered.

The advantage of blind receiving is that it forces the receiving clerk to verify all amounts received. The disadvantage is that should an error have occurred (overage or shortage) the merchandise will still be accepted. This is particularly important if less than the ordered amount was delivered. A shortage or stock out may occur that may prove to be disastrous. Note that with blind receiving a rerouting of invoices should be made. Invoices should first be sent to the purchasing agent so that he can verify amounts delivered with amounts ordered.

Storage

The primary responsibilities of the storeroom manager are to insure against theft or unauthorized issuing of merchandise, to properly rotate stocks, and to inform the purchasing agent of amounts on hand so that adequate stocks may be maintained. In some establishments it is also the duty of the storeroom clerk to maintain various records in order to establish dollar amounts on hand or to determine amounts consumed daily. Several types of control systems and methods of issuing may be used. All, however, are designed to provide the information and controls needed by management.

Methods of Inventory Control

Perpetual Inventory. The most common method for controlling and recording beverage inventories is the perpetual inventory system. In this system a constant count is kept of all merchandise in stock. Any new merchandise is added to the count. Issues are subtracted from the total. Every brand, every size, and every type of item must be recorded, and separate records kept for each item. Generally, a master sheet (Figure 3-7) or record is maintained by the inventory clerk and, in addition, bin cards (Figure 3-8) may be used.

Some operations keep no records. Whenever liquor is needed, the manager (usually the owner himself) merely goes to the storeroom and takes whatever merchandise is needed. When orders are to be placed, the salesman and the owner may enter the storeroom and visually examine stocks to determine what is needed. Orders are placed based on estimates of expected consumption along with stock on hand.

Bin Cards—Master Record. Bin cards are normally placed where the merchandise is stored. The master record is kept in the inventory clerk's office or in the accounting department. At any given moment the amounts on the bin card, the master record, and the actual physical count of merchandise should be equal. The records must be kept up to date at all times. Any discrepancies (which are normally noted when physical counts are taken) naturally must be investigated, but with a tightly controlled system and insistence by management that records be kept current, few errors should occur. Figure 3-9 shows a typical bin card, January through June. The other side of the card (July through December) would be similar, with a section for totals included.

Reordering. In conjunction with perpetual inventories, minimum stock reorder points should be established. (See Figure 3-10.) These minimum amounts to be kept on hand must allow for amounts used, delivery dates, and waiting times. For example, an establishment may determine that during any week the most scotch it has ever used is three cases. Delivery of this product normally takes two weeks, thus it becomes obvious that this product must be ordered whenever there are only six cases on hand. A safety factor may also be used to allow for the fact that unusual business may warrant an extra case (or a percentage of normal consumption established by management) being kept on hand. Thus the reorder point may be seven cases. Note that by the

FIGURE 3-7

PERPETUAL INVENTORY MASTER RECORD

Reorder at _____

Brand _____

Stock # _____ Size _____

Date	In	Issued To	Amount Issued	Balance	By

FIGURE 3-8

BIN CARD

Brand _____   Size _____

Reorder Point _____   Stock # _____

Date	In	Out	Balance On Hand	By

time the shipment arrives, the amount left should only be about one case. If less than six cases were ordered there would not be enough merchandise to carry over till the next delivery date.

Minimum reorder amounts are equal to the maximum stock used during delivery period, less anything over that amount still in stock, plus the extra case or percentage used as a safety factor.

Minimum Amount to Order = cases used during delivery time + safety factor — excess in stock over maximum usage.

Example

Amount to order = $6 + 1 - 4 = 3$

If 10 cases were on hand when it came time to order, the amount of the order would be the cases needed for maximum usage (6), reduced by the inventory above the maximum usage (4). Then 1 case would be added to the order as a safety factor. This means that 3 cases would be ordered. Allowing two weeks for delivery, normal maximum use would account for six cases by the time the order arrived. Thus, four cases would remain, three cases would

FIGURE 3-9

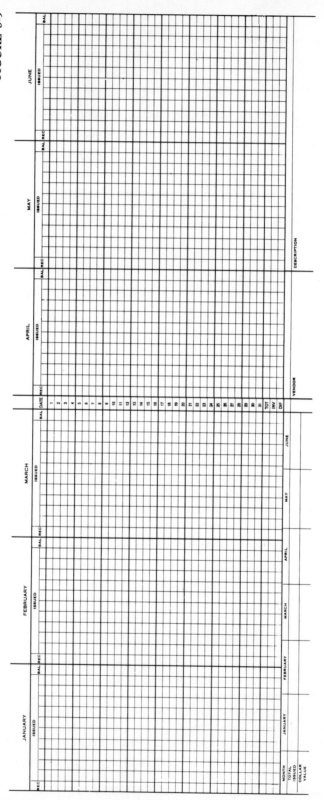

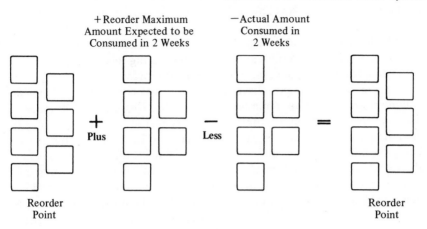

FIGURE 3-10 *Minimum Stock System*

+ Reorder Maximum
Amount Expected to be
Consumed in 2 Weeks

− Actual Amount
Consumed in
2 Weeks

Plus

Less

=

Reorder
Point

Reorder
Point

FIGURE 3-11 *Minimum-Maximum Stock System*

+ Maximum for 2–
Week Delivery

− Actual Amount
Consumed in 2 Weeks

Plus

Less

=

Reorder
Point
7 Cases

Order
24

25 Cases

have arrived, and stock would now be down to seven cases. The next order would be for six cases less any inventory over maximum usage (6) on hand, plus a safety factor.

Sometimes it is advantageous to order more, due to special sales or discounts that a purveyor may give. Future reordering then would be delayed until your stock once again reached the minimum point.

Some establishments have a slightly different system, in which minimum and maximum amounts are used. (See Figure 3-11.) Whenever a stock reaches a minimum point an order is placed. Instead of using the minimum base, however, a maximum amount to be kept on hand is used. Using the same amounts as above, an establishment may say that whenever their stock of XXX Scotch reaches seven (maximum consumption plus safety factor) an order is placed. The maximum amount desired to be on hand is 25 cases. In this case, the amount to order would be the maximum amount less any inventory over the maximum (6) consumed during the delivery period.

Master records and bin cards may differ slightly, since only the count is needed on the bin card, whereas the dollar amounts are normally also recorded on the master record. An "issued to" column may be useful, so a simple tally may be made directly from the master record that will give the exact amounts of each brand issued to different bars in the same establishment. This additional information may be used for the purpose of determining par stocks, variances in consumption at private parties, or simply as a preference indication for a particular bar or specialty room in a large establishment. Its use is somewhat limited, however, and the column may be eliminated. Note that costs (issues) for each bar are determined from a separate requisition slip (one for each bar). (See Figure 3-12.) The preference information could be determined from these requisitions but would involve more clerical work.

Inventory clerks may be responsible for determining dollar amounts of merchandise on hand, as well as physical amounts. (In some establishments this function is left to the accounting department.) A current price list of all beverages must be kept by the inventory clerk. He must also keep track of the dollar amounts of any additions to or subtractions from the inventory. Therefore, one copy of an extended invoice should be given to the inventory clerk so that he may keep his records current.

Other information necessary for accurate control would be:

Bottle size	Stock Number	Issued To
Brand	Date In and Date Out	Initialed In and Out
Reorder Points		

A number of variations of these forms may be designed, depending upon the needs of the establishment. In some operations one book is used. Each type of liquor has perhaps one page, with a number of columns, so that

FIGURE 3-12

		Beverage Requisition		

Requisition # _____ Department _____ Date _____

Quantity	Size	Brand or Item	$ Unit Value	Total

Authorized by: _____

a continual record may be maintained for periods up to one year. No matter which forms are used, the reason for the bin card and the master record remains the same—to determine the exact amounts of merchandise that should be on hand.

In smaller operations, it is just as important to maintain formalized records. Although normally bin cards are not maintained, a master record may be kept by the storeroom manager (bar manager) or, preferably, by the accounting office. To simplify the ordering, each liquor should be kept in one area and reorder points posted so that the bar manager can quickly determine by visual inspection those items that need to be ordered. Since a storeroom clerk is normally not available, record-keeping becomes the task of the bar manager, the bookkeeper, or even the manager. The system must be designed for the particular structure of the company.

Issues. No merchandise should be taken out of the liquor storeroom without a proper requisition signed by an authorized person. Three copies of this form are needed, one for the accounting office, one for the storeroom, and one for the originating department. The information required on the issue slip is the brand, size, amount requested, authorized signature, department requesting the item, and the date. In some cases, the dollar amount may be noted to facilitate daily costing procedures, and code numbers may also be used.

Breakdowns in the system usually occur during periods of stress when merchandise is needed by one department immediately and established procedures are ignored due to the urgency of the situation. It is the responsibility of the inventory clerk, and ultimately the responsibility of the food and beverage controller, to insure that established procedures are followed at all times. A summary of daily issues may be performed by the storeroom manager or by the accounting department to determine total daily issues. (See Figure 3-13.)

Merchandise for any bar, or for the kitchen, must come from storeroom issues. Normally one department should not be permitted to borrow from another. If exchanges are permitted, a special issue or exchange form should be used.

ALTERNATIVE METHODS FOR RECEIVING, STORAGE, INVENTORY CONTROL, AND ISSUING

The objective in instituting controls in any area is to firmly fix the responsibility for merchandise upon one individual. If the function areas for personnel within an organization change, then the methods of control must be altered to allow for these changes and to reestablish new spheres of control. To fully understand the function areas, a list of the normal duties for each area is shown below:

Receiving 1. Inspects merchandise for quantity and quality.
2. Accepts and transfers ownership of merchandise from purveyor to establishment.
3. Transports and distributes merchandise to appropriate area of use or storage.

Storage 1. Accepts responsibility for merchandise.
2. Maintains records of stock on hand.
3. Stores and rotates stock; secures stock from unauthorized personnel.
4. Transports stock to authorized individual or department.
5. Maintains records of merchandise issued to departments.

When receiving and storage are under the jurisdiction of separate personnel, Step 1 under storage must be performed and some record of this

FIGURE 3-13 *Summary of Daily Beverage Issues*

FILLED BY _____ DATE: _____ REQ. NO. _____

BRAND	SIZE	ORDER BAR ROOM SHOW	ORDER BAR EMB. ROOM	ORDER BAR STEAK	ORDER BAR STR. LINER	ORDER BAR LOUNGE	ORDER BAR CAFE	TOTAL
BIN. NO.								
BAR BOURBON	QTS							
ANCIENT AGE	QTS							
JIM BEAM	QTS							
CANADIAN CLUB	QTS							
JACK DANIELS	QTS							
EARLY TIMES	QTS							
I.W. HARPER	QTS							
OLD BUSHMILLS	5TH							
OLD CHARTER	QTS							
OLD FITZGERALD	QTS							
OLD FORESTER 86	QTS							
OLD GRANDAD 100	QTS							
OLD OVERHOLT	QTS							
OLD TAYLOR 100	QTS							
SEAGRAMS SEVEN CROWN	QTS							
SEAGRAMS V.O.	QTS							
SEAGRAMS CROWN ROYAL	5TH							
WALKERS DE LUXE	QTS							
BAR SCOTCH	QTS							
BALLANTINES	QTS							
BLACK & WHITE	QTS							
CHIVAS REGAL	5TH							
CUTTY SARK	QTS							
DEWARE'S WHITE LABEL	QTS							
GRANTS 8 YR OLD	QTS							
HAIG & HAIG PINCH	5TH							
J.&B.	QTS							
J.W. BLACK	QTS							
J.W. RED	QTS							
100 PIPERS	QTS							
TEACHERS	QTS							
BAR VODKA	QTS							
SMIRNOFF VODKA	QTS							
CACAO DARK	QTS							
CACAO WHITE	QTS							
GREEN MENTHE	QTS							
WHITE MENTHE	QTS							
COMPARI	5TH							
CHARTREUSE GREEN	5TH							
CHARTREUSE YELLOW	5TH							
CHERRY HERRING	5TH							
COINTREAU	5TH							
DRAMBUIE	5TH							
GALLIANO	5TH							
GRAND MARNIER	5TH							
KAHLUA	5TH							
KIJAFA	5TH							
PERNOD	5TH							
SOUTHERN COMFORT	5TH							

transfer of ownership (responsibility) must be maintained. For example, the receiving clerk may sign for 200 bottles of liquor. He will have checked the shipment to insure that 200 bottles came in, but in transporting the merchandise to the storeroom, two bottles may disappear. Unless the storeroom clerk again verifies the quantity, these two bottles will be accepted on the books as having arrived when in fact they never entered the storeroom. (See Figure 3-14.) It is not necessary for new forms to be made out (although often a receiving sheet is used) but a copy of the invoice should be signed by the storeroom clerk as he accepts responsibility for the goods. In this case, much time and effort may be wasted since both the storeroom clerk and the receiving clerk must physically count all the merchandise.

An alternate plan would be for the storeroom clerk to receive all merchandise, bypassing the receiving clerk. (See Figure 3-15.) With this plan the need to double count merchandise is eliminated. One difficulty may be that the storeroom clerk may not be able to leave the storeroom if he has to be constantly present to issue merchandise (particularly if he is also responsible for food). This may be solved by requiring deliveries to be made at certain hours or even by permitting the liquor purveyors to make deliveries directly to the storeroom.

In very small organizations, a storeroom clerk may not even be used or employed. Instead, the bar manager is responsible for the merchandise up until the time that it is issued to each bartender or to various bars. (See Figure 3-16.) It is mandatory in all cases that the ultimate user (the individual bartender) sign for the merchandise and thus acknowledge responsibility.

FIGURE 3-14 *Routing of Merchandise with Control Forms*

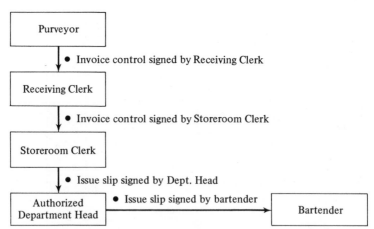

FIGURE 3-15 *Alternate Routing of Merchandise with Controls (1)*

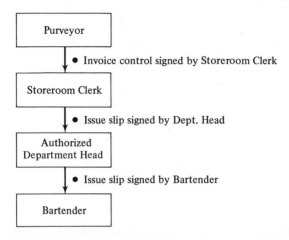

FIGURE 3-16 *Alternate Routing of Merchandise with Controls (2)*

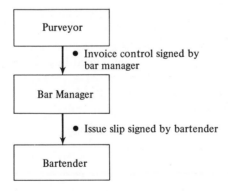

With all systems, management must be able to determine the amount of goods that should be on hand at any time. This is readily accomplished, no matter which system is used, by the formula:

Beginning Inventory + Purchases (Invoices) — Issues = Goods on Hand

In actual practice, the figures are often obtained and verified by referring to a master record maintained by the storeroom clerk or to the bin cards, which should have been posted daily. A physical count of the merchandise is thus made. *This is incorrect. A separate master record should be maintained by the accounting office for auditing purposes.* The master record or the bin cards that are maintained within the storeroom should only be used for ordering purposes. (For further discussion of this, see Case 2, page 56.)

PHYSICAL FACILITIES

Naturally, the volume of an operation and the types of merchandise carried will dictate how much space is allocated for storage. (See Figure 3-17.) For most operations some refrigeration for beer storage is required, a cool room for the storage of wines (approximately 50°-55°F.), and a clean, well-lit, and ventilated storeroom for distilled beverages (plus ample working areas). All areas must be under tight security with authorized entry (keys) issued to

1.   Inventory Control Clerk
2.   Food and Beverage Controller—access to emergency key only
3.   Beverage Manager—access to emergency key only. (In some operations the term bar manager is used, and he may or may not have access to the storeroom.)

Emergency keys may be kept in the manager's office, or perhaps at the front desk. They should be placed in a sealed envelope. When an emergency key is issued to an authorized individual, the individual would be permitted to enter the secured area only if accompanied by another person, usually an assistant manager or someone with equal authority. All merchandise obtained would be signed for by both individuals, as well as by the person receiving the merchandise (usually the bartender). A copy of this requisition

FIGURE 3-17 *Storeroom Layout*

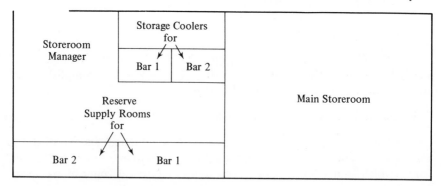

should be left in the storeroom so that the storeroom manager may immediately adjust his records.

Even with operations that maintain bars that are open for more than one shift (in Nevada, for example, it is legal to sell liquor 24 hours a day), the liquor storeroom need not stay open for these long periods of time. The primary objective of any type of control system is to fix the responsibility for goods or merchandise on one individual. Should more than one person have access to the liquor much of the effectiveness of a system will be negated. It may become necessary to have several persons maintaining the storeroom, due to the amount of work and volume of sales. Then, security measures should be installed so that no merchandise can be removed without the permission of the one individual who is held accountable for the entire storeroom. In order to accomplish this, the storeroom must be laid out in such a manner that there is only one exit door. If fire regulations require an emergency exit, it can be constructed in such a manner that an alarm will sound if it is used at any time. Issuing times can be firmly regulated so that the storeroom manager can carefully control all merchandise leaving the storeroom.

If sufficient supplies cannot be stored at the various bars, a reserve supply may be set up either in a separate area or perhaps on portable locked carts that can be easily transported whenever needed. The main storeroom, however, would be locked after regular hours.

Access to the reserve storeroom would be limited to one or two persons. Separate keys would be required for each bar's reserve supply. The reserve supply for each bar could even be set up on a par basis (this will be discussed more fully in a later chapter) for each bar.

Coolers for wine and beer may be combined due to the cost of installing separate ones for each bar. Preferably, however, either separate coolers should be used or a partition with separate locks for each bar could be installed in the cooler. Normally the items requiring refrigeration would be champagne, white wines, and beer. It may be feasible to separate only the higher value items (champagne and some white wine) and allow joint access to the beer. Ideally, sufficient storage space should be available at the individual bars so that a restocking problem does not occur, and thus separate coolers are not required. The actual physical construction and facilities of each operation, coupled with the volume of business and operating hours, will govern the type of controls that must be installed. Normally bar business is at its lowest ebb early in the morning hours (7 A.M. to 11 A.M.). Main issues could be made at this time, and a secondary daily issue may be made later in the day just prior to the closing of the storeroom. With two issues each day, even poorly laid out plant facilities can be adapted to enforce the tight security system suggested. Deliveries can be arranged from about 10 A.M. to 3 P.M. Thus the receiving and issuing can be done by one individual or one shift.

BOTTLE STAMPING

Bottle stamps may be used as a device to prevent persons from selling merchandise other than that ordered by the establishment. Every bottle issued out of the storeroom is stamped with a special seal. By insuring that every bottle has a seal on it, no merchandise may then be used in the establishment that has not been officially purchased.

A ploy perpetrated by dishonest bartenders is to bring in their own bottle, sell their own merchandise, and pocket the money. Although the use of a bottle seal, or stamp, will not eliminate this practice, it does make it cumbersome for the dishonest bartender, since he is forced to pour his own liquor into a stamped bottle (preferably with a number on it) and also dispose of his own bottle that he has emptied.

The use of the seal will also help to prevent unauthorized unopened bottles from being sold (as in room service), making it much more difficult for the dishonest bartender to use and transfer his own merchandise. A spot bottle count (see Chapter 4) of the par stock at irregular times will also help to prevent these dishonest practices, even when bottle stamps are not used.

A variation of the bottle stamp method is to have gummed labels that are not reusable and that cannot be removed from the bottles. Additional security may be achieved by numbering each label and by dating them at time of issue. (See Figure 3-18.) Bottle checks will then quickly expose bottles that are being reused or that have apparently been around for extended periods of time. If fraud is suspected, a quick comparison of the number with the stub (or duplicate) of the bottle label will reveal if the seal is on the wrong bottle. Some automated systems incorporate a bottle seal into the inventory control portion of the systems.

FIGURE 3-18 *Bottle Label*

DATE _____

BRAND _____

#100 _____

SIGNATURE _____

A modification of this form would enable it to be combined with the master record sheet. This system would be similar to the payroll systems used in some small establishments, in which the weekly payroll, the employee's individual payroll card, and an information slip are all filled out at the same time. In the beverage system, the master record compares to the employees payroll card, the daily issue sheet is comparable to the weekly payroll card, and the bottle labels can be compared to the employee's information sheet.

The Master Record Card for each brand is inserted under the form shown (Figure 3-19) and all the information recorded at the same time.

FIGURE 3-19

MASTER RECORD–ISSUES–BOTTLE LABEL SYSTEM

#	Date	Brand	Amount	Price	Total	Label Date	Label Brand	Label Number	Signature
101	4/7	J & B	2	6.00	12.00	4/7	J & B	101	
102		"			—	4/7	J & B	102	
103	4/7	C C	1	6.00	6.00	4/7	C & C	103	
104	4/7	V.O.	1	6.00	6.00	4/7	V.O.	104	
105	4/8	Dewars	4	6.00	24.00	4/8	Dewars	105	
106		"			—	4/8	Dewars	106	
107		"			—	4/8	Dewars	107	
108		"			—	4/8	Dewars	108	

CASE STUDIES

Case 1. The ——— Hotel is an exceptionally large organization doing approximately $100,000 per month in liquor sales. A full-time liquor storeroom clerk is employed. The clerk is responsible for the receipt of merchandise, the storeroom, and the issuing of merchandise. At the end of each month the storeroom clerk performs a physical count of the number of bottles or cases of each item. The results of this count are sent to the accounting department, which compares it to the master record balance that it maintains. They find that the liquor cost is normal, the amount on hand balances out, and on pricing out the inventory, no shortage is noted. After one year an audit is performed and again no shortages are noted. Six months later the storeroom clerk resigns, a physical count is taken, and over $2,500 in merchandise is missing.

Management during the intervening six months had become complacent and neglected to perform the usual month-end inventory. The clerk after several months realized that there was no one auditing the actual physical inventory and took advantage of this lapse in the control system.

Case 2. The ——— Inn is also large, with approximately the same organizational structure and with the same volume of business. At the end of each month a physical count of merchandise is performed by the accounting department. The tally is compared with the records maintained by the storeroom clerk on both bin cards and a master record. Daily issue slips are kept and recorded on the bin cards and master record. Liquor cost is 34%, which is accepted by management as a normal operating cost. This figure is obtained by the accountant by computing the total issues of each liquor from the master record.

The storeroom clerk is later discovered to have been systematically stealing over $1,000.00 per month from the organization. This was accomplished by merely increasing the amount of issues recorded on the master record and bin cards. The accounting department did not maintain a record of issues. The monthly audit never referred directly back to the issue slips but instead utilized the tally entered by the storeroom clerk, as shown in Figure 3-20.

In actuality, the issue slip for 12/3 only called for 9 bottles. The bar was charged for the extra bottle. Since management was unsure as to the exact liquor cost that should be obtained, the difference went unnoticed—but 1% of $100,000 is $1000 a month. By using only the figures furnished by the storeroom clerk, no real audit was ever performed, although physical counts were actually taken by the accounting department.

Case 3. In Hotel ——— there are several persons working in the liquor storeroom. Merchandise is received by the receiving clerk. One of the workers from the storeroom is then summoned to transport the merchandise to the storeroom. When merchandise is issued to the various bars, again a storeroom worker is used to take the merchandise to each individual bar, where the person in charge of the shift signs for the goods.

An audit at the end of the year indicates a shortage in the inventory of over $10,000. Management is unable to pinpoint responsibility for the lost merchandise, as no actual count of the goods was made by the storeroom manager when the items were brought to the

FIGURE 3-20

Master Record:							
Qts. ____(J & B SCOTCH)____					Reorder at 12 cases		

Date	In	Out	Bal.		Cs. Price	Btl.	Total Value
			Cases	Btl.			
12/2	20 cs.	—	20		66.00	5.50	1320.00
12/3		10B	19	2			1265.00

storeroom. Several persons had access to the merchandise, and although the bar manager signed for the merchandise when it was transported from the storeroom, no record was maintained of the exact amounts received by each bartender.

Case 4. The bar manager for ——— Country Club was responsible for the receiving, storing, and issuing of merchandise, as well as for cash receipts. In an examination of the storeroom by the food and beverage controller, some invoices marked COD were found among the manager's papers. Beverage costs were normal, yet sales were low in proportion to the volume of business in the other departments. It was found that the beverage manager was pocketing a fairly substantial amount of the cash receipts. This loss had not been noted, since the bar manager was in effect selling his own merchandise and the beverage cost percentage was normal.

Chapter 3

I. *Class Exercise*

For each of the above cases, suggest a control system to remedy the situation.

II. *Study Questions:*

   1. Why are bid sheets not used in purchasing alcoholic beverages?
   2. What types of controls should be used for purchasing beverages?
   3. What are the primary functions of the liquor purchasing agent?
   4. Discuss the various laws governing the purchasing of liquor from vendors.
   5. List and discuss the advantages and disadvantages of serving malt beverages in bottles.
   6. List the advantages and disadvantages of serving malt beverages in kegs.
   7. Explain the advantages and disadvantages of a house policy that
      a. limits wine selection to 3 or 4 kinds.
      b. offers an extensive selection of wines.
   8. Make up a purchase requisition form also to be used for the purchasing of liquors, including all necessary information on the form.
   9. Compare the forms required to purchase liquor in a large hotel with those needed for a small neighborhood tavern.
   10. Discuss the various methods used to account for the return or shortage of merchandise.
   11. List the possible reasons for issuing credit memos. In each instance point out the person or department who initiates the credit memo.
   12. What is the advantage of having the storeroom clerk also perform the receiving function?
   13. List the functions of the storeroom clerk.
   14. Discuss the purposes of bin cards and master records. Why must a master record be maintained by the accounting department?
   15. Discuss the various purposes of issuing slips and issuing controls and the information provided by them.
   16. Make a list of all the forms and controls that could be utilized for a large bar operation.

4

Beverage Service

Several types of control systems may be used to determine dispensing costs, record sales, and insure that all merchandise has been accounted for. Systems may be used independently or may be combined, depending upon the needs of the establishment.

Basically, the systems may be outlined as follows:

1. Automated systems—merchandise is automatically counted when sold.
2. Ounce or drink control.
3. Par stocks—bottle control.

AUTOMATED SYSTEMS

Automated systems have mechanical or electronic control devices placed on the bottles themselves. Each time a drink is poured, the system automatically counts what has been consumed. Equally as important is the fact that automated systems are designed to pour exact measured amounts, usually within 1/8 of an ounce. The exact amount consumed is thus readily determined. This type of system has several advantages: the customer always gets the same drink, there is no waste from spillage, personnel cannot pour free drinks, and underpouring or overpouring can be reduced or eliminated.

At first, simple systems used a locked pourer that was attached to each bottle. With further advancements, the systems now allow for separate pumps for each liquor, pressurized tanks, the recording of the sale on a guest check, the pouring of several liquors from one spout, and machines that will actually mix the drinks and make cocktails. (See Figure 4-1, a-h.)

In several systems the bartender does not handle bottles of liquor at all—the basic filling of the units is conducted by the storeroom keeper. Under this method, no transfer or record of transfer of control is required

FIGURE 4-1

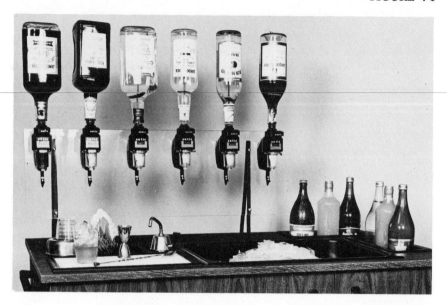

Portable Bar, Gravity Feed with Automatic Counters
Reproduced by permission of Radial/Autic Sales, Evergreen, Colorado

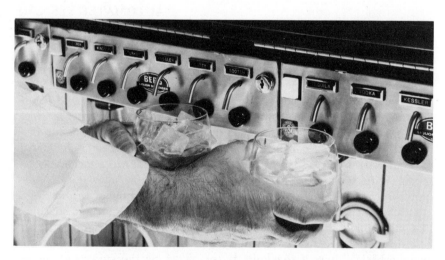

Electronic Bar with Multiple Dispenser and Optional Tie-in to Cash Register
Reproduced by permission of Berg Company, Madison, Wisconsin

FIGURE 4-1 (*continued*)

Electronic Bar with Single Dispenser and Tie-in to Cash Register
Reproduced by permission of NCR, Dayton, Ohio

Beermatic II Solid State Dispenser, A Piston Type Beer Pouring System
Reproduced by permission of Auto Bar Systems Corporation, Red Bank, New Jersey

FIGURE 4-1 (*continued*)

THE GUN DISPENSER

Provides you the dispensing capabilities of the under bar plus the mobility and speed of a gun — every product and portion control at your fingertips.

- Unique non-drip design incorporated in polished aluminum gun

- Six products with same selective portion control as in the under-bar dispenser

- Rugged construction

- Solid State electronic P.C. switch pak provides "plug-in" servicing ease

- Integral seal construction protects gun from moisture

- Gold plated contacts replace delicate micro-switches

- Illuminated push buttons

- Extremely flexible hose gives full six foot reach

If you prefer the hand type dispenser, our gun dispenser is sure to suit your needs

Pushbutton Hose Dispenser
Reproduced by permission of Diverse Ventures Corp., Phoenix, Arizona

Remote Inventory System—
Serves Several Bars from Central Location
Reproduced by permission of Diverse Ventures Corp., Phoenix, Arizona

FIGURE 4-1 (*continued*)

NUMBER OF DRINKS PER BOTTLE COMPARISON CHART

	SIZE OF DRINKS (OUNCES)	⅝	⅔	¾	⅞	1	1⅛	1¼	1⅓	1½	1⅔	1¾
FIFTHS	NUMBER OF DRINKS BERG DELIVERS	40.9	38.4	34.1	29.2	25.6	22.7	20.4	19.2	17	15.3	14.6
	NUMBER OF DRINKS OWNERS AVERAGE	33 to 35	30 to 32	27 to 29	23 to 25	20 to 22	18 to 19	16 to 17	14 to 15	13 to 14	11 to 12	10 to 11
QUARTS	NUMBER OF DRINKS BERG DELIVERS	51.1	48.0	42.66	36.5	32	28.4	25.6	24	21.33	19.2	18.3
	NUMBER OF DRINKS OWNERS AVERAGE	42 to 45	40 to 42	35 to 37	29 to 31	25 to 27	22 to 25	20 to 22	19 to 21	16 to 18	14 to 16	13 to 15

BERG LIQUOR DISPENSERS CAN BE ADJUSTED TO SERVE ANY FRACTION OF AN OUNCE

BERG'S MECHANICAL SIMPLICITY MEANS- ● FEWER SERVICE CALLS ● LOWER MAINTENANCE COSTS

- No positive displacement pumps for each brand.
- No factory man needed to adjust portions.
- No pressure on bottles—no explosions.
- No gasses to buy for operating equipment.
- No shutdown to change bottles.
- No valves to open or close.
- No critical limits on distance, or location of liquor inventory room.
- No screens, filters or wells to clean.

STANDARD EQUIPMENT INCLUDES-

- ● Dual portions on each brand.
- ● Lock in or out of dual portions.
- ● Dual counters for each brand.
- ● Cash register plug in.
- ● Lighted brand names.

Drinks-per-Bottle Comparison Chart
Reproduced by permission of Berg Company, Madison, Wisconsin

FIGURE 4-1 (*continued*)

NCR Electra–Bar controls quality, inventory, money

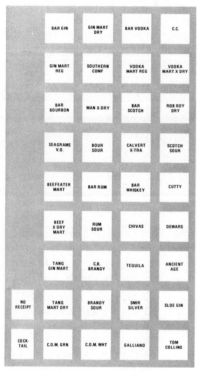

The NCR Electra-Bar provides management with a complete bar control system:

- Electronically controls amount of liquor(s) served as straight shots or mixed drinks and charges the inventory for liquor dispensed to the nearest 1/8th ounce.
- Controls amount of money charged for these drinks, through automatic selection of the proper preset amount.
- Automatically dispenses a drink of uniform quality.
- Eliminates over-pouring and spillage.
- Dispenses drinks at a faster rate than hand-pouring.

Automatic Drink Keys

Thirty-six drink keys (programmable to each user's needs) automatically dispense highball and cocktail portions and prime ingredients for over 600 drink combinations.

An Auxiliary Cocktail Key, used in conjunction with the 36 drink keys, expands the capability of the Electra-Bar. Depression of this Cocktail Key permits a complete change of portions and prices for the cocktail hour or entertainment.

Two–Column Guest Check

You and your customers will appreciate the accuracy and legibility of two-column guest check printing provided by the NCR Electra-Bar. When your system requires a guest check, Electra-Bar prints the items in the left column and the totals in the right. Creates customer confidence when you present a guest check which is easy to read and understand. Permanent, unchangeable, machine-printed figures simplify auditing procedures.

Electronic Bar with Sample Automatic Drink Keys and Guest Check and Cash Register Tie-in
Reproduced by permission of NCR, Dayton, Ohio

from the storeroom to the bar, since at no time is the control of the liquor under the supervision of the bartender. The bartender does not have access to the liquor unless he punches a button, which records the consumption and dispenses the liquor.

The bartender thus only becomes accountable for the cash for the number of sales that are recorded on the automatic counters, which are an integral part of the system. Other merchandise is vended in a normal fashion since it is not practical to have every brand of liquor incorporated into the system. Separate controls must be established for other merchandise, and either of the other types of control systems may be used. With almost all automated systems about 85% of the liquor consumed can feasily be incorporated into the system.

The storeroom clerk or manager is responsible for all merchandise in the storeroom. Thus any sales recorded by the automatic counters would be treated in the same manner as issues. The other merchandise not incorporated into the system must be handled by issue slips. In order to determine liquor costs, or the amount that should be in the storeroom, three records must be maintained: the master record of the issue slips or requisitions, the amount of merchandise sold as indicated on the automatic counters, and finally the amount of merchandise still remaining in the system and in the storeroom.

Computation then becomes:

$$
\begin{array}{l}
\text{Opening Inventory} \\
+ \text{Purchases} \\
\hline
\text{Goods Available For Sale} \\
- \text{Issues (Master Record)} \\
- \text{Sales Indicated by Automatic Counters} \\
\hline
\text{Inventory Remaining}
\end{array}
$$

This is compared with a physical count of full bottles plus merchandise in the system. The two figures should be the same. The cost of goods sold is the issues plus the tally of the amounts on the counters. (The effect of par stocks will be discussed later in this chapter.)

Newer automated machines also compute the number of drinks sold, amount of cash received, amounts of liquor in the system, plus other accounting data. This greatly simplifies the task of the beverage controller.

Certain disadvantages are apparent when completely automated systems are used. In some types of operations, however, they are amazingly effective, when used with additional controls. It is impossible to change the recipe in some machines. The guest who wishes an extra extra dry martini or an extra sweet pink lady may not be able to get the drink that is desired. A major goal of operations is to please the guests' taste; this may be impossible with some automated systems. If locked pourers are used, a sufficient number must be available, and they are expensive. The initial investment for adequate control may be prohibitive. Atmosphere and personal service are difficult to create when the customer is faced with the knowledge that his drinks are from an "assembly line." Some automated machines have proved to be too slow (in volume operations) and are unable to keep up with the orders.

Additional problems of acceptance by employees may become apparent, particularly if machines are installed in already operating units. Resistance to these units by individual bartenders as well as unions has slowed down widespread adoption of automated units. This resistance includes the sabotaging of units to discourage the use of the system. The need for reeducation of employees in the use of the new systems is mandatory prior to installation. The need for more efficient control systems, however, has compelled many operators to install these types of units. The companies marketing these systems and operators who have installed them are almost unanimous in their praise as to the effect of the systems in reducing liquor cost percentages. Part of the savings are said to be attributable to the reduction in the amount of theft. The fact that machines are much more accurate in pouring exact amounts of liquor is another major contributing factor. The advantages of the system far outweigh the disadvantages, as the following summary shows:

1. Systems provide measured pouring, which eliminates problems of underpouring, spillage, and overpouring.

2. Customers are assured of receiving the amount they pay for and get a consistant drink.

3. Many systems are designed to utilize half-gallon bottles, which saves the operator an additional $3.00 to $5.00 per case (averaging about 7%).

4. Merchandise cannot be dispensed without automatically being counted.

5. Most, though not all, systems incorporate accounting and record-keeping machinery, so that these tasks are greatly simplified.

6. In some cases the systems are faster than manual-operated ones, particularly in the making of mixed drinks.

Automated systems are being adapted to establishments other than simple bar service. One new system is designed specifically for airline service. Under the system being used by many airlines, each drink is served in an individual bottle, which greatly increases the cost per drink and also requires special handling. With the new system, a unit is loaded aboard the airline and just as in the operation of a regular bar, drinks are measured and counted from a single unit. The airline unit is small (about the size of a portable TV set) and can be easily transported from one area to another or wheeled down the aisle of a plane.

Larger portable units are desired for use by hotels for private parties. A portable bar that is not completely automated can be used for each private function, or the full controls of an automated system can be made available. If there is a host bar the unit need not have a cash register. All bottles are locked in and the drinks are poured, measured, and counted automatically. Total consumption at the end of the function can quickly be determined from the totals on the counters. Extra bartenders and other personnel do not have access to liquor supply. With a no-host bar, a cash register can be added and the bartender then becomes responsible for the collection of cash. However, since no drinks can be poured without being automatically recorded, the amount due to the house can be carefully controlled. As in the first system, there is no direct access to the liquor supply.

With increased acceptance, the number of manufacturers producing equipment and the types of equipment becoming available is growing. Units with improved dispensing systems are now being produced for different size operations. Additional features being incorporated into the systems so that bottle labels, immediate inventory counts, and even a count of the mix of sales (see Glossary) are all integral parts of the systems package.

OUNCE OR DRINK CONTROLS

The most accurate method for determining the amount of liquor sold is the drink control or count system. It is also the most complicated, as well as the most difficult to establish and operate. In order for the ounce control system to function effectively, the following steps are necessary:

1. Every type of drink must be analyzed to determine the exact amount of each type of liquor used.

2. Every check must be examined and a tally kept of each drink sold.

3. The amount of liquor consumed is determined by multiplying the type of drink sold by the amount of liquor in the drink.

FIGURE 4-2 *Ounce Control System*

Quantity	Drink	Gin	Vermouth	Total Gin	Total Vermouth	Indiv. Price	Total Price
5	Tom Collins	1 1/2 oz.	0	7 1/2 oz.	0	1.25	6.25
6	Martini	2 oz.	1/2 oz.	12 oz.	3 oz.	1.25	7.50
6	Martini X Dry	2 1/2 oz.	1/4 oz.	15 oz.	1 1/2 oz.	1.35	8.10

The total costs of the consumption of gin and vermouth are determined by calculating the number of bottles consumed and adding up the total costs for those bottles. The total beverage cost percentage is then determined by dividing sales into total cost.

$$\text{Beverage Cost \%} = \text{Beverage Cost} \div \text{Beverage Sales}$$

The total amount that should have been sold is compared with actual amounts sold. Any deviations indicate a failure somewhere in the system.

As can be seen, this becomes an extremely cumbersome process, since every drink must be tallied along with consumption by brand names. This type of system is normally only feasible if a computer is available, or if, as the drinks are tallied on the cash register (or by a beverage checker), the information is fed into a computer that will do the tallying, or if automated systems are used.

A slight simplification would be to have all drinks in the same category tallied together regardless of the brand of liquor called, providing they are priced the same. Some cheating, of course, may be done by dishonest employees, by pouring less than the required amounts of liquor or substituting bar liquors for call liquors. Requiring bartenders to adhere to recipes and to use measuring devices will help alleviate short pouring.

Unlike automated systems, in which little variation will occur, the ounce control system cannot correct intentional or unintentional underpouring or overpouring. The basic principal of the ounce system is that by accurately determining what was sold, an establishment can relate this figure to what should have been used and investigate differences.

PAR STOCK—BOTTLE CONTROL

A simple but effective method for beverage control is by installation of par stock. The procedure is as follows:

1. Determine the maximum amounts consumed daily for each type of liquor.

2. For each liquor add a small safety factor. The amount consumed daily plus the safety factor is issued to each bar. This is the par stock—the amount that should be on hand at any bar at the beginning of every day. To simplify the system further, only a bottle count is used. That is, if consumption of a particular type of liquor normally is less than a bottle per day, one bottle (preferably two bottles, which builds in a safety factor) would be counted as the par stock. Half bottles or partial bottles are not measured.

3. All empty bottles are saved to be turned in at the close of the day or shift. (Space limitations may limit strict adherence to this procedure.)

4. The number of empties, by brand, automatically become the issues, and a requisition form is filled out based on the empties.

5. A standard sales value for each type of liquor and brand is calculated. Standard sales are determined by running a test sample for a period of time. This sample records the actual type of liquor and multiplies this by the sales value of each drink to determine the total revenue obtainable. For example, a quart of rye normally may be used for 10 highballs at $1.00 each (1-ounce portions). Five manhattans at $1.25 each (1 1/4-ounce portions), 15 whiskey sours at $1.10 each (1-ounce portions). This totals 31 1/4 ounces; 3/4 ounce is allowed for spillage, and thus a return of $32.75 per bottle is expected. If the bottle costs $6.00, the optimum percentage for this type of liquor would be:

$$\$6.00 \div \$32.75 = 17\%$$

Deviations from this percentage would be investigated.

6. Standard sales are based on amounts consumed and compared with actual sales to determine if all sales have been recorded. Some variations will occur daily, since amounts in partly consumed bottles are not recorded on a daily basis. This factor should average itself over a span of one week.

The advantages of this system are the simplicity in establishing it and the ease of operation. At any given moment an individual bar should have a certain number of bottles on hand. Any deviation from this bottle count indicates a breakdown in the system. Verification of sales can be made immediately, based on bottle consumption. The amount of issues times standard sales value should equal income for the previous day. Thus, instantaneous information is available to management. With other systems, an inventory must be taken before a determination and comparison of sales and consumption can be made.

This system assumes that the stock of partly consumed bottles remains relatively constant (after the system has been operating for a short period of time), so that it becomes superfluous to count each bottle's contents to determine sales.

Standard sales values for different brands of liquor are determined by actually counting drinks poured and revenues for each brand during a test period. In effect, the procedure outlined for the ounce system is used for a short period of time.

With the use of the par stock and bottle control system the effectiveness of the control is based upon *what has been used*. By determining the amount consumed, it can calculate how much revenue there should have been. The ounce control system bases its conclusions on *how much revenue there has been* and then *determines how much should have been consumed.*

NECESSARY CONTROLS FOR ALL SYSTEMS—PORTION CONTROL

No matter which system is used, certain rules must be followed by an establishment for any system to work.

1. Recipes must be standardized. If one bartender pours 2 ounces of gin and 1 ounce of vermouth into a martini and another pours 3 1/4 ounces of gin and 1/2 ounce of vermouth, it is obvious that each bartender will operate with a different beverage cost percentage. Just as in making various items of food, standardized recipes must be used by all bartenders. Even changing the shape of the ice cubes will affect the quantities of liquor required and the recipe itself.

   Of course, with automated systems, not every drink or liquor will come from a mechanical measuring device. For example, no bar has a measuring control for cream used in Brandy Alexanders and few have mechanical controls for the orange juice used in making screwdrivers. Yet unless these amounts are measured, drinks poured by different bartenders will taste different, and may cause customer complaints as well as alter beverage costs.

   Standardized recipes may be selected from one or more bartenders' guides or may be designed for an individual operation.

   Standardized recipes in beverage operation are particularly important where large quantities of premixed drinks are made. This would normally be done (when legal) either for parties or for rush periods in which a large number of various cocktails (martinis, whiskey sours, daiquiris, etc.) are sold. The minute variations that may be undetectable when cocktails are made individually become quite noticeable when mixing 50-100, or 1,000, drinks at one time.

2. All glassware must be standarized. (See Figure 4-3.) Strange as it may seem, many taverns operate with various size glasses for the same drinks. It is true that a collins glass and a highball glass normally have a distinct difference in their capacities, but no bar should have two different-sized collins glasses nor two different-sized highball glasses. Care must be taken by the beverage manager that all glasses, when purchased, are of the capacities requested. It is almost impossible to look at any glass and determine its capacity. The thickness of the glass, its shape, the type of bottom, and other factors all influence its capacity. Two glasses that look alike may actually hold different amounts.

   Sometimes the same drink may be served in different glasses, such as drinks served on the rocks and straight up (stem glassware). Often the net capacities of the glasses are different. A martini straight up may be served in a four-ounce glass, but if it is served

FIGURE 4-3 *Common Sizes and Shapes of Liquor Glassware*

STEMMED COCKTAIL GLASS: (Martini, Manhattan, etc.) ranges in capacity from 3 to 4½ ounces.

ALL-PURPOSE WINE: 4 to 8 ounces; stemmed glass.

WHISKY SOUR: 3½ to 4½ ounces.

STANDARD WINE: from 3 to 4 ounces; stemmed glass.

OLD-FASHIONED: 6 to 9 ounces; average size is 8 ounces; Used for "on the rocks."

CORDIAL: sometimes called a Pony; 1-ounce capacity is normal.

ROLY POLY: adaptable for many drinks; ranges from 5 ounces to 15 ounces in size. May be used for "on the rocks."

BRANDY SNIFTER: designed to enhance aroma; 6 to 12-ounce capacity.

STANDARD HIGHBALL OR TUMBLER: 8 to 12-ounce capacity; straight sided shell or sham.

SHERRY: 2-ounce capacity is normal.

COOLER: tall, slim glass for summer beverages, (Zombie, Collins, etc.), varied capacity, 14 to 16 ounces are popular. Often frosted.

SHOT GLASS: lined or unlined; 1 to 2-ounce capacity with ¾ to 1½-ounce line.

PILSNER: 8 to 12 ounces; 10-ounce size is most popular.

SHAM PILSNER: 8 to 12-ounce capacity.

STEIN OR BEER MUG: 8 to 12-ounce capacity.

TAPERED CONE PILSNER: 8 to 12-ounce capacity.

TULIP CHAMPAGNE: 6 to 8-ounce capacity; sometimes hollow-stemmed.

STEM PILSNER: 8 to 12-ounce capacity.

SAUCER CHAMPAGNE: ranges from 4½ to 7½ ounces.

GOBLET: 6 to 10-ounce capacity.

on the rocks, ice must be used and the total capacity of the glass may be more. If the glass is filled completely with ice, the amount of liquor that may be added may be more or less than for the stem glass. A knowledgeable guest will sometimes select one or the other because he knows in which one he will get more.

3. All transactions must be recorded. Any transfer of "ownership" from the receiving clerk to the storeroom clerk, or between bars, or from the bartender to the waiter or guest must be recorded. The slightest weakness in enforcing this policy will negate the value of the control system.

No matter how well each system is designed, it is apparent to the astute and experienced operator that there are flaws in any of the systems. There must be continuing checks on the system as a whole, as well as on each employee. The possibility of siphoning off of either merchandise or revenue always exists.

STANDARD COST OR POTENTIAL SALES

Care should be taken to occasionally recheck potential sales values to determine if there has been any change. For example, when the sales value of a bottle of rye is first calculated, the type of clientele at that particular time may have had taste preferences differing from those at another time. As an example, during the first test period you may have had an unusually large number of customers who preferred whiskey sours, as compared to a clientele that may prefer highballs or manhattans. The potential sales value per bottle will be different, and the eventual liquor cost percentage will vary. (See Figure 4-4.)

The operator of any beverage establishment should be keenly aware that despite all precautions that may be taken, despite the effective management techniques he uses, and despite the fact that his establishment serves only quality products, he is never able to attain the maximum sales value for the products consumed. Perfection is beyond the grasp of any operator. The optimum in sales would mean that at all times the staff is working at peak efficiency, no employee ever spills a drink, overpours, or mixes a drink that the customer finds unpalatable, and that all standards that have been established are followed. Obviously, this is an impossibility. Realistically, the operator estimates what his sales *should be* after determining what they *could be*.

In practice the procedure is as follows:

1. Establish sales prices and cost percentages based on data relating to desired profits, fixed and other operating costs, and other incidental expenses.

2. Set standards for recipes and glassware.

FIGURE 4-4 Potential Sales Value per Bottle

4/5 QUART (25.6 oz.)

PRICE PER DRINK

Glass Size	No. Drinks	.50	.60	.70	.75	.80	.85	.90	.95	1.00	1.05	1.10	1.15	1.20	1.25	1.30	1.35	1.40	1.45	1.50
5/8oz	40.9	20.45	24.54	28.63	30.67	32.72	34.77	36.81	38.86	40.90	42.95	44.99	47.04	49.08	51.13	53.17	55.22	57.26	59.31	61.35
3/4oz	34.1	17.05	20.46	23.87	25.57	27.28	28.99	30.69	32.40	34.10	35.81	37.51	39.22	40.92	42.63	44.33	46.04	47.74	49.45	51.15
7/8oz	29.2	14.60	17.52	20.44	21.90	23.36	24.82	26.28	27.74	29.20	30.66	32.12	33.58	35.04	36.50	37.96	39.42	40.88	42.34	43.80
1 oz	25.6	12.80	15.36	17.92	19.20	20.48	21.76	23.04	24.32	25.60	26.88	28.16	29.44	30.72	32.00	33.28	34.56	35.84	37.12	38.40
1-1/8oz	22.7	11.35	13.62	15.89	17.02	18.16	19.30	20.43	21.57	22.70	23.84	24.97	26.11	27.24	28.38	29.51	30.65	31.78	32.92	34.05
1-1/4oz	20.4	10.20	12.24	14.28	15.30	16.32	17.34	18.36	19.38	20.40	21.42	22.44	23.46	24.48	25.50	26.52	27.54	28.56	29.58	30.60
1-3/8oz	18.6	9.30	11.16	13.02	13.95	14.88	15.81	16.74	17.67	18.60	19.53	20.46	21.39	22.32	23.25	24.18	25.11	26.04	26.97	27.90
1-1/2oz	17.1	8.55	10.26	11.97	12.82	13.68	14.54	15.39	16.25	17.10	17.76	18.81	19.67	20.52	21.38	22.23	23.09	23.94	24.80	25.65
1-5/8oz	15.7	7.85	9.42	10.99	11.77	12.56	13.35	14.13	14.92	15.70	16.49	17.27	18.06	18.84	19.63	20.41	21.20	21.98	22.77	23.55
1-3/4oz	14.6	7.30	8.76	10.22	10.95	11.68	12.41	13.14	13.87	14.60	15.33	16.06	16.79	17.52	18.25	18.98	19.71	20.44	21.17	21.90
1-7/8oz	13.6	6.80	8.16	9.52	10.20	10.88	11.56	12.24	12.92	13.60	14.28	14.96	15.64	16.32	17.00	17.68	18.36	19.04	19.72	20.40
2 oz	12.8	6.40	7.68	8.96	9.60	10.24	10.88	11.52	12.16	12.80	13.44	14.08	14.72	15.36	16.00	16.64	17.28	17.92	18.56	19.20

QUART (32 oz.)

PRICE PER DRINK

Glass Size	No. Drinks	.50	.60	.70	.75	.80	.85	.90	.95	1.00	1.05	1.10	1.15	1.20	1.25	1.30	1.35	1.40	1.45	1.50
5/8oz	51.2	25.60	30.72	35.84	38.40	40.96	43.52	46.08	48.64	51.20	53.76	56.32	58.88	61.44	64.00	66.56	69.12	71.68	74.24	76.80
3/4oz	42.6	21.30	25.56	29.82	31.95	34.08	36.21	38.34	40.47	42.60	44.73	46.86	48.99	51.12	53.25	55.38	57.51	59.64	61.77	63.90
7/8oz	36.5	18.25	21.90	25.55	27.38	29.20	31.03	32.85	34.68	36.50	38.33	40.15	41.98	43.80	45.63	47.45	49.28	51.10	52.93	54.73
1 oz	32.0	16.00	19.20	22.40	24.00	25.60	27.20	28.80	30.40	32.00	33.60	35.20	36.80	38.40	40.00	41.60	43.20	44.80	46.40	48.00
1-1/8oz	28.4	14.20	17.04	19.88	21.30	22.72	24.14	25.56	26.98	28.40	29.82	31.24	32.66	34.08	35.50	36.92	38.34	39.76	41.18	42.60
1-1/4oz	25.6	12.80	15.36	17.92	19.20	20.48	21.76	23.04	24.32	25.60	26.88	28.16	29.44	30.72	32.00	33.28	34.56	35.84	37.12	38.40
1-3/8oz	23.3	11.65	13.98	16.31	17.48	18.64	19.81	20.97	22.14	23.30	24.47	25.63	26.80	27.96	29.13	30.29	31.46	32.62	33.79	34.95
1-1/2oz	21.3	10.65	12.78	14.91	15.98	17.04	18.11	19.17	20.24	21.30	22.37	23.43	24.50	25.56	26.63	27.69	28.76	29.82	30.89	31.95
1-5/8oz	19.7	9.85	11.82	13.79	14.78	15.76	16.75	17.73	18.72	19.70	20.69	21.67	22.66	23.64	24.63	25.61	26.60	27.58	28.57	29.55
1-3/4oz	18.3	9.15	10.98	12.81	13.73	14.64	15.56	16.47	17.39	18.30	19.22	20.13	21.05	21.96	22.88	23.79	24.71	25.62	26.54	27.45
1-7/8oz	17.1	8.55	10.26	11.97	12.83	13.68	14.54	15.39	16.25	17.10	17.96	18.81	19.67	20.52	21.38	22.23	23.09	23.94	24.80	25.65
2 oz	16.0	8.00	9.60	11.20	12.00	12.80	13.60	14.40	15.20	16.00	16.80	17.60	18.40	19.20	20.00	20.80	21.60	22.40	23.20	24.00

1/2 GALLON (64 oz.)

PRICE PER DRINK

Glass Size	No. Drinks	.50	.60	.70	.75	.80	.85	.90	.95	1.00	1.05	1.10	1.15	1.20	1.25	1.30	1.35	1.40	1.45	1.50
5/8oz	102.4	51.20	61.44	71.68	76.80	81.92	87.04	92.16	97.28	102.40	107.52	112.64	117.76	122.88	128.00	133.12	138.24	143.36	148.48	153.60
3/4oz	85.3	42.65	51.18	59.71	63.98	68.24	72.51	76.77	81.04	85.30	89.57	93.83	98.10	102.36	106.63	110.89	115.16	119.42	123.69	127.95
7/8oz	73.1	36.55	43.86	51.17	54.83	58.48	62.14	65.79	69.45	73.10	76.76	80.41	84.07	87.72	91.38	95.03	98.69	102.34	106.00	109.65
1 oz	64.0	32.00	38.40	44.80	48.00	51.20	54.40	57.60	60.80	64.00	67.20	70.40	73.60	76.80	80.00	83.20	86.40	89.60	92.80	96.00
1-1/8oz	56.9	28.45	34.14	39.83	42.68	45.52	48.37	51.21	54.06	56.90	59.75	62.59	65.44	68.28	71.13	73.97	76.81	79.66	82.51	85.35
1-1/4oz	51.2	25.60	30.72	35.84	38.40	40.96	43.52	46.08	48.64	51.20	53.76	56.32	58.88	61.44	64.00	66.56	69.12	71.68	74.24	76.80
1-3/8oz	46.5	23.25	27.90	32.55	34.88	37.20	39.53	41.85	44.18	46.50	48.83	51.15	53.48	55.80	58.13	60.45	62.78	65.10	67.43	69.75
1-1/2oz	42.7	21.35	25.62	29.89	32.03	34.16	36.30	38.43	40.57	42.70	44.84	46.97	49.11	51.24	53.38	55.51	57.65	59.78	61.92	64.05
1-5/8oz	39.4	19.70	23.64	27.58	29.55	31.52	33.49	35.46	37.43	39.40	41.37	43.34	45.31	47.28	49.25	51.22	53.19	55.16	57.13	59.10
1-3/4oz	36.6	18.30	21.96	25.62	27.45	29.28	31.11	32.94	34.77	36.60	38.43	40.26	42.09	43.92	45.75	47.58	49.41	51.24	53.07	54.90
1-7/8oz	34.1	17.05	20.46	23.87	25.58	27.28	28.99	30.69	32.40	34.10	35.81	37.51	39.22	40.92	42.63	44.33	46.04	47.74	49.45	51.15
2 oz	32.0	16.00	19.20	22.40	24.00	25.60	27.20	28.80	30.40	32.00	33.60	35.20	36.80	38.40	40.00	41.60	43.20	44.80	46.40	48.00

3. Determine a "normal" tolerance percentage to allow for spillage, waste, errors, breakage, and incidental losses. This may be done on a per bottle basis or on a straight percentage of total costs. A spillage factor of one ounce per bottle in effect amounts to a 3% + loss. This is a considerable amount if one considers that the sales price may be three times that amount or more.

4. Deduct tolerance calculations from optimum sales to determine potential sales. This then becomes the standard and expected return based on consumption.

With par stock beverage sales using a fixed percentage system, a typical weekly work sheet (see Figure 4-5) gives a daily recapitulation of beverage costs and potential sales based on a standard beverage cost percentage of 33.3%. The cost is determined from issues.

In determining beverage cost from the requisition form and potential bottle sales system, a typical work sheet (see Figure 4-6) gives the standard sales to be expected based on issues and potential sales of each bottle of liquor.

Note that if these figures were 100% accurate (ignoring variations that occur due to partially filled bottles), the shortage for February 1 is only $10.00 according to the straight percentage method (Figure 4-5) but $32.00 when the potential bottle sales value method (Figure 4-6) is used.

BOTTLE SALES

The sale of merchandise by the bottle differs considerably in price from the revenues normally obtained when selling drinks individually. Bottle sales must be recorded and treated apart from normal beverage sales.

To control bottle sales, the operators must first determine what the selling price should be for whole bottles. Consideration must be given to the convenience offered to the guests, as well as the additional items included in the sale (ice, glasses, mixers, etc.), as compared to the price at which the same bottle can be purchased in liquor stores. If the sale is made in a restaurant, then obviously no other source of supply is available. For hotel guests, the guest may decide to purchase liquor elsewhere if the differential is too great. It may also become profitable for employees (room service, waiters, or bellhops) to offer the same merchandise at a lower price if the profit warrants the risk. Without a control system this can easily be done. When the liquor is delivered to the room, if the guest pays in cash, the bellhop then merely places the liquor back into inventory and pockets the money. The liquor actually sold to the guest came, of course, from the bellhop's own stock.

To prevent guests from purchasing liquor elsewhere, the prices charged, including set ups, must be in line with competitive markets— roughly two times the retail cost of the liquor.

Date	Day	Beverage Today	Cost To Date	Sales Today	To Date	Potential Today	Sales* To Date	Beverage Today	To Date
Feb. 1	M	100.00	100.00	290.00	290.00	300.00	300.00	34.4	34.4
2	T	200.00	300.00	625.00	915.00	600.00	900.00	32.0	33.2
3	W	300.00	600.00	1000.00	1915.00	900.00	1800.00	30.0	31.3
4	Th								
5	F								
6	S								

* Potential sales figure based on a 33% cost.

FIGURE 4-6 *Typical Work Sheet for Beverage Cost Determined From Requisition Form and Potential Bottle Sales System*

Date Feb. 2

Size Quarts	Brand	Cost	Total Cost	Bottle Sales Value	Standard Sales
2	WW Gin	5.00	10.00	15.00	30.00
1	BB Rye	4.00	4.00	12.00	12.00
3	VO	6.00	18.00	20.00	60.00
4	CC	6.00	24.00	20.00	80.00
8	Seg 7	5.50	44.00	17.50	140.00
	Standard Sales Total $322.00*				

*This amount should equal (or come close to) the sales receipts for Feb. 1.

To prevent dishonesty on the part of employees, all liquor used for bottle sales should be specially labeled. Separate inventories for bottle sales must be utilized. The cost of sales should be treated separately from other beverage income and costs. A prechecking system should be utilized. As orders are given by guests, they should be recorded on a sales check and rung up on a register, and the waiter or bellhop must return with either the cash or a signed check after delivering the beverage. Most room sales are charged to the guest's account. The prechecking of sales will deter the employees from pocketing the cash in the few instances when a guest pays cash.

FRAUD AND SPECIAL PROBLEMS

Short Pouring

With any of the systems, it is still possible for the dishonest or unscrupulous bartender to cheat both the house and the customer by pouring less than the desired amount. Should the dishonest bartender wish to take merchandise home or pocket money, it is possible by pouring only 1/4 of an ounce less per drink to sell or take home a bottle a day with as small a volume of sales as 125 drinks per day.

Even in mechanical systems, a bartender may place a glass under the pourer and siphon off a portion of the measured amount. This is particularly easy to accomplish in service bars or when bottles are hidden or concealed so that the customer is unable to view the bartender's actions. The bartender might even place the merchandise that has accumulated into a soda bottle (no deposit) and take it home when his shift is over. Should he have access to cash, it becomes apparent that without ringing up a sale he could collect money from a customer and sell him some of the stolen liquor and still show the desired beverage cost percentage.

In those systems where there is no mechanical device he simply has a surplus in his bottles that he may use himself or sell to a customer at his own convenience.

The experienced dishonest bartender attempting this type of fraud may try to keep track of the amounts due him by recording it somewhere. Signs of broken matches, toothpicks, etc., may mean that he is counting how much he has stolen and thus knows how much he can take without affecting the beverage cost percentage. With a par stock system, this merchandise cannot stockpile for too long a period of time, as bottles are turned in regularly. Short pouring is most frequently done in those places where the bartender also collects the cash.

Substitutions

The substitution of cheap bar or not as well stock for call brands is also done most frequently in those establishments where the bartender collects cash. He simply collects a higher price for a cheap drink, rings up the lower price, and pockets the difference.

With both short pouring and substitution, the best method of control is to force each ringup immediately after pouring each drink. The bartender also should be required to give the customer a receipt for the amount collected.

In cases where cash is pocketed, the volume of receipts would be the best indicator that some type of fraud was being perpetrated by employees. If sales drop without any noticeable change in other areas of business and the cost percentages remain the same, then this type of chicanery may be occurring. It cannot readily be practiced in systems utilizing bottle pourers with counters.

Dilution of Merchandise

After opening any bottle (and sometimes even without opening) it is possible to remove some of the liquor and water it down so that shortages of inventories would not be noticeable. Gin and vodka would be particularly susceptible to this type of theft since the liquor is colorless. A large amount of dilution of other liquors would discolor the liquor.

In systems in which all liquor is opened at the bar service area, then the bartenders would be the ones responsible. In cases in which the merchandise is fed into a system from the storeroom, then of course it is the storeroom clerk who is the culprit. In the case of the bartender, the substitution is made to cover theft of actual money. In the case of the storeroom clerk, the substitution covers up the theft of liquor. In both cases, detection is difficult if excess amounts of water are not added. Customers cannot normally differentiate to a fine degree.

Testing of alcoholic content and proof isn't normally done in the vast majority of liquor service operations and only rarely by state inspectors. Fraud of this nature is more readily accomplished in operations in which there is little supervision by management.

Theft of Merchandise

In any operation it is possible for employees to take merchandise out of the establishment without being noticed. Even in those large hotels where security guards are posted at the employees' exit, merchandise may be removed via other exits or under the guise of garbage, returned merchandise, through collusion with guests or delivery men, etc.

Since it is impossible to stop this type of theft, it must be controlled in some fashion. This is accomplished by limiting the number of employees that have access to the merchandise and by pinpointing the area of control of theft by accurate recordkeeping. The prohibiting of packages from being taken out of the establishment unless they are inspected is a good rule to follow. In addition it may become necessary to occasionally inspect the "garbage dump" or the empty soda bottles that are removed by the bartender.

The receiving clerk is held responsible for any merchandise "lost" between the time he receives it and the time he transfers the control to the storeroom clerk, who must sign for the merchandise. The clerk in turn is responsible for any merchandise from the storeroom, since only he is permitted to enter the storeroom or allow merchandise to be removed. In turn, the bartender is responsible for the merchandise under his jurisdiction and he must have either cash or receipts (dupes) from the waitress for the merchandise he has dispensed. The waitress should be required to turn in a dupe (further discussion of alternative controls for waitresses will be discussed in later chapters). She assumes responsibility for that merchandise and must, in turn, either show a waitress receipt or cash for the amount she has received from the bar.

With all systems, irregular as well as scheduled physical counts must be taken to verify actual counts. Although more records must be maintained, larger operations having many persons involved in beverage control (a separate receiving clerk, inventory clerk, etc.) have a good chance of preventing theft. The areas of responsibility are more clearly defined and there may be less chance of collusion.

In restaurants or hotels where one person buys the merchandise and controls it to the point of also taking cash, there is absolutely no control. At any point in the system substitutions may be made, merchandise removed, or cash pocketed without management being aware of any wrongdoing. Simply by buying his own liquor and putting it in stock, a dishonest bartender having complete freedom, as outlined above, can sell the bottle, not record the cash, and pocket the receipts. With another person taking cash there is still an excellent possibility for theft and collusion between the bartender and the cashier, since only two persons are involved. With still another person involved in receiving or storing merchandise the possibility of collusion still exists but is lessened, as more and more people have to record and transfer merchandise.

Cash receipts for beverage sales will be covered in a later chapter, since the controls for food and beverages are quite similar and involve the same types of problems.

Complimentary Drinks

All drinks served complimentary to a guest or for employees who are authorized to consume beverages must be recorded in the same manner as a regular sale. They are merely handled as a regular charge and then debited to the appropriate account by the accounting department.

Returns of Merchandise Issued to Private Parties

A common practice in hotels and restaurants is to charge private parties either only for the merchandise consumed by the guests or for all bottles opened. In some cases the guest may be charged for all merchandise ordered, whether opened or not. The first two instances present considerable control problems, particularly since the sales figures are based on the amounts consumed.

Normally, excess merchandise is issued, as it is impossible to determine exactly how much liquor a party will consume and also which particular brands or types of liquor will be preferred. To prevent the possibility of running out during rush periods it is customary to estimate how much will be consumed and issue about 25% more to make sure that no shortages occur.

A percentage of sales is usually added to the bill as a gratuity for the staff. This encourages the staff to free pour (without measuring devices) and to pour on the "heavy" side. Often the staff is composed of "temporaries" or "extras" who are not concerned with either the policies of the house or its good name. They may partake of some of the refreshments or attempt to carry some out and are not concerned with any of the regular control systems of the house. Since they will be gone by the time losses may be discovered, unusual and much stricter control systems should be used:

1. A regular employee must be in charge and no extra employee should be allowed to work alone or unsupervised.
2. Immediate counts must be made of merchandise, both prior to service and before the departure of employees.
3. Immediate counts of cash (if a cash system is involed) must be made.
4. Independent controls for each employee must be set up.

In practice, this means that a separate inventory control for each bartender (including steady employees) is necessary. When cash sales are recorded, the amounts of monies turned in must equal the potential sales or the amounts of merchandise consumed.

No bartender should be allowed to take cash, as this would permit a bartender to control both inventory and receipts, negating the whole control system. For example, a bartender pouring five drinks and shorting each drink slightly would be able to pour a sixth and pocket the money without any possibility of detection unless another individual was watching.

Since another person must watch anyway, it would be better to use the second person to take the cash, and then unless there was collusion, cash receipts should equate to amounts consumed. One cashier may be able to take cash for a number of bartenders, providing a separate record of sales for each bartender can be kept. The cashier should be a regular employee rather than an extra.

In those systems where there is an open or host bar (the host pays for everything) and no cash is involved, the exact amount of merchandise issued to each bartender must be recorded. All full and empty bottles must be returned immediately after the function. All bottles should have a special house stamp or label. Mechanical controls (locked pour tops with counters or perhaps completely automated systems) may be easily incorporated into these systems as a further check on cashiers and bartenders.

Often in private functions, the host or person booking the party will request that a specific size drink should be served (1 1/4 ounce) rather than the normal one utilized by the house. For this reason it is desirable to have automated systems in which the portion size may be adjusted easily (but not by the bartender).

Methods of Payment and Types of Service for Private Parties

The service for private functions must be tailored to meet the needs of those persons attending the affair. For this reason several methods of accounting for merchandise consumed have been developed. All are specifically designed for the guests rather than for the establishment. Each method varies slightly and may have built-in advantages or disadvantages that must be closely examined to eliminate possibilities of error or fraud.

Host Bars. A host bar (one in which all the guests may consume beverages and the host pays for the amount consumed at the end of the function) may be operated either by drink count or bottle count.

Drink count. Under this method an accurate (hopefully) count of each drink served is kept. The host normally pays a fixed price per drink. Beer and soft drinks may be separately recorded and priced. This system is most often used whenever a complete line of beverages is desired by the host (all brands, including afterdinner drinks, etc.) or where it is inconvenient to set up a separate bar or separate stock.

The advantage of this method is that there is no need to open additional bottles, no record or system needs to be set up to record returns of unused merchandise, and normally a lower beverage cost percentage may be achieved, since the total return per bottle (based on drink cost) is higher.

A disadvantage of the system is that there is no sure method of determining whether the host is charged for all the drinks consumed, or in some cases, whether or not he is being overcharged in that an excessive number of drinks may be tallied against his account. Undercharging may occur by error—the bartender may forget or be unable to keep an accurate account. Overcharging may be by either the bartender (who in turn sells the merchandise to others and pockets the money or actually keeps the merchandise plus the additional gratuity that may be charged) or may in fact be performed by unscrupulous management.

Bottle count. When this method is used a separate par stock must be established for each private function. The host normally is charged for only the amount consumed, or in some cases, for all bottles that have been opened, even if some of the bottle still remains. A simple count of the empty and full bottles at the end of the affair will determine the amount consumed.

Obviously there is still room for fraud should a dishonest bartender either pour liquor into other bottles or even throw it away to increase his gratuity. Adequate supervision should prevent this type of theft.

Either of these two methods may be utilized for the entire duration of the affair, or time limits may be specified. If a time limit is specified in the contract, the bar may be closed permanently at that point, or an inventory or count taken and then the bar may reopen as a no-host bar.

No-Host Bars. Under certain circumstances (particularly with service clubs, some convention functions, and meetings) each person attending the function must pay for any beverages he wishes to consume. Payment may be effected by cash collection or coupon sales.

Cash collection. The guest may either pay the bartender or a cashier when the receives his drink.

Coupon sales. Guests purchase tickets or coupons from a cashier ahead of time. They give these to the bartender when the drink is served. The advantage of this system is that the coupons may be sold either by the management (eliminating the need for a cashier at the bar and also preventing the use of cash at the bar) or by the host organization. This is sometimes done (providing it is permitted by state law) when the host organization receives a portion of the revenue for its own use (fund raising).

Guests may be given a specific number of coupons prior to service (one or two drinks included in the price of the meal), which are given to the bartender at time of service.

Additional drinks may be purchased by using either cash collection or coupon sales. With allotted coupons, another guest not using his allotment may give the tickets away.

Any of the above systems must be audited and controlled by normal management and supervisory accounting procedures.

BEER AND WINE

Bottled beer and bottled wine are much easier to control than other forms of liquor. It is impossible for the bartender to short the customer, since a bottle is normally sealed and, of course, a guest would immediately notice a bottle that was only partially full. Substitutions are also improbable in that the customer buys a name brand that can readily be identified. Unit sales and the quantity of units sold should equal an exact dollar return. Any variances from this amount would be detectable.

In most cases, shortages in inventory (particularly in beer) can be attributed to free drinks issued to employees but not recorded. Separate house checks (a check chargeable to a house account or an employee such as the kitchen manager or the chef) should be kept. These are handled in the same manner as guest checks. Thus the bartender becomes responsible for any shortages.

The most difficult problems arise in that several bartenders (whether they be on the same shift or separate shifts) normally use the same coolers for the stocking of beer, and thus they work out of the same inventory. Shortages cannot be specifically pinpointed to one individual. Inventories are not normally taken at the close of a shift. No feasible solution can be offered, but should there be a large shortage of merchandise it may become necessary to install controls so that each bartender has his own stock.

Draught beer cannot be as accurately counted, since there are some variations in the exact yield from barrels or kegs. Even the type of glassware used will alter the yield. For example, the expected yield from a 1/2 barrel of beer is 330 seven-ounce glasses. This yield occurs if a shell-type glass is used. If a bar uses a seven-ounce sham pilsner glass, the expected yield would be 418 glasses. Expected yield computations are derived from the *Modern Beertender*, a retailers chart of draught beer glassware, published by the Anheuser-Busch Company.

The beverage controller must determine the expected yield and potential sales value of a 1/2 barrel based on the size and type of glassware used and on the sales price of the glass. If several sizes are used, then a weighted value for average sales must be determined by actual testing for a period of time.

The manner in which the bartender pours the beer will also affect sales, since a larger or smaller head (normal is one inch) will raise or lower yields per barrel. New piston type beer pouring systems (see Figure 4-7) have been designed that are able to measure exact quantities and keep accurate counts of glasses sold.

Wine sales by the glass should be controlled in the same manner as hard liquor sales. The methods and techniques of service and the possibilities for deception and fraud are identical.

BAR CHECKING SYSTEMS

Except for nightclubs and for some types of operations in which the bar sales are of unusually high dollar value, an individual assigned solely for the purpose of checking waiters' or waitresses' drinks is normally not desired. The savings effected may not pay for the additional salary of the bar checker.

With the new automated dispensing systems now available, it may not even be necessary to have bar checkers for large operations. For example, with the newer systems a drink cannot be dispensed without being automatically counted; with the more advanced and complex models, drinks will not be dispensed unless they are rung up on a check. Thus should a server wish a drink she would merely hand her check (which has been assigned to her and accounted for) to the bartender. He inserts the check into the cash register and then pours the drinks that are ordered. As each drink is

FIGURE 4-7 *Piston Type Beer Pouring System*

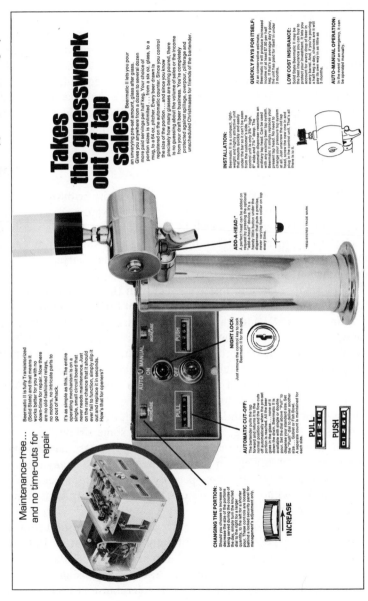

Maintenance-free... and no time-outs for repair

Beermatic II is fully Transistorized (Solid State) and that means it works better for you with no down-time for repair. Now there are no old-fashioned relays, no motors, no intricate parts to go out of whack.

It's as simple as this. The entire operating mechanism is on a single, small circuit board that never needs maintenance. Just on the rare chance that it should ever fail to function, simply slip it out and replace it in seconds. How's that for openers?

Takes the guesswork out of tap sales

Beermatic II lets you pour an unvarying pre-set amount, glass after glass. Gives you anywhere from a dozen to several dozen more paid servings per half keg. Your choice of portion sizes is unlimited . . . from a six oz. glass, to a mug, to a 64 oz. pitcher. Every beer drawn is registered on the automatic counter. Since you control the size of the portion . . . and since you know precisely how many glasses are being poured, there is no guessing about the volume of sales or the income from your draft beer business. You're completely protected against spillage, overpour, pilferage and unscheduled Christmases for friends of the bartender.

INSTALLATION:

Beermatic II is a compact, lightweight and highly attractive unit that mounts quickly and easily underneath the bar so it can't be seen from the customer's side. The control unit is only 3½" high, 6" wide and 7½" deep. The automatic dispenser resembles an ordinary beer head. Can be used with any existing beer tap system. Beermatic II simply replaces your present tap head. No need to change your present tap system at all. Just unscrew the old tap head, screw the new one in and plug in the control unit. That's all there is to it.

ADD-A-HEAD:*

A perfect head can be added on request by pressing the optional "add-a-head" device. It's a handy little button under the dispenser that puts a precise head of foaming beer on top every time.

*REGISTERED TRADE MARK.

QUICKLY PAYS FOR ITSELF:

At an conservative estimate, Beermatic II will produce increased income of at least $7.50 per half keg. If that's an average day's pour, the unit has paid for itself in 3 months.

LOW COST INSURANCE:

Solid State Beermatic II may be the best insurance you can buy to protect your investment. It lets you account for every drop of beer in every barrel. And, if you're pouring a half keg a day, chances are it will pay its own way in as little as 3 months.

AUTO-MANUAL OPERATION:

In the event of an emergency, it can be operated manually.

NIGHT LOCK:

Just remove the control key to lock Beermatic II for the night.

AUTOMATIC CUT-OFF:

The bartender pulls the tap forward and returns it to the normal position and the flow cuts off automatically when the pre-set portion is reached. All the beer goes in the glass . . . none of it down the drain. Beermatic II is available with single or double pour. Set the dial above "Pull" to dispense your standard size. Set the "Push" dial to deliver another size . . . Goblet or Fish Bowl. A separate count is available for each size.

CHANGING THE PORTION:

Should you choose to increase or decrease the size of the portions being served during the course of the day, simply turn the knurled dial to the right for a larger quantity, to the left for a shorter pour. These controls are located behind a locked security panel for management's adjustment only.

INCREASE

PULL

PUSH

poured it is automatically recorded on the check, thus eliminating the need for a checker.

In very large operations in which there are many service bartenders, one bartender (and checker if desired) can be assigned to pour and record those drinks that are not incorporated into the system.

Registers can be so designed as to record the amounts issued to each server. The individual server would be responsible for turning in that amount at the end of the shift. The bartender in turn would be accountable for all the merchandise used at his station. This total should equal the amount charged to each of the waiters he served. Thus, merchandise consumed equals amounts charged to each waiter. Cash receipts should equal this figure. Without an automated system, of course, this method cannot be used.

SUMMARY

Beverage dispensing systems must of necessity be designed individually for any given organization. Primarily, the design must overcome the service needs of the organization as well as insure that payment is received for all merchandise dispensed. Other highly important variables are accuracy in following recipes and avoidance of either underpouring or overpouring (intentional or otherwise).

For smaller bars, intimate contact with the customers, the absence of responsible supervisors, and the combining of functions make it exceedingly difficult to install adequate control measures. A bartender may be responsible for the sale of merchandise, which includes dispensing and the receipt of cash. Unless continually watched, he may be able to bring his own merchandise into the establishment to substitute, short pour on merchandise, or pocket some of the receipts. Even more subtle kinds of chicanery may be accomplished: favoring customers who are known to tip by dispensing a little extra and making up the difference by shortchanging strangers or poor tippers; overcharging for some drinks.

In larger organizations, if adequate controls are not maintained and areas of responsibility clearly defined, theft may occur anywhere along the system. Several bartenders may operate out of the same stock. Only one may be stealing, but without a tight system, the responsibility for this theft cannot be determined.

Finally, the kinds of services offered within the establishment may be so varied as to necessitate several different kinds of control. In heavy volume operations, the pace of service may be so hectic it precludes the use of some automated systems that are more accurate in dispensing exact amounts of liquor. Some additional spillage may be tolerable and necessary in order to insure prompt service. Larger operations have the advantage of being able to separate the function of dispensing from that of cash receipts. This separation eliminates some of the avenues in which dishonest employees are able to steal without being detected.

In essence, beverage control systems are designed to prevent shortages in either merchandise or cash. Methods of controlling cash will be discussed in Chapter 5.

No matter how well designed a system may be, there are methods of "beating" any system. Thus, continual inspection and vigilance are essential. The manager who states or believes that his system is foolproof, all his employees are honest, or that his system prevents theft is operating under a halo of innocence or ignorance. He soon may be rudely made aware that blind faith in one method or in people has no place in beverage control systems.

Chapter 4

1. List the 3 basic methods of beverage service.

2. Discuss the advantages and disadvantages of each system.

3. In what size (volume) operation are automated bars advantageous? What volume(s) of sales would necessitate different control systems?

4. Describe the ounce or drink control system. What are its advantages and disadvantages?

5. Discuss the advantages and disadvantages of par stock control systems.

6. Discuss the procedure required to establish a par stock system.

7. Describe basic procedures required for all control systems.

8. Discuss optimum sales, standard costs, potential sales, standard sales, and actual sales.

9. Discuss methods to prevent
   a. short pouring.
   b. substitutions.
   c. theft of merchandise.

10. Set up a control system for a private no-host bar—serving 300 people.

11. Establish a control system for a private host bar to be set up for a wedding—serving 100 people.

5

Cash Receipts

Although this chapter is titled "cash receipts," it must be realized that in today's modern society, cash itself no longer accounts for all the exchanges that occur when any individual wishes to pay for the meal or beverage that he has consumed. A large number of transactions are charged through various systems or separate credit companies.

In any case, the owner or operator of a food and beverage establishment is concerned only with the fact that in some manner he has been reimbursed for all the food and beverage services that he has rendered. The operator is aware that many times, in fact, he does not receive full reimbursement, either due to unintentional errors on the part of his employees or through dishonest acts on the part of either the employees or the guests. An attempt is made, therefore, to devise systems that will eliminate errors and minimize fraud.

Accounting for cash (or charges or credit cards) is only meaningful when the totals relate in some manner to actual goods issued, consumed, or sold. Since the mechanical methods of cash collection are to a great extent automated, these correlations and the reasons for utilizing one system of control over another are the primary interests of the food and beverage controller.

A system that automatically records purchases, issues, and cash collection would be ideally the most efficient. Unfortunately, no system has yet been devised that can incorporate all the variables involved with food and beverage service. (See Figure 5-1.)

As a result, cash collection systems are designed to incorporate and guard those areas in which the danger of losses is greatest. Even in these areas, the cost of accounting for all transactions may become prohibitive and as a result some leakage will still occur.

Newer systems however, are constantly being improved. A number of cash register companies and computer companies have developed mini-computers that enable the operator to perform many of these functions.

FIGURE 5-1 *Tranti System 21*

Reproduced by permission of Tranti Systems, Inc., Tewksbury, Massachusetts

Figures 5-2(a) and (b) illustrate the Tranti System 21, which allows up to 192 menu items to be included on the keyboard. It records sales, cash or charges, reports sales on an item-by-item basis, either by dollar volume or as a percentage of total sales, and updates inventories. Menu items (and sales prices of each) can be changed in a matter of seconds. Other features, including customer receipts and automatic calculation of sales tax, are also part of this system.

Figures 5-3, 5-4, and 5-5 illustrate the NCR electronic cash register system and some of its features.

Cash collection is an area in which there is a great possibility for theft and error. Fortunately it can be automated to a great extent, so that leakage in this area should be minimal.

TYPES OF FRAUD AND AREAS OF LOSS WITH CASH COLLECTION

Customers

The primary kind of customer fraud is the customer walking out without paying the check. However, a customer may also cheat an establishment by a number of other methods. He may claim that the food was un-

FIGURE 5-2 *Menu Items for Tranti System 21*

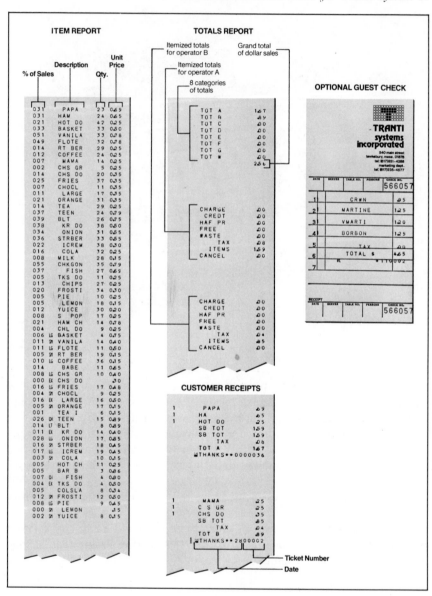

FIGURE 5-2 *(continued) Keyboard for Tranti System 21*

The Keyboard

The keyboard on the Tranti Cash Control System is designed for maximum efficiency and ease of use. Clear item descriptions and color coding act as a guide to the machine's operation. Unique to the Tranti System are the condiment and modifier keys that allow for standard order variations. The Tranti keyboard can be individualized by you to meet your special menu requirements.

Total and control keys
provide for the machine's tabulation of individual orders as well as cash control entries. Totals, no charge, half price, credit and delete entries are all printed in red on the customer's sales check and evaluation reports for easy identification. Two sets of operator totals, with eight categories of sales summary reports are available to keep track of sales by cash, room charge, charge card, waiter etc.

Mode Control Keys
change machine operating modes from order taking to report generating, changing menu items and prices or calculating.

Shift Keys
enable the owner to shift to new item keys. There are a total of 192 items available utilizing the shift keys.

Subtotal

Total

Total and control keys
provide for the machine's tabulation of individual orders as well as cash control entries. Totals, no charge, half price, credit and delete entries are all printed in red on the customers sales check and evaluation reports for easy identification. Two sets of operator totals, with eight categories of sales summary reports are available to keep track of sales by cash, room charge, charge card, waiter etc.

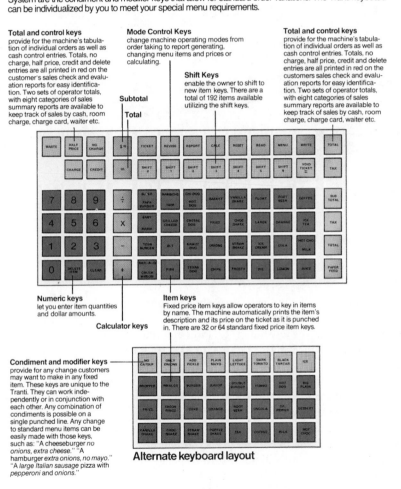

Numeric keys
let you enter item quantities and dollar amounts.

Calculator keys

Item keys
Fixed price item keys allow operators to key in items by name. The machine automatically prints the item's description and its price on the ticket as it is punched in. There are 32 or 64 standard fixed price item keys.

Condiment and modifier keys
provide for any change customers may want to make in any fixed item. These keys are unique to the Tranti. They can work independently or in conjunction with each other. Any combination of condiments is possible on a single punched line. Any change to standard menu items can be easily made with those keys, such as: "A cheeseburger *no onions, extra cheese.*" "A hamburger *extra onions, no mayo.*" "A *large Italian sausage* pizza with *pepperoni and onions.*"

Alternate keyboard layout

FIGURE 5-3 *The NCR Electronic Cash Register System*

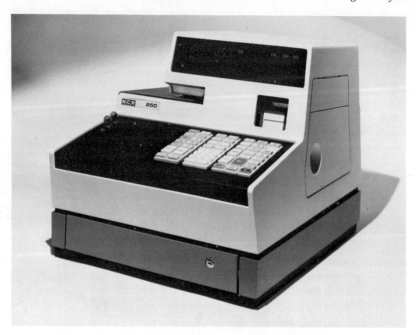

Reproduced by permission of NCR, Dayton, Ohio

satisfactory and thus indicate (usually the manager or host will make the suggestion) that he will not pay for it. Another possibility, which has occurred frequently, is for the customer to indicate that his food contained some foreign matter such as glass or china, or even an insect (perhaps even brought in by the customer).

These complaints are generally made to the waiter, who should in turn call the manager or host to resolve the problem. Since there is always the possibility that the event did in truth occur, the normal policy is to grant a free dinner or dinners to the guest to avoid embarrassment, to prevent possible lawsuits, and of course, to encourage the customer to return. In most cases of fraud the guest will not return to perform the same type of fraud nor will he return merely to buy a dinner.

In the case of falsified complaints, the establishment has no recourse except to treat the affair as a normal business expense. In cases of walkouts, the house may have legal recourse, and of course it can set up a control system that minimizes the chances of this type of theft.

Customers normally cannot perpetrate any other type of theft, since they do not have access to food or beverages. Disputes may arise, however, as to the exact number of drinks that were served. In the cases of parties where

FIGURE 5-4

Two basic keyboards provide push-button operation

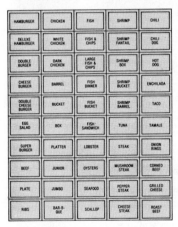

NCR 250-6000

This Keyboard has 46 function keys surrounding a 10-key cluster of numeric keys. Light key action eliminates operator fatigue and improves efficiency. Even during regular peak periods or unexpected business surges, operators are able to maintain speedy register operation. Keys are preprogrammed to perform specific functions. Simplicity in design and ease of operation reduce operator training time and promote accuracy.

NCR 250-6500

This keyboard has 90 function keys that surround the 10-key cluster of numeric keys. With the exception of added function keys, the optional keyboard is identical to the standard keyboard. In either keyboard, design, color-coded keys, and ease of operation promote accuracy.

Reproduced by permission of NCR, Dayton, Ohio

FIGURE 5-5

Information aids management... control prices, control taxes, control inventory, and control people

Automatic Reporting

Daily reports aid management in successfully planning sales, controlling inventory, balancing money and records, and calculating profits. Various reports are available at any time of the day . . . just index the number of the report required and through a preprogrammed cycle the NCR 250 automatically prints the report.

How quickly and accurately management receives this information many times determines success or failure of the business. With the NCR 250, this vital information is just a key depression away.

Each report shows number of customers served, number of "No Sales," consecutive number, store number, register number, and date.

Portion Control

This system aids management in establishing portion control to offset rising food costs and bigger payrolls. Item count aids management in making crucial decisions regarding food portions. Wise decisions, good food, and reasonable prices promote repeat business.

Inventory Control

Inventory Control can begin at the earliest possible moment of the sale, even before the products leave the preparation areas. This eliminates opportunities for unintentional and intentional errors. Actual machine-printed prices on the receipt can become a requisition. Dollar and department information printed on the receipt also displays publicly at the top of the register and accumulates in management-controlled totals.

A book inventory can be maintained by subtracting-individual daily unit counts from current inventory figures. Spot checking readily reveals any out-of-balance condition that, if neglected, could seriously inflate food costs and reduce expected profit.

NET REGISTER TOTAL			
START #50 PROGRAM CHANGE/RESET COUNTER CUSTOMER COUNTER/NO SALE	X	51	361 A
	X	621	22 A
NET ACCOUNTABILITY	X	1	925.25 A A
CONSECUTIVE #/STORE & REGISTER #/DATE	2278	12	4/02/7–

REGISTER FINANCIAL REPORT		TRANS COUNT	REGISTER TOTALS
START #51 PROGRAM CHANGE/RESET COUNTER CUSTOMER COUNTER/NO SALE		X 51	361 B
		X 621	22 B
CURRENT TIED-UP GROUP	1B	X	30637.45 1B
GROSS SALES TODAY	2B	X	971.15 2B
DEPARTMENT VOIDS	3B	X 0	.00 3B
DISCOUNTS	4B	X 0	.00 4B
NET SALES	5B	X	971.15 5B
PAID OUT	6B	X 5	45.90 6B
CASH CALLED FOR	7B	X	925.25 7B
INSIDE SALES TOTAL	8B	X 461	648.93 8B
CARRYOUT SALES TOTAL	9B	X 160	322.22 9B
CONSECUTIVE #/STORE & REGISTER #/DATE		2279	12 4/02/7–

TAXABLE GROUP TOTAL REPORT			
START #53 PROGRAM CHANGE/RESET COUNTER CUSTOMER COUNTER/NO SALE		X 51	361 D
		X 621	22 D
TAXABLE GROUP TOTAL	1F	X	338.57 ID
CONSECUTIVE #/STORE & REGISTER #/DATE		2281	12 4/02/7–

A. At any time of the day, a net sales total is instantly available. This makes it easy to take hourly readings, quickly establish cash balancing information, or determine sales activity for special promotions.

B. A preprogrammed printout provides varied information for financial control. This report simplifies cash balancing, aids in maintaining control over credit transactions, and pinpoints sales activity by type.

C. A Taxable Group Total establishes total tax accountability. The register automatically captures all taxable amounts and stores them in memory for this printout. This total is instantly available at any time desired.

payment is based on headcounts, lower figures may be presented by the guests. However, verification can readily be made by staff members.

Only one or two systems of cash collection can eliminate the walkout fraud. Cash collected either by a cashier stationed at the beginning of the food service (single-price dinners or buffets) or a cashier at the end of the line of cafeterias would eliminate customer frauds of this nature. A COD system comparable to those used for beverages is occasionally used in food service.

In every other system there remains a possibility that the customer will walk out despite precautions by management and by employees. It is impossible for a waiter or waitress to continually watch a table. Even with team systems in which two waiters work together—one remaining in the dining room and the other placing orders and relaying food from the kitchen—the team cannot continually watch every customer. A team system, however, certainly is an improvement over the individual waiter system. Likewise, a cashier cannot be expected to stop every customer to determine if the check was paid, particularly during busy meal hours.

Customers may also use credit cards that are worthless or attempt to pay by checks that are not honored by banks. Unless customers are known, the best policy to follow in cashing of checks is to avoid it wherever possible. If a check must be cashed, adequate identification should be provided, and no checks should be honored for more than the value of the dinner. In the case of credit cards, a quick check of the current lists provided by the various credit card companies or a call to the company's office should provide verification of the current status of the cardholder. Of course, all signatures should be compared.

Occasionally customers will attempt, either intentionally or unintentionally, to give to cashiers counterfeit currency. In most cases this currency will be easy to detect if proper cash handling procedures are followed. All bills should be quickly examined on both sides and placed on the ledge of the register. Hopefully this cursory examination will detect most of the counterfeit money, although in some cases reproductions will be of such quality that only an expert will be able to detect the fraud.

Newer registers will determine the exact change. If this feature is not available, change to be given must be calculated by the cashier. Change should be counted out twice by the cashier, once upon withdrawing it from the register and the second time while placing it on the counter (not in the hands of the customer). If a twenty-dollar bill is presented and the check was $14.75, the cashier should count up from $14.75 to arrive at the amount tendered. Upon completion of the transaction to the satisfaction of both the cashier and the customer, the twenty-dollar bill is placed in the proper receptacle in the register and then the drawer is closed. The amount tendered by the customer should always be announced by the cashier. In the example above upon receipt of the twenty the cashier should announce "$14.75 out of $20.00."

Waiter or Waitress Theft

Depending on which system of cash collection is utilized by an establishment, various methods of fraud or chances for error on the part of service personnel arise.

Intentional Omission of Items. Items are omitted from the bill in order to establish a rapport with customers, to increase tips, or perhaps to give free merchandise to friends or fellow employees. This type of fraud occurs when inadequate dupe systems or validating systems are utilized. In the case of small items with low values, such as beverages, rolls, etc., the cost of instituting full controls may outweigh any savings effected. A full control system in organizations having full services (complete dining facilities with waiter service) is impractical since accounting for items with a retail sales value of 10¢ or 15¢ would be too costly. Bookkeeping costs would become a high percentage of income.

However, food establishments with limited menus and those featuring items of low sales value must establish these controls, since the majority of their sales may be in this price range. In these operations normally the menus are limited, and mechanical or electronic controls for these specialized stores may be installed. Without adequate controls, the chances of large-scale thefts are great and occur frequently. It is essential that some type of control or automated systems be installed, to record all sales no matter how low a value.

In some cases, the items that are to be sold are already under the control of the service staff, as in the case of milk in individual containers or a 6-gallon refrigerated carton in the service area. No record is maintained whenever a waitress pours a glass of milk. Should this charge be omitted from the check it would be impossible to track down the guilty party, since a number of personnel may have access to the milk supply.

For high-value items, the transfer of the merchandise to the waitress or waiter can be recorded, since the cost of bookkeeping for each order remains a small percentage of the overall costs. The item sold has a relatively high dollar value in relationship to bookkeeping cost.

Reusing of Checks. This type of theft may occur in any type of establishment. For high-volume operations, it is possible that a large number of sales may be of the same dollar amount. Thus a customer presented with a particular check would have no way of verifying whether it was his own or not, since the dollar amount was correct and the items may be the same. With the abbreviations normally used on checks it may be impossible for a customer to read a check without an interpreter. So long as the dollar amount is correct, he is satisfied. In fact, unless the dollar amount is higher, most customers do not care if it is their check. Certainly in cases where the check is lower and the customer realizes that it is not his check, a comment may not be made, since the customer knows he has saved some money.

Pocketing Checks or Using Unauthorized Checks. It is often possible to reproduce the checks that are used by an establishment. Certainly if stock checks (not specially imprinted ones) are being used, they may be readily purchased by anyone from dealers.

It is also possible when checks are not numbered or recorded (and in those cases where the numbers are recorded but not audited) for a waiter to simply pocket the check and the cash received, if other control systems are not being utilized. (See Figure 5-6.)

Two basic methods are used for the issuing of checks. In operations in which there is a high customer count per server, the normal practice is to issue a book or partial book of checks to each server. Figure 5-6 illustrates a method of recording this type of system. Unused checks are returned at the close of the shift. Another system may be utilized for operations in which there is a lower customer count per server. Each server signs for the check or is issued a check when a party is seated at his or her station. In this method the recording of checks and the numerical sequence is simplified, since checks are only issued when a party is already within the establishment and ready to be served.

In noncash operations (such as clubs in which all services are charges), the numbering of checks may not be required unless it is felt that staff members may be "buying" for members (i.e. giving away merchandise). For one thing, it is possible to lose a check. This could readily be noticed by keeping track of all the numbers, but the amount of work and costs involved with this type of verification as compared to simple head counts after each meal indicate that numbering systems for *total charge* operations are unwarranted.

In total charge areas, the possibility for employee theft of cash is greatly reduced. Payments are normally made by members or guests at the end of a specific period of time (usually monthly). Payments are made by checks made out to the establishment. These cannot be cashed by employees. Although more costly to operate (since there are additional bookkeeping expenses), the charge system, in fact, eliminates the need for most types of cash control since employees cannot directly benefit from theft. Unintentional errors, however, will still occur. Management must maintain control systems to guard against this possibility.

Checks can now be counted automatically by the utilization of a check numbering system similar to that being used by banks. Each check is imprinted with a magnetic number that can be read by a machine. If a number is omitted the machine will report this omission. Such a system is primarily designed for high-volume (customer) operations.

Overcharging. This practice may occur when staff members are allowed to make corrections on checks without supervision. The customer may be charged for merchandise not received, or higher prices may be entered on the check. After the customer has paid the staff member, the correct

FIGURE 5-6

RECORD OF WAITERS CHECKS
(IN GROUPS)

CASHIER _____ DEPARTMENT _____ DATE _____

| NUMBER OF CHECKS ISSUED | | WAITER'S SIGNATURE | NO. | NUMBER OF CHECKS RETURNED | | WAITER'S SIGNATURE | NO. | CHECKER'S INITIALS |
BEGINNING NUMBER	ENDING NUMBER			BEGINNING NUMBER	ENDING NUMBER			

prices and amounts are entered, the check is retotaled, and the difference pocketed by the waiter.

Incorrect Addition. Intentionally adding a dollar to each check and pocketing the money when the check is properly totaled can readily be performed, particularly if amounts are handwritten on the checks. Should the error be discovered by the customer it is normally excused, since an error in over-adding can be quickly explained away as simply poor arithmetic.

Substitutions. In some establishments with fairly tight systems of control, it may be impossible for a waitress to supply friends with free merchandise. However, substitutions can be made by ordering from the kitchen higher-priced items and charging for lower ones. Or the reverse may be true if the substitution is to be made to a customer and the cash collected by the waitress.

In the first case, a higher-priced item is ordered from the kitchen but the waitress records a lower-priced item on the check. The friend is presented with a check for the smaller amount.

In the second case (which may occur even when a food checker is used) the waitress orders the higher-priced item from the kitchen, but the food checker may not be able to verify each item on the tray. This negligence may occur either because the physical layout is poor or because the delay caused by examining each plate would be too great. The waitress tells the checker that it is a lower-priced item but collects the full amount from the customer. In high-volume operations (either food or beverage) the food checker often can only verify the number of orders on a tray. He cannot identify each order. Thus the substitution can be made either way by the server. Substitutions are normally done in conjunction with reusing of checks.

Falsification of Tips or Other Charges. In some areas of the country, notably Las Vegas or Reno, where many food and beverage sales are complimentary, other incidents occur, where a dinner is being paid for by someone other than the guest. Extra amounts of beverages or food may be placed on the checks to increase the value of sales. This extra food can then be sold to other guests, and the entire cash received pocketed by the waiter. This padding of the bill may also be done whenever the tip may be a fixed proportion of the total bill. If sales are increased by ten dollars then the tip may go up $1.50 or more. When given a free dinner the guest normally does not closely inspect the items on the bill. Instead he merely gives it a brief inspection and signs for the full amount.

In Nevada, complimentary dinners are an accepted practice. In some cases a server will even add an extra tip to the bill. Again, when the guest (gambler) checks out of the hotel, very little attention is paid to each and every item. Thus the waiter or waitress has been able to defraud the house, the guest, or both.

Finally, in some types of operations, no check is used. Amounts are either rung up on the cash register by the waiter or waitress or cash is collected and pocketed by the waitress (see "Methods of Cash Collection," in this chapter). With this system of control—or rather, the absence of it— employees may attempt any of the aforementioned methods of fraud, as well as "bunching of sales." Bunching is the practice by which the total of several checks or amounts may be rung up on the cash register at one time, but an incorrect total is rung up and the difference is pocketed by the waiter or waitress.

Incorrect Change. Shortchanging of customers is possible no matter what system is used. It cannot be prevented without a shopper system, which may or may not be able to detect the fraud. Certainly if repeated complaints by customers occur, immediate action must be taken.

A shopper system is one in which a person unknown to the regular employees is hired to come into the store and, posing as a customer, check on various segments of the system. A report is forwarded to management, and errors in the system, poor service, inferior maintenance, etc. may be detected. Normally employees will give better service to their superiors and be even more careful with portion sizes. Thus errors are not normally detected by management. The shopper, however, receives the same service as a regular customer. He may be able to notice defects in the system that are hidden from supervisors.

Cash registers that record the amount tendered and then indicate the correct change will alleviate shortchanging errors on the part of the staff. Deliberate fraud on the part of the waitress, however, is extremely difficult to detect.

Split Rings. When waitresses also handle the cash registers, split rings may occur. This situation arises when, for example, a check for $2.75 is rung up as $.65 and then $.10. The owner has lost $2.00, which the waitress pockets.

By ringing the second time, the waitress prevents the customer from seeing the actual amount of the first ring-up. The customer usually presumes there was a simple error. Should anyone question the two rings for one check, the waitress merely states that she made an error on the first ring and rang $2.65 by mistake. A cash register with a tape will help to alleviate this type of fraud.

Waiter or Waitress Errors

In addition to all the possibilities for fraud, waiter and waitress errors also occur. Almost any of the previously mentioned types of fraud may occur inadvertently. The server may also commit the following:

Incorrect Addition on Checks. Incorrect addition, both in favor of the house and against the house, may occur. When errors are made in favor of the house, they may quickly be noted by customers and the server's attention is brought to the error. A correction is then made, and all parties are aware of the errors. Errors in favor of the customer may be noted by the guest, but in many cases the guest accepts the error and does not report it. The frequency of errors in favor of the customer seems to be higher than those in favor of the house (according to conversations with representatives of cash register companies).

Incorrect Addition in Ringing. Should a number of items be rung up, extended, or combined by the waitress at the time of ringing, mathematical mistakes may occur. Three hamburgers costing $.75 each may be rung up erroneously by the waitress as $2.15, or two items such as pie and coffee, at 25¢ and 15¢, may be rung up as 35¢.

Omission of Items. During the normal course of service to a guest, extra items may be ordered at intervals during the meal and erroneously omitted from the check. Perhaps the guest wishes an extra salad or dessert, and due to the rush of business and the need to serve other customers, the waitress forgets to include this item on the check. The customer may call the waitress' attention to the item. More than likely, however, if the omission is even noted by the guest, no mention of it will be made either to the waitress or the cashier, and the house will lose this income.

Incorrect Pricing. If waitresses are permitted to enter prices on the check without verifying the selling price, if prices are changed, or even if prices are entered by some type of cash register, there is the possibility for an incorrect price to be charged. Overcharging of the customer again may be noted by the guest, but the tendency for customers not to verify totals allows this type of error to occur frequently. Even if the customer totals and reviews the check, he may not be aware of the exact price. Incorrect pricing, either undercharging or overcharging, is equally damaging for the establishment. With overcharging the customer may decide that the total costs were too high and may not return. With undercharging, of course, the revenues are lost.

Incorrect Change. If waitresses are handling cash either by using the cash register directly or by collecting from the customer and paying the amount to a cashier, the possibility of giving incorrect change occurs. Again the error may be made either in favor of the house or in favor of the guest. Whether honest or dishonest, the error is still costly.

Bartender Fraud or Errors

A bartender that handles cash (using a register) has the same opportunity for theft as a waiter or a waitress—and the same chance of error. Controls that are effective for one type of employee may be applied to the other, with slight variances due to the nature of the merchandise sold, the method of service, and the type of cash collection.

Cashier Theft or Error

The possibility of theft or error for cashiers is more restricted than with either bartenders or waitresses, since they normally do not handle the products sold. If the cashier is responsible solely for cash collection, errors or theft may occur under any of the following categories:

1. Cashier keeps the money and pockets or destroys a check.
2. Cashier changes the total of check after collection.
3. Cashier bunches sales, split-rings, or underrings.
4. Cashier gives incorrect change.
5. Cashier performs incorrect addition.
6. Cashier falsifies payout or adds items to complimentary checks and removes them from other checks.

Previous Balance Fraud

If a cashier is also responsibile for food checking, another type of fraud may occur. On some cash registers, a previous balance figure may be entered on a machine, and then an entry is printed on the check. The entry may be utilized instead of an actual sale. The printed figure is registered on the check and either the waiter or the customer pays this amount without realizing that, in fact, the figure means nothing, since it has never been recorded as a sale. (See Figure 5-7.) The check may or may not be destroyed by the cashier.

This type of fraud also occurs when the food checker-cashier and the food server are conspiring to defraud management.

FIGURE 5-7 *Previous Balance Fraud*

			Dollar amounts printed by cash register
1 R.B.	I	4.00 ◄	Sale not recorded—previous balance key used. (# I Key)
1 Stk	II	5.00	Sale recorded (# II Key)
1 Fish	II	4.00	Sale recorded (# II Key)
			Total
	Total	13.00	Waiter or customer pays $13.00. Only $9.00 in sales is recorded.
	Cash Received		
	III	9.00	Cashier pockets $4.00, or splits it with waiter.

Variations of this method may be used even when a cashier does not perform food checking, if complete control systems are not being used.

In the case where the cashier-checker is pocketing the money for himself, the check can be destroyed *if it is also the function of the cashier to verify the checks turned in.* In cases where verification of the check is not performed by another department (*as it should be done*), the cashier does not have to destroy the check.

The only method of detecting this fraud is if each check is verified by another party to determine that a previous balance key has not been rung up in the space allocated for a sale item or to verify the total on the check with the cash-received key. In the example in Figure 5-7, #I key is a previous balance key. The roast beef should have been rung up on the #II key. The #III key for cash receipts is actually rung up after the guest and the waiter have paid the cashier. A clerk auditing the check must examine all items and the total key (cash received, #III key).

To simplifiy this checking, the cash receipts key (#III) should be rung on the front of the check. Thus, when an audit is performed, the auditor need only look at the one side of the check. Previous balance keys should either not result in a printed entry on the check or, preferably, the entry should clearly be denoted as "previous balance."

Methods of Cash Collection

There are five basic methods for the handling of either charges or cash:

1. The customer pays the cashier.
2. The customer pays the waitress, who has already paid the bartender or food server—the "cash bank" method.
3. The customer pays the bartender.
4. The customer pays the waitress, who in turn pays the bartender.
5. The customer pays the waitress, who in turn pays a cashier. Variations of cash collection and dispensing of beverages are illustrated later. (See page 106.)

Customer Pays the Cashier. With the first system, only two persons are involved in the handling of cash: the customer and the cashier, who turns in her receipts at the end of the day. In order for this system to be effective, customers must be prevented from walking out without paying their checks. Only one entrance and exit should be used, and (in some manner) customers must be forced to be counted automatically.

It is extremely difficult for a cashier in a busy operation to determine how many people are walking out to go to the restrooms, make a telephone call, or buy some cigarettes. When more than one order is written up on a check and five people pass the cashier's stand, she must somehow insure that all five of those persons are actually the ones whose orders are on that particular check. Practically, this is almost impossible.

This type of system is really most effective for operations in which customers pay at the end of a service line, as in cafeterias, or at the beginning of the line, as in fixed price operations (buffets, smorgasbords). In some types of operations possible additional methods of control would be to incorporate into the system the device of having a separate check for each person and to have guest facilities located in a position that would not require guests to pass by the cashier's station. Thus, every person passing the cashier's station would be required to present a check.

Unless an operation falls into one of the aforementioned categories, or uses individual checks as a control, the operator is relying upon the honesty of the customer as a means of guaranteeing receipts of all amounts due.

The basic advantage of this system is that it separates those handling cash receipts from those entrusted with the issuing of merchandise and the responsibility for the charging of the customer for that merchandise.

Insuring that every item consumed by the customer has, in fact, been placed on the check is normally the responsibility of the waitress. Only in some cases, such as a cafeteria line or when a food checker is used, is the cashier or checker responsible for this task. Obviously, unless there are further controls in the system that make it mandatory for the waitress or checker to charge the full amount, there is a distinct possibility for error or fraud.

Waitress Pays Food or Beverage Server and Then Customer Pays Waitress. This system usually operates under a "bank" policy. At the start of a shift, each waitress is issued a small bank from which she makes change and pays for any merchandise as she receives it from either the cooking area or the beverage area. Thus, if the waitress picks up three drinks worth $3.00, she pays the bartender as she receives the merchandise. Then she collects from the customer. Collection, in most cases, is made at the time the order is delivered to the table.

One advantage of this system is that a customer cannot walk out without paying for merchandise received. Another is that errors in making change are normally absorbed by the waitress, since at the end of the shift the full amount of the bank must be turned in. Since tips and the bank are mixed together in most cases, the shortages are made up out of the tips received.

In many states it is illegal for the operator to charge the waitress or cashier for cash shortages. With this system, it is possible to "charge" her without violating the law. In some cases, the waitress will run a tab for the customer, but this is not recommended.

Customer Pays the Bartender. Under this system, which is most commonly used at bars in which the customer is seated at the bar, the customer receives his drinks and pays immediately, or he may run up a tab, according to the policy of the house. Normally, this system is used in establishments when the normal pattern and volume of business does not warrant the hiring of another person as a cashier. Unfortunately, this system is fraught with loopholes that would enable dishonest employees to defraud the owners and management.

The one advantage of a bartender collecting cash is that it eliminates one person from the payroll. Normally a bartender is able to perform this function without being overworked. Since a minimum of one bartender is required for many operations even though the volume of business may not warrant it, the function of cashier is most conveniently transferred to the bartender.

The disadvantage of this type of system is that the bartender then has control over both the issuing of merchandise and the collection of cash. He may have the opportunity to perpetrate all areas of fraud that may be done by the waitress, as well as those available to cashiers.

Every attempt should be made to prevent this type of collection. Should the volume and the nature of the business necessitate this type of system, other controls are mandatory. Additional validation controls, mechanical or automatic systems for inventory control, shopping services, and spot checking should be performed as often as possible.

Customer Pays Waitress Who in Turn Pays Bartender. With this system, the waitress merely transports the money from the customer to the bartender. The bartender operates the cash register as well as serving drinks. In this system, the bartender usually can also receive cash directly from customers. A bartender may receive cash directly from either customers sitting at the bar or in some cases from those who have received table service.

The advantage of the system is that it again eliminates the need for a cashier and thus the extra salary. If the customer must pay the waitress, there is less chance of the customer walking out without paying, since it is relatively simple for each waitress to know which of her customers has paid prior to their leaving the table. It is still possible, though, for the customer to walk out without paying while the waitress is involved with other duties. A distinct disadvantage of this system is that the waitress' prime function is to serve food, and in many cases she must wait while the bartender finishes mixing drinks.

With this system, a waitress receipt should be used, since this will pinpoint the responsibility for "lost" checks. As the waitress gives the money and check to the bartender the receipt is stamped with the amount paid. Thus, should money or check fail to be turned in, the waitress can produce the receipt, which indicates that the loss was due to an error on the part of the bartender. If she cannot produce a receipt, then the presumption must be made that either the customer walked out without paying or that the waitress "lost" the check and/or the money.

If the waitress is paying the bartender, there is once again the disadvantage of having the person responsible for the issuing of merchandise also having control of the cash receipts. Any system allowing this to occur has a built-in disadvantage, and is a poor procedure in that it precludes accurate separate comparisons of receipts and issues.

If this system or the previous one (customer pays bartender) must be used, as in the case of many small taverns, alternate or additional controls must be used:

a. Require all sales to be rung up. Require all tabs to be recorded as sold.

b. Require a receipt to be given to all customers and waitresses.

c. Post prices.

d. Have a shopper (a hired customer) come in, without the knowledge of the employees, to verify that the system is in fact being followed.

e. Red Star the customer's receipt to add an incentive for him to watch ringups. Under this system whenever a customer receives a receipt with a red star on it, a free drink (or other award) is given to him.

f. Require the bartender to use a measuring device (preferably a clear shot glass) to prevent short pouring, and also require him to pour and measure in front of the customer.

g. Place the cash register in a prominent position so that the customer can clearly see the amount being rung up.

h. Use a mechanical dispensing system. This may be ideal for places such as ball parks or racetracks, which have small bars located throughout the park.

i. Spot check all parts of system frequently.

Customer Pays the Waitress, Who in Turn Pays the Cashier. This system incorporates all the advantages of the previous system, plus it follows the basic precept that those persons receiving money should be separate and distinct from those issuing merchandise. The same practice of issuing receipts to the waitress must also be used. Although seemingly more complicated, this system, which separates the controls, i.e. the duties of the bartender or cook from the waitress and from the cashier, in practice becomes the most effective and efficient method for accurate cost accounting and control systems.

At the end of the cashier's shift a report must be turned in that summarizes the transactions that took place at the register. This report will vary, depending upon the capabilities of the register being used and the assigned responsibilities of the cashier. One type of report is illustrated in Figure 5-8. Each establishment should design its own form for its own needs.

In some cases the cashier will turn in the entire cash drawer, which is counted in her presence, and then the amounts are recorded on a separate sheet. In other cases the cashier will count out the drawer and place the

FIGURE 5-8 *Sample Cashier's Report for Register Transactions*

CASHIER'S AND CHECKER'S RESTAURANT REPORT

PLACE _____ SHIFT _____ DATE _____ CHECKER _____

REGISTER KEY READINGS	CASH AND CHARGES		
	CASHIER	TAPES	CASH TURN IN

KEY _____

    READING $ _____

    VOIDS $ _____

        TOTAL _____

KEY _____

TOTAL CASH $

    READING $ _____   SHORTAGE (PLUS) $

    VOIDS $ _____   OVERAGE (MINUS) $

        TOTAL _____   CASH TOTAL $

KEY _____

    READING $ _____   CHARGES

    VOIDS $ _____

        TOTAL _____ $ _____

KEY _____ $ _____

    READING $ _____

    VOIDS $ _____

        TOTAL _____   COMPS.

KEY _____ $ _____

    READING $ _____ $ _____

    VOIDS $ _____

        TOTAL _____   COMP. TOTAL _____

TOTAL TO BE ACCOUNTED FOR $ _____   TOTAL ACCOUNTED FOR _____ entire amount (or perhaps withdraw the original bank and place the remaining amount) in a sealed envelope. The summary of the transactions may be placed on the face of the envelope, which has been imprinted with the necessary information, or a separate form may be placed inside the envelope. Any of the methods are acceptable.

FIGURE 5-9 *Possible Systems or Routes of Beverage Dispensing and Cash Collection*

1. Bartender------Customer ∤∤∤ Bartender
2. Bartender------Customer ∤∤∤ Cashier
3. Bartender------Customer ∤∤∤ Bartender ∤∤∤ Cashier
4. Bartender------Waitress------Customer ∤∤∤ Cashier
5. Bartender------Waitress------Customer ∤∤∤ Waitress ∤∤∤ Bartender
6. Bartender------Waitress------Customer ∤∤∤ Waitress ∤∤∤ Cashier
7. Bartender------Waitress------Customer ∤∤∤ Waitress

                ∤
                ∤
                ∤
          Bartender

*8. Customer ∤∤∤ Cashier/ticket/Customer/ticket/Bartender------Customer
*9. Customer ∤∤∤ Cashier/ticket/Customer/ticket/Waitress/ticket/Bartender------Waitress------Customer

------ Beverage
∤∤∤ Cash

* Customer buys ticket for drinks from cashier and then gives ticket to bartender. A waitress may take ticket and give ticket to bartender or checker. With numbers 8 or 9 the sequence of events may be changed but the basic elements of control and issuing remain the same.

BASIC PRINCIPLES FOR CASH CONTROL

No matter which method of collection is used by an operator, there are basic principles for the collection of cash or for the charging of accounts that should be adhered to by an operator.

The most basic principle is that those persons responsible for the issuing of food or beverage—that is, the waiter, waitress, or bartender— should not be allowed to also receive cash.

General Rules

1. With all the systems, any check should be added by and rung up on a cash register, or totaled by an adding machine. No matter how efficient a waitress, bartender, or cashier may be, errors in addition occur with astonishing frequency. For the most part, errors in favor of the house are quickly brought to the attention of the person responsible, whereas errors that favor the customer are often quietly ignored and the earned revenue lost forever.

It may be desirable for management to place a small hand calculator or adding machine at each waitress station. The cost of these machines is approximately $50.00, and their operating costs are infinitesimal. If a station is used by several waitresses or waiters, the savings effected by the use of these machines should pay for the machines within a very short period of time. In addition, once personnel are familiar with the operation of the machine a great deal of time can be saved, since not only are they more accurate but they are also much faster. Any server having a check to add in which there may be ten or more items will save at least one minute.

2. All checks should be rung up individually, and the cash drawer closed after each check is rung up. Without this type of control in all systems it is possible for the person operating the register to underring the check and pocket the difference or to make just one ringup when two checks are presented. A check for $16.00, for example, may be rung up as $15.00, and $1.00 is pocketed by the cash register operator. This type of fraud would be a distinct possibility in those systems not using a method of control or stamping the "cash received" amount on the checks.

3. Use a dual method. Under this system, all merchandise taken from the bar is first rung up by the bartender (prechecked) on a separate key. When the cash is received by the cashier it is again rung up. The two totals should be equal. (Food may also be prechecked.)

4. Do not allow alterations to be made on checks, and have all checks individually priced by machine for each item.

New improvements in cash registers allow menu or bar items to be imprinted on the cash register keys. (See Figures 5-1 through 5-4, at the beginning of this chapter.) Instead of the cashier ringing up dollar amounts, the sale is recorded as the actual menu item, and the register automatically records the correct dollar amount. Extensions are also done automatically. For example, if a customer orders three steaks, at $7.25 each, the food checker and/or the cashier may record 3 x steaks and the correct amount of $21.75 is imprinted on the check. Under the older systems, the cashier would have to either ring $7.25 three times or multiply the amount in her head. An additional advantage is that the cashier need not look at the menu for the correct price. She merely has to punch the correct key and the correct price is locked into the machine.

On most new cash registers the prices can be changed without much difficulty. Some systems can also change the entire menu by the insertion of one card, so that the cash register can be used for breakfast, lunch, and dinner without adding additional controls. These new registers will also record inventories and keep customer counts. They also have many other features that simplify the tasks of all personnel involved with food and beverage control.

5. Never allow more than one person to be responsible for the cash register. When two persons are needed (relief of shifts), separate banks must be issued and readings must be taken each time the operator is changed.

6. Do not allow registers to be cleared. Clear keys must be handled only by top management, but preferably the master cash record on registers need not be cleared at any time. Machines should also have tapes for permanent records. Register tapes should be torn, not cut.

7. Checks should be specially imprinted, numbered, issued, and recorded. The verification of issuing of checks and the recording of this should be done by the accounting department, not by the manager or person responsible for actual cash receipts.

8. The responsibility for the issuing of different types of merchandise should be placed so that if any given type of merchandise is missing or if receipts are short, the individual responsible for shortages can be pinpointed. Separate inventories for each bartender should be required.

9. Automate and integrate the entire collection and issuing systems so that bookkeeping is kept to a minimum, and so that each control point serves as a check upon other parts of the system.

As part of the controls that must be integrated with the cash collection systems, separate counts of customers and items served should be maintained. Other responsible department heads should correlate the customer and party count maintained by the hostess and the count indicated by checks issued.

To verify honesty of cashiers, shoppers (hired by management) should be instructed to present the exact amount of bill and immediately leave the cashier station. The shopper should then note if the actual amounts were rung up by cashier and if the check was handled in the proper manner. Often a cashier will use this type of situation to pocket the money, reuse the check (in conjunction with waitress), or destroy the check. If, for example, the cashier is charged with the responsibility of verifying that all checks issued have been accounted for, then there is really no system at all. She is merely checking on herself, and if the check is not rung up, no one can detect the loss.

10. Insist that all procedures be followed by all personnel, with no exceptions made. Any change in pricing, alteration of checks, refunds, or allowances for unsatisfactory merchandise must be approved by an authorized individual only, and noted on appropriate records.

11. Cash registers should be designed so that each check can be stamped when the money is received. The auditing department should then verify that every check has been stamped. Preferably the cash receipts stamp or ring should be clearly and easily distinguished from other types of rings made on checks.

12. Adopt a system specifically designed to suit each of the needs of your organization. One type of system is normally not sufficient for an operation. Systems should change with variances in shifts, types of services, etc.

13. A receipt should be given to all customers whenever a system is used that does not incorporate actual checks.

14. Review procedures and verify systems at least once a month.

CASE PROBLEMS

Case 1. Justine, a waitress, has several favorite customers with whom she is friendly. Whenever they want a steak, or an extra portion, she substitutes a much lower priced item in place of the steak, or she chooses to charge them only for the single portion. Even with an individual check for each customer, there would be no way for management to observe this type of fraud without some other type of control.

Case 2. Mary, an excellent and honest waitress, handles more customers than most of the other waitresses. However, since she is always pressed for time, somehow she never manages to remember to write on the checks all the dessert items and beverages she has served. An honest mistake, but very costly for management.

Case 3. Susan, one of ten waitresses in a large restaurant serving over two hundred persons, always charges her customers for every item that she has served them and never substitutes lower prices. The customers normally pay the cashier. The manager has called her into the office, since in a routine spot check of all checks for one day several of hers are found to be missing. She insists she gave the customers the checks; the cashier insists that he never received the money. Perhaps no one is guilty of dishonesty, yet management has lost over twenty dollars in receipts.

Case 4. Charles, a very excellent mixologist with a charming personality, is well liked by his customers, at least his favorite customers. Charles always pours the better brand labels for these individuals and charges for the cheaper brands. He substitutes the cheaper brands on the waitresses' orders and charges them for the more expensive ones. Charlie makes a lot of tips and all the sales are rung up.

Case 5. Sam goes one step farther than Charles. He short pours all his drinks. Since he also collects the money, he is able to pocket quite a bit of extra change from those customers who pay the bill but don't wait or don't bother to see if it is rung up. No one is watching him, so he doesn't bother to ring these up. The owner is unaware and unable to notice any shortages, since by short pouring, Sam is able to keep his liquor cost percentage right where it should be. For every five or six dollars that the owner takes in, Sam takes one for himself, with no overhead or cost.

Case 6. Alice is Charles' girlfriend and has learned quite a bit from him. The two of them work on different shifts. Thus the boss has at least prevented any collusion. Alice works a cash bank. She pays the bartender for each and every drink that she receives. Her specialty is charging the full amount for the call liquor (name brand) ordered by the customer, but ordering a cheaper brand for him from the bar and paying the bartender for the cheaper brand. If a customer orders a regular brand but he is not a regular customer, she raises the price a nickel or a dime and pockets the difference. But she works hard!!

Chapter 5

I. *Class Exercise*

Discuss methods of eliminating the errors or frauds in the six cases above.

II. *Study Questions*

1. List the primary tasks of the cash receipts function area.

2. What additional information or tasks can be programmed into new "computer type" cash registers?

3. List the types of customer fraud. For each type indicate a method of prevention.

4. List and discuss intentional errors or theft by waiters and waitresses. Illustrate methods required to prevent each type of fraud.

5. Discuss the differences that may occur if the personnel committing the fraud or errors are
   a. bartenders.
   b. cashiers.

6. What is the "previous balance" fraud? Discuss means of preventing it.

7. Discuss the 5 basic methods for handling cash collection.

8. Discuss the basic principles for cash control.

9. What would be an ideal system of cash collection?

6

Food Purchasing Principles

GENERAL PURCHASING POLICIES

For some operations, the primary role of the purchasing agent is to insure that the establishment has all the food required. This role, however, is only part of the true function of the purchasing agent.

As today's technology improves and the selection of products increases in quality as well as variety, the purchasing agent is faced with the difficult task of determining which products should actually be used in an operation. He must make his decisions based on the varying degrees of quality, the needs of the establishment, and the true costs of the products.

In earlier days the purchasing agent (steward, dietician, food and beverage manager, or whatever title he or she may have held) had little choice in buying many products. For example, if french fried potatoes were on the menu, he had to purchase fresh whole potatoes, perhaps limiting the purchase to a specific variety. Today, however, he may purchase fresh whole potatoes, fresh peeled potatoes, frozen or fresh potatoes already cut, frozen or fresh potatoes already partially cooked, fully cooked french fried potatoes that merely have to be reheated, or perhaps a powdered instant potato mixture. The purchasing agent's decision must be based on a number of factors, such as the quality of the final product, the skill level of his employees, the costs of the products, and overall costs of production (including such factors as space allocation, equipment depreciation, building costs, labor costs) and of course employee and customer acceptance.

Every day the average food service establishment uses hundreds of products. The purchasing agent must make decisions relating to each of the products. Three interdependent factors govern which products he eventually selects. His decision is based on obtaining the best quality product for a specific purpose, bearing in mind that he should obtain it at the lowest possible price.

Quality, however, may be a rather loose term. Quality for one type of operation may be completely different from that in another establishment. The quality hamburger for a 59¢ hamburger shop may differ completely from the quality hamburger in a higher-priced restaurant.

Even the determination of quality may differ from one establishment to another or from one guest to another. For example, a quality pie crust with lard used as the shortening agent may be unacceptable to individuals who have a dislike for the distinctive taste imparted by this product. Or perhaps the taste of aged meat is an unfamiliar one to certain clientele but desired by others. Even the fact that quality meat has an extensive fat covering and marbling may be considered unacceptable in certain areas of the country.

The quality of service in the coffee shop also differs from the standards established in a French service restaurant. Each however, may be the best for the purpose and according to the standards established by management.

Just as quality differs from operation to operation, it may also change within an operation. The best quality AA eggs may be purchased for service directly to the customer, such as in an omelette, or poached eggs. However, an AA quality egg may not be deemed necessary if the eggs are merely to be used for a cake mixture. Nor should the purchasing agent purchase the finest quality peeled whole tomatoes if the chef is to use them in making a tomato sauce in which they are to be ground up in the cooking process. Among the finest beef cuts is the tenderloin, yet few, if any, operations would even consider using this cut of meat for hamburger, even for a superior quality hamburger.

Thus, in discussing quality the standard varies with the purpose for which the product is used, as well as the type of operation. Basically, then, the statement that the purchasing agent's function is to purchase the best quality for a specific product purpose at the lowest possible price must be followed.

In order to accomplish his tasks, the buyer must be aware of all factors influencing the quality of the product outside the establishment. He must also be alert to the conditions within his own operation that will alter or influence the quality of the end product that is to be served.

It would be foolish for a buyer to purchase a whole side of beef if within his operation there was no person with the required skills to cut it into the correct cuts of meat. Nor should he purchase unpeeled potatoes if the necessary equipment for the operation (a potato peeler) was not available, either because the establishment never owned one or because it was out of service due to a breakdown or malfunction.

Often an establishment will change chefs or cooks, and the new personnel will prefer to use different types of products or techniques. The purchasing agent who may be unaware of this change and continues to purchase in his normal fashion may soon be overstocked with unwanted and unusable merchandise. One chef may use large quantities of soup bones. The next may prefer to fortify his stocks with good soup bases. Some chefs or storeroom clerks are meticulous about rotating their inventories and utilizing all leftovers. Others may be careless and stockpile foods that eventually must be discarded. The food buyer, although perhaps not directly responsible for these inefficiencies, must be made aware that unnecessary waste and, in turn, unnecessary purchases are occurring. Corrective action should be taken.

Although the receiving clerk is directly responsible for insuring that all goods that are delivered conform to the specifications and purchase orders, the purchasing agent must provide the necessary materials and copies of information regarding the quality and quantity ordered. In addition, the buyer should verify occasionally that the procedures for the receiving of merchandise are actually followed for all types of merchandise.

Conditions in the general economic community that appear to have no direct bearing upon a food service establishment may greatly affect the products that are available for use. The buyer who is unaware of weather conditions in various parts of the country may suddenly find that the cost of raw materials has unexpectedly either risen or fallen due to the change in harvest conditions. A sudden freeze in the producing areas may cause the price of lettuce and other similar products to double within just a few days. A good harvest of corn or grains this year might affect the cost of beef next year, as feed costs are lowered to cattle breeders.

Transportation costs are an integral part of overall raw products' costs. A raise for teamsters may add a considerable amount to the total purchase price of materials. A strike by transportation workers may cause a shortage or a complete absence of products from the market.

The devaluation of the dollar causes a price rise for all imported products. The alert buyer may stock up on some items just prior to a devaluation.

An efficient buyer must get his information from many sources. He must not become so wrapped up in the needs of his own organization and the daily pressures of work that he ignores some of the basic tools necessary to perform his tasks. He should be able to utilize government agricultural bulletins, stock market reports, commodity bulletins, and wholesale daily reports.

Information regarding new products, price changes, and special sales of each individual purveyor should be conveyed to the buyer by the salesman of the vending companies. Too often the salesman, however, becomes merely an order taker, either because of his own lack of foresight or due to the attitude of the buyer who clearly demonstrates that he merely wishes to place an order and get the task over with. This lack of interest by both parties often creates undue costs for management as opportunities for discount buying or special purchases are overlooked. This does not mean that the buyer needs to devote a great deal of time to every salesman that comes, but he should indicate a willingness to listen and be receptive to new ideas and be interested in information on sales or other important changes.

At the same time, and in the course of doing business with the various salesmen, the buyer will develop an awareness as to which salesmen do indeed pass on information and which ones are merely trying to sell or take orders. A good salesman will be aware of the needs of the food service establishment that he is servicing. He may have a number of products on sale during a week, but omit mentioning them as he realizes that they do not fit the needs of the food service establishment. Thus he saves the buyer's time as well as his own and in turn, earns the respect and appreciation of the buyer. When a product that may be useful to the establishment is on sale or other information may be useful, the buyer will listen more closely, since he knows the information is germane to his establishment.

Simply because the chef orders a particular item does not mean that the buyer should always purchase it. A close working arrangement between the chef (or other person planning the menus) and the buyer is essential. Items not in season are often placed on the menu if they are ordered by customers without regard to the added expense that may be incurred, such as shipping costs if they must be shipped in by special carrier. Placing seasonal items on the menu during the season is fine. However, often the menu planner will place them on too early in the season or continue to leave them on the menu at the close of the season. This not only adds considerably to the cost of the item, but also may tend to lower the quality of the food, since the peak times for the growing or catching of certain produce or seafood directly affect the quality of the item.

The buyer must also inform the chef regarding the availability of products. In many cases it is possible for the chef to alter the recipe or substitute one item in place of another, without detracting from the quality of the finished product.

PURCHASING PRACTICES

As in any field, there are many practices within the food service industry that may apply to all operators, regardless of the type of food served or the degree of service offered by the institution. The buyer must be aware of certain approved industry practices and at the same time be alert to deviations from these policies and practices that are frowned upon.

For example, under certain conditions it is permissible for purveyors to refund to the house a percentage of the sales. This discount (discussed below) is an accepted and industry-wide practice. However, this refund is made to the food service establishment and not to the purchasing agent. In practice, several other acceptable types of refunds are also made.

Rebates

A rebate is a type of refund made to a company, based normally upon the volume of purchases made by that company. It normally occurs under circumstances in which a purveyor does not wish to vary his basic price structure at the time of delivery. This often occurs when the person delivering the product makes out a bill or invoice at the time of delivery, and the amounts delivered vary. No previous order need to have been given; the driver leaves enough to replenish the stock of the food service establishment. Bread, milk, and ice cream are typical types of products that may be supplied under this arrangement. The driver prices all his customers' bills in the same manner and at the same fixed price. At the end of a specified period of time, the purveyor determines how much of the product the food service establishment consumed and gives a refund based upon the total volume of consumption.

Discounts

Prompt Payment. Under this practice, a food service establishment often is able to save some percentage of a bill by paying promptly. The invoice or statement of the purveyor might contain the notation "1/10 net 30." This means that if the operator pays within 10 days of the date of the invoice or statement he will be able to subtract 1% of the sales price.

Quantity Purchase. A discount may also be used when the food service establishment buys a specified quantity that is larger than a normal order. For example, a case of an item may cost $5.00; but if the buyer purchases five cases at one time he may receive a 10% discount. Thus, each case would cost the establishment $4.50. This net price of $4.50 is normally the amount placed on the invoice.

Kickbacks

The kickback is a practice that is frowned upon. In this case, the purchasing agent and the purveyor agree that the purveyor will give directly to the buyer a certain amount of money or goods as long as the purchasing agent continues to buy the purveyor's products. This practice is illegal and it is possible to prosecute the purchasing agent.

Kickbacks may take the form of special preferential treatment given to the buyer or purchasing agent. Perhaps the vending company will take the purchasing agent and his family out to dinner or even send gifts to his home. Christmas presents may be considered an acceptable form of appreciation, but if the cost of the gifts becomes excessive, then perhaps it would be wise for management to place a dollar limit on gifts that may be accepted. Gifts over that amount must be returned. Many large companies today limit the dollar value to approximately $25.00.

Kickbacks, whether they take the form of gifts, preferential treatment, or actual cash refunds, are difficult to control. Therefore, managements must set up adequate controls to insure that all purchasing agents are performing their functions solely for the establishment rather than for their own benefit.

Date of Purchase

Besides taking advantage of discounts and rebates the purchasing agent may also save additional money for the establishment by timing his orders so that the purveyor, in effect, "carries" the establishment for a period of time by extending credit. This may occur when a buyer times his orders so that he buys most of the products at the beginning of the credit period, uses up the products during the period, and pays at the expiration of the cycle. An example is given below:

> Company A purchases most of its products from XXX Co. Company A's statement from the XXX Co. is rendered at the end of each month, and a 1/10 net 30 policy is in effect. All purchases made during the month are placed on the statement. Buyer A purchases most of his items at the beginning of the month, so that at the end of the month his inventories are low. He reorders for delivery on the 1st or 2nd of the following month. He thus is able to use the products free of charge for one month, and still receive a 1% discount for prompt payment.
>
> Company B purchases from the same company. However, the buyer's orders are placed at the end of the month. Thus he only has the use of the products for a short period of time prior to the actual date when he must make payment.

Suppose both companies consume $5,000 worth of goods each month. Buyer A purchases the $5,000 worth at the beginning of the month. The food is sold throughout the month (with a 50% food cost he would receive $10,000). The company retains the use of the money during the month, and then pays the purveyor. In effect, every month the buyer is using the purveyor's money. He also deducts 1% and is able to save $50.00. One could also presume that there were no other expenses and that over the month's period the buyer banked the money and received an additional dividend by placing the money in a savings account.

Buyer B, however, has to pay immediately. Each month he would, therefore, be using his own money. This adds to the total cost of the operation. If buyer B is unable to pay on time he loses the $50.00 discount. He also is unable to use any of the purveyor's money. Since the cost of borrowing money is approximately 12% a year, another 1% is lost.

By the proper timing of orders the astute purchasing agent has saved about $100.00, or 2% of the total order for the month.

Specifications

A specification is a detailed description of a product that enables the purveyor to understand exactly what the purchasing agent desires. Specifications may also include information concerning how the product is to be delivered. They may even include conditions of the sale, such as how it is to be paid for, and any other special conditions that may affect the purveyor. Normally, when referring to specifications we consider only those terms that directly concern the product.

Specifications are essential. Without them neither the buyer nor the seller can be sure that they are, in fact, talking about the same product. The simple table below compares various types of specifications for a meat product and an automobile.

1. Automobile	1. Steak
2. Ford	2. Strip Loin
3. 4 door	3. Bone-in
4. LTD	4. U.S.D.A. Prime
5. Air conditioning	5. 1/4-inch outside fat
6. Bucket seats	6. 2-inch tail

Obviously, in purchasing an automobile one does not simply say "I want a car." If that were the case the buyer might be talking about and pricing a Cadillac and the seller a Volkswagen. As we progress from items 1 through 6 in the table, the specific product that we are referring to becomes clearer and clearer. Of course, with both products many more bits of information still must be given that will further clarify exactly what is desired. With the automobile no mention has been made of color, braking system, etc., and with the steaks we have omitted information regarding aging, degree of marbling, weight, and other pertinent data. No purchasing agent can compare the prices and qualities of purveyors unless he knows that the purveyors are quoting on exactly the same product. One obviously does not expect a car dealer to sell you an air-conditioned car for the same price as a car without air conditioning, nor should a buyer expect one purveyor to sell steak for a much lower price unless there are markedly different characteristics or specifications in the products.

Sources of Specifications

Specifications for each type of product are available from various state, federal, or local governments, as well as from industry associations and some textbooks.

Some excellent sources are:

U.S. Department of Agriculture, Agricultural Marketing Service, for produce, milk, poultry, meat, fresh and processed products, Agriculture Handbook 341.

National Association of Meat Purveyors, *Meat Buyers Guide to Standardized Meat Cuts* and *Meat Buyers Guide to Portion Control Meat Cuts* (NAMP, Chicago, Ill.)

Lendell H. Kotshchevar, *Quantity Food Purchasing,* (John Wiley and Sons, Inc., New York 1975).

Home Economics—Consumer Services, National Canners Association, 1133 20th St. N.W., Washington, D.C. 20036.

National Restaurant Association, Chicago, Ill.

U.S. Department of Commerce, National Marine Fisheries Service, Washington, D.C.

Specifications must be carefully written and tailored to the needs of each establishment. The purchasing agent may use the specifications of other institutions as a guide. But he must adapt them to his own particular needs.

An example (see Figure 6-1) of complete specifications for grades of lemons as listed by the U.S.D.A. illustrates the great detail that must be shown. An establishment might select certain attributes and list those for its own specifications. For example, §51.2805 may be included in its entirety, but most likely one paragraph, (a), might be used along with §51.2806, §51.2807, and others.

The National Live Stock and Meat Board, the U.S.D.A., and the National Association of Meat Purveyors all have general guidelines for primal as well as retail cuts of meats. Figure 6-2 shows a number of steaks, with some information and specifications.

With the specifications given in Figure 6-2 for the various tenderloin, top sirloin, and strip loin steaks, additional details must be formulated for a specific operation. No mention is made within the general specifications as to the size of the steak, nor are any instructions given or required as to the amount of aging desired. These further details must be determined by management and included in the final written specifications that are forwarded to all vendors.

METHODS OF BUYING

Quotations

Various segments of the food service industry tend to prefer to use different methods to obtain merchandise. Generally speaking, hotels and restaurants normally operate on the quotation or daily bid system. In this system the purchasing agent either receives a call from the purveyor or calls the purveyor directly to inquire as to the prices of the various products that he must order on that day. In some cases the buyer may actually visit the market to determine the quality of the products of the vendors, while at the same time obtaining the selling prices. For products that do not fluctuate

FIGURE 6-1 *Sample of U.S. Specifications*

UNITED STATES STANDARDS

FOR GRADES OF

LEMONS

EFFECTIVE SEPTEMBER 1, 1964

U. S. DEPARTMENT OF AGRICULTURE
AGRICULTURAL MARKETING SERVICE
WASHINGTON, D. C.

FIGURE 6-1 (*continued*)

2

UNITED STATES STANDARDS FOR GRADES OF LEMONS [1]
(29 F.R. 11328)
Effective September 1, 1964

GRADES

Sec.
51.2795 U.S. No. 1.
51.2796 U.S. Export No. 1.
51.2797 U.S. Combination.
51.2798 U.S. No. 2.

UNCLASSIFIED

51.2799 Unclassified.

TOLERANCES

51.2800 Tolerances.

JUICE CONTENT

51.2801 Juice content.

APPLICATION OF TOLERANCES

51.2802 Application of tolerances.

STANDARD PACK

51.2803 Standard pack.

STANDARD SIZING AND FILL

51.2804 Standard sizing and fill.

CONDITION STANDARDS FOR EXPORT

51.2805 Condition standards for export.

DEFINITIONS

51.2806 Firm.
51.2807 Fairly well formed.
51.2808 Well formed.
51.2809 Reasonably smooth.
51.2810 Smooth.
51.2811 Contact spot.
51.2812 Internal evidence of Alternaria development.
51.2813 Membranous stain.
51.2814 Damage.
51.2815 Fairly well colored.
51.2816 Well colored.
51.2817 Fairly firm.
51.2818 Reasonably well formed.
51.2819 Fairly smooth.
51.2820 Serious damage.
51.2821 Moderately well colored.

AUTHORITY: The provisions in this subpart issued under secs. 203, 205, 60 Stat. 1087, as amended, 1090 as amended; 7 U.S.C. 1622, 1624.

---

[1] Packing of the product in conformity with the requirements of these standards shall not excuse failure to comply with the provisions of the Federal Food, Drug and Cosmetic Act or with applicable State laws and regulations.

GRADES

§ 51.2795 U.S. No. 1.

"U.S. No. 1" consists of lemons which are firm, fairly well formed (unless specified as well formed), reasonably smooth (unless specified as smooth), which have stems which are properly clipped, and which are free from decay, contact spot, internal evidence of Alternaria development, unhealed broken skins, hard or dry skins, exanthema, growth cracks, internal decline (endoxerosis), red blotch, membranous stain or other internal discoloration, and free from damage caused by bruises, dryness or mushy condition, scars, oil spots, scale, sunburn, hollow core, peteca, scab, melanose, dirt or other foreign material, other disease, insects or other means.

(a) Color: The lemons are fairly well colored (unless specified as well colored): *Provided,* That any lot of lemons which meets all the requirements of this grade except those relating to color may be designated as "U.S. No. 1 Green" if the lemons are of a full green color, or as "U.S. No. 1 Mixed Color" if the lemons fail to meet the color requirements of either "U.S. No. 1" or "U.S. No. 1 Green" (See § 51.2800.)

(b) Lemons have the juice content specified in § 51.2801.

§ 51.2796 U.S. Export No. 1.

"U.S. Export No. 1" consists of lemons which are firm, fairly well formed, reasonably smooth and which are free from decay, contact spot, internal evidence of Alternaria development, unhealed broken skins, exanthema, growth cracks, internal discoloration and free from damage caused by bruises and dryness or mushy condition.

(a) At least 50 percent of the lemons are free from damage caused by scars, oil spots, scale, sunburn, peteca, scab, melanose, dirt or other foreign material, other disease, insects or other means, and the remainder of the lemons are free from serious damage by any cause.

FIGURE 6-1 (*continued*)

3

(b) Color: Lemons are moderately well colored. (See § 51.2800.)

(c) Lemons have a juice content of not less than 28 percent by volume.

§ 51.2797   U.S. Combination.

"U.S. Combination" consists of a combination of U.S. No. 1 and U.S. No. 2 lemons: *Provided,* That at least 40 percent, by count, of the lemons meet the requirements of U.S. No. 1 grade.

(a) Color: The lemons are fairly well colored (unless specified as well colored) : *Provided,* That any lot of lemons which meets all the requirements of this grade except those relating to color may be designated as "U.S. Combination Green" if the lemons are of a full green color, or as "U.S. Combination Mixed Color" if the lemons fail to meet the color requirements of either "U.S. Combination" or "U.S. Combination Green". (See § 51.2800.)

(b) Lemons have the juice content specified in § 51.2801.

§ 51.2798   U.S. No. 2.

"U.S. No. 2" consists of lemons which are fairly firm, which are reasonably well formed and fairly smooth, which have stems which are properly clipped, and which are free from decay, contact spot, internal evidence of Alternaria development, unhealed broken skins, hard or dry skins, exanthema, internal decline (endoxerosis), and red blotch, and free from serious damage caused by bruises, membranous stain or other internal discoloration, dryness or mushy condition, scars, oil spots, scale, sunburn, hollow core, peteca, growth cracks, scab, melanose, dirt or other foreign material, other disease, insects or other means.

(a) Color: The lemons are fairly well colored (unless specified as well colored) : *Provided,* That any lot of lemons which meets all of the above requirements of this grade except those relating to color may be designated as "U.S. No. 2 Green" if the lemons are of a full green color, or as "U.S. No. 2 Mixed Color" if the lemons fail to meet the color requirements of either "U.S. No. 2" or "U.S. No. 2 Green". (See § 51.-2800.)

(b) Lemons have the juice content specified in § 51.2801.

UNCLASSIFIED

§ 51.2799   Unclassified.

"Unclassified" consists of lemons which have not been classified in accordance with any of the foregoing grades. The term "unclassified" is not a grade within the meaning of these standards but is provided as a designation to show that no grade has been applied to the lot.

TOLERANCES

§ 51.2800   Tolerances.

In order to allow for variations incident to proper grading and handling in each of the foregoing grades, the following tolerances, by count, are provided as specified:

(a) *U.S. No. 1 grade*—(1) *For defects.* Not more than 10 percent of the lemons in any lot may fail to meet the requirements of this grade, but not more than one-half of this tolerance, or 5 percent, shall be allowed for decay, contact spot, internal evidence of Alternaria development, internal decline (endoxerosis), unhealed broken skins, growth cracks, and other defects causing serious damage, including not more than one-tenth of this latter amount, or one-half of 1 percent, for lemons affected by decay at shipping point: *Provided,* That an additional tolerance of 2½ percent, or a total of not more than 3 percent, shall be allowed for lemons affected by decay en route or at destination.

(2) *For color.* Not more than 10 percent of the lemons in any lot may fail to meet the requirements relating to color.

(b) *U.S. No. 2 and U.S. Combination grades*—(1) *For defects.* Not more than 10 percent of the lemons in any lot may fail to meet the requirements of the U.S. No. 2 grade, but not more than one-half of this tolerance, or 5 percent, shall be allowed for decay, contact spot, internal evidence of Alternaria development, and internal decline (endoxerosis), including not more than one-fifth of this latter amount, or 1 percent, for lemons affected by decay at shipping point: *Provided,* That an additional tolerance of 2 percent, or a total of not more than 3 percent, shall be allowed for lemons affected by decay en route or at destination.

(2) *For color.* Not more than 10 percent of the lemons in any lot may fail to meet the requirements relating to color.

(3) When applying the tolerance for U.S. Combination grade individual packages may have not more than 10 percent less than the percentage of U.S. No. 1 required: *Provided,* That the entire lot averages within the required percentage.

(c) *U.S. Export No. 1.* (1) *For defects:* 10 percent for lemons which fail to meet the requirements of the grade:

FIGURE 6-1 (*continued*)

4

Provided, That not more than the following percentages of the defects enumerated shall be allowed:

1 percent for decay;
3 percent for contact spot;
3 percent for broken skins which are not healed;
3 percent for growth cracks;
3 percent for internal evidence of Alternaria development;
3 percent for internal discoloration;
5 percent for soft; and,
5 percent for damage by dryness or mushy condition.

(2) For color: 10 percent for lemons which fail to meet the requirements relating to color.

(3) The contents of individual containers may have not more than 10 percentage points less than the percentage specified to meet the requirements in § 51.2796(a): *Provided,* That no container shall have more than double the percentage specified for any one of the defects enumerated in sub-paragraph (c)(1) of this section.

JUICE CONTENT

§ 51.2801 Juice content.

Lemons in the U.S. No. 1, U.S. Combination and U.S. No. 2 grades shall have a juice content of not less than 30 percent, except when designated as "U.S. No. 1 Green for Export", "U.S. Combination Green for Export" or "U.S. No. 2 Green for Export". When so designated, the lemons shall have a juice content of not less than 28 percent, by volume.

APPLICATION OF TOLERANCES

§ 51.2802 Application of tolerances.

(a) Except when applying the tolerances for "Condition Standards for Export", and the tolerances set forth in sub-paragraph (c)(1) of § 51.2800, the contents of individual packages in the lot, based on sample inspection, are subject to the following limitations: *Provided,* That the averages for the entire lot are within the tolerances specified for the grade:

(1) For packages which contain more than 10 pounds, and a tolerance of 10 percent or more is provided, individual packages in any lot shall have not more than one and one-half times the tolerance specified. For packages which contain more than 10 pounds and a tolerance of less than 10 percent is provided, individual packages in any lot shall have not more than double the tolerance specified, except that at least one decayed lemon may be permitted in any package.

(2) For packages which contain 10 pounds or less, individual packages in any lot are not restricted as to the percentage of defects: *Provided,* That not more than one lemon which is seriously damaged by dryness or mushy condition may be permitted in any package and, in addition, en route or at destination not more than 10 percent of the packages may have more than one decayed lemon.

STANDARD PACK

§ 51.2803 Standard pack.

(a) Lemons shall be fairly uniform in size and shall be packed in boxes or cartons and arranged according to the approved and recognized methods. Each wrapped fruit shall be fairly well enclosed by its individual wrapper.

(b) All such containers shall be tightly packed and well filled but the contents shall not show excessive or unnecessary bruising because of overfilled containers. When lemons are packed in standard nailed boxes, each box shall have a minimum bulge of 1¼ inches; when packed in cartons or in wire-bound boxes, each container shall be at least level full at time of packing.

(c) "Fairly uniform in size" means that when lemons are packed for 165 carton count or smaller size, or equivalent sizes when packed in other containers, not less than 90 percent, by count, of the lemons in any container shall be within a diameter range of four-sixteenths inch; when packed for sizes larger than 165 carton count, or equivalent sizes packed in other containers, not less than 90 percent, by count, of the lemons in any container shall be within a diameter range of six-sixteenths inch.

(1) "Diameter" means the greatest dimension measured at right angles to a line from stem to blossom end of the fruit.

(d) In order to allow for variations incident to proper packing the following tolerances are provided:

(1) 10 percent for wrapped fruit in any container which fails to meet the requirement pertaining to wrapping; and,

(2) 5 percent for containers in any lot which fail to meet the requirements for standard pack.

STANDARD SIZING AND FILL

§ 51.2804 Standard sizing and fill.

(a) Boxes or cartons in which lemons are not packed according to a definite pattern do not meet the requirements of standard pack, but may be certified as meeting the requirements of standard

FIGURE 6-1 *(continued)*

5

sizing and fill: *Provided*, That the lemons in the containers are fairly uniform in size as defined in § 51.2803: *And provided further*, That the contents have been properly shaken down and the container is at least level full at time of packing.

(b) In order to allow for variations incident to proper packing, not more than 5 percent of the containers in any lot may fail to meet the requirements of standard sizing and fill.

CONDITION STANDARDS FOR EXPORT

§ 51.2805 Condition standards for export.

(a) Not more than a total of 10 percent, by count, of the lemons in any container may be soft, affected by decay or contact spot, or have broken skins which are not healed, growth cracks, internal evidence of Alternaria development, internal decline (endoxerosis), or serious damage by membranous stain or other internal discoloration, or dryness or mushy condition, except that not more than the following percentages of the defects enumerated shall be allowed:

(1) One-half of 1 percent for decay;
(2) 3 percent for contact spot;
(3) 3 percent for broken skins which are not healed;
(4) 3 percent for growth cracks;
(5) 3 percent for internal evidence of Alternaria development;
(6) 3 percent for internal decline (endoxerosis);
(7) 5 percent for soft;
(8) 5 percent for serious damage by membranous stain or other internal discoloration; and,
(9) 5 percent for serious damage by dryness or mushy condition.

(b) Any lot of lemons shall be considered as meeting the condition standards for export if not more than a total of 10 percent, by count, of the lemons in any container have defects enumerated in the condition standards for export: *Provided*, That no sample shall have more than double the percentage specified for any one of the defects enumerated.

DEFINITIONS

§ 51.2806 Firm.

"Firm" means that the fruit does not yield more than slightly to moderate pressure.

§51.2807 Fairly well formed.

"Fairly well formed" means that the fruit shows normal characteristic lemon shape and is not materially flattened on one side. Lemons having moderately thickened necks at the stem end shall be considered as fairly well formed unless the appearance is materially affected.

§ 51.2808 Well formed.

"Well formed" means that the fruit is typically normal in shape with well centered stem and stylar ends.

§ 51.2809 Reasonably smooth.

"Reasonably smooth" means that the appearance of the lemon is not materially affected by protrusions or lumpiness of the skin or by grooves or furrows. Coarse pebbling is an indication of good keeping quality and is not objectionable.

§ 51.2810 Smooth.

"Smooth" means that the skin is of fairly fine grain and that there are no more than slight furrows radiating from the stem end.

§ 51.2811 Contact spot.

"Contact spot" means an area on the lemon which bears evidence of having been in contact with decay or mold.

§ 51.2812 Internal evidence of Alternaria development.

"Internal evidence of Alternaria development" includes red or brown staining of the tissue under the button in the core, or in the fibro-vascular bundles.

§ 51.2813 Membranous stain.

"Membranous stain" is a brown or dark discoloration of the walls of the fruit segment.

§ 51.2814 Damage.

"Damage" means any specific defect described in this section; or an equally objectionable variation of any one of these defects, any other defect, or any combination of defects, which materially detracts from the appearance, or edible or shipping quality of the fruit. The following specific defects shall be considered as damage:

(a) Dryness or mushy condition when affecting all segments of the fruit more than one-fourth inch at the stem end, or more than the equivalent of this amount, by volume, when occurring in other portions of the fruit;

(b) Scars (including sprayburn and fumigation injury) which exceed the following aggregate areas of different types of scars, or a combination of two or more types of scars the seriousness of which exceeds the maximum allowed for any one type:

FIGURE 6-1 (*continued*)

6

(1) Scars which are very dark and which have an aggregate area exceeding that of a circle one-fourth inch in diameter;

(2) Scars which are dark, rough or deep and which have an aggregate area exceeding that of a circle one-half inch in diameter;

(3) Scars which are fairly light in color, slightly rough, or with slight depth and which have an aggregate area exceeding that of a circle 1 inch in diameter; and,

(4) Scars which are light in color, fairly smooth, with no depth and which have an aggregate area of more than 20 percent of the fruit surface;

(c) Oil spots (Oleocellosis or similar injuries) which are more than slightly depressed, soft, or which have an aggregate area exceding that of a circle one-half inch in diameter;

(d) Scale when more than ten medium to large California red or purple scale adjacent to button at stem end or scattered over fruit or any scale which affects the appearance of the fruit to a greater extent;

(e) Sunburn which causes appreciable flattening of the fruit, drying of the skin, material change in the color of the skin, appreciable drying of the flesh underneath the affected area or affects more than 25 percent of the fruit surface;

(f) Hollow core which causes the fruit to feel distinctly spongy; and,

(g) Peteca when more than two spots or when having an aggregate area exceeding that of a circle one-fourth inch in diameter.

§ 51.2815 Fairly well colored.

"Fairly well colored" means that the area of yellow color exceeds the area of green color on the fruit.

§ 51.2816 Well colored.

"Well colored" means that the fruit is yellow in color with not more than a trace of green color. Fruit of a decided bronze color shall not be considered well colored.

§ 51.2817 Fairly firm.

"Fairly firm" means that the fruit may yield to moderate pressure but is not soft.

§ 51.2818 Reasonably well formed.

"Reasonably well formed" means that the fruit is not decidedly flattened, does not have a very long or large neck and is not otherwise decidedly misshapen.

§ 51.2819 Fairly smooth.

"Fairly smooth" means that the skin is not badly folded, badly ridged, or very decidedly lumpy.

§ 51.2820 Serious damage.

"Serious damage" means any specific defect described in this section; or an equally objectionable variation of any of these defects, any other defect, or any combination of defects, which seriously detracts from the appearance, or the edible or shipping quality of the fruit. The following specific defects shall be considered as serious damage:

(a) Membranous stain, or other internal discoloration which seriously affects the appearance of the cut fruit;

(b) Dryness or mushy condition when affecting all segments of the fruit more than one-half inch at the stem end or more than the equivalent of this amount, by volume, when occurring in other portions of the fruit;

(c) Scars (including sprayburn and fumigation injury) which exceed the following aggregate area of different types of scars, or a combination of two or more types of scars the seriousness of which exceeds the maximum allowed for any one type:

(1) Scars which are very dark and which have an aggregate area of more than 5 percent of the fruit surface;

(2) Scars which are dark, rough or deep, and which have an aggregate area of more than 10 percent of the fruit surface;

(3) Scars which are fairly light in color, slightly rough or of slight depth, and which have an aggregate area of more than 25 percent of the fruit surface; and,

(4) Scars which are light in color, fairly smooth, with no depth, and which have an aggregate area of more than 50 percent of the fruit surface;

(d) Oil spots (Oleocellosis or similar injuries) which are soft, or which have an aggregate area exceeding that of a circle 1 inch in diameter;

(e) Scale when California red or purple scale is concentrated as a ring or blotch, or more than thinly scattered over the fruit surface, or any scale which affects the appearance of the fruit to a greater extent;

(f) Sunburn which causes decided flattening of the fruit, marked drying or dark discoloration of the skin, material drying of the flesh underneath the affected area, or which affects more than one-third of the fruit surface;

FIGURE 6-1 (*continued*)

(g) Hollow core which causes the fruit to feel excessively spongy;

(h) Peteca when more than five small spots, or when having an aggregate area exceeding that of a circle three-fourths inch in diameter; and,

(i) Growth cracks that are leaking, gummy or not well healed.

§ 51.2821 **Moderately well colored.**

"Moderately well colored" means that the area of greenish-yellow or yellow color exceeds the area of green color on the fruit.

The United States Standards for Grades of Lemons contained in this subpart shall become effective September 1, 1964, and will thereupon supersede the United States Standards for Lemons which have been in effect since March 15, 1959, as amended, January 15, 1961 (7 CFR, §§ 51.2795–2819).

Dated: August 3, 1964.

ROY W. LENNARTSON,
Associate Administrator.

[F.R. Doc. 64–7915; Filed, Aug. 5, 1964; 8:51 a.m.]

greatly in price over a period of time, weekly quotation sheets may be sent out by the purveyor, or a salesman may call upon the establishment and present the latest price quotations. This practice is generally followed for frozen or canned items. Produce, meats, and seafood may be quoted on a daily basis.

Since dealers in canned or frozen items normally carry many products, the quotation sheet may include only the items that are on special for that week or period. A presumption may be made that the prices for the remaining products have not changed. If this is not the case, then normally the salesman will bring the new price to the attention of the buyer.

Larger restaurant, hotel, and food organizations may prefer to buy in part by one of the other available methods.

Contract Buying

Bid System. This system is used more often by hospitals, schools, governmental agencies, and larger commercial operations. Under this system, bids are submitted by purveyors to supply a product or group of products, for a specified period of time and for a specific amount of merchandise. Normally, when submitting the contract for bid, the buyer indicates other pertinent data, such as method of delivery, payment, and place of delivery. Deliveries may be made at intervals during the life of the contract.

In some cases there may be an escape clause that allows the purveyor to cancel the contract should certain conditions arise. A typical situation would be one in which the purveyor's costs exceed the selling price. This might occur due to crop failure or a sudden shortage of a product.

Bids are usually submitted sealed and opened at one time so that all purveyors are given an equal opportunity to obtain the contract.

FIGURE 6-2 *Specifications for Steaks*

FOUR FABRICATED CUTS FROM THE TRIMMED FULL LOIN

1. **Full Tenderloin, Special.** All surface fat is removed in making this cut but it may be trimmed three ways . . . 1) Leave both the "silver skin" and the "side strap" on the tenderloin, 2) Remove the "side strap" but not the "silver skin" or 3) take off both the "side strap" and the "silver skin" as pictured.

2. **Strip Loin, Boneless, 4 x 3.** Strip loins are sold on their overall width (9″, 10″, 11″) or on the length of the flank meat (tail) measured from the eye of the loin. A strip loin, regular, includes 6 inches of flank on the rib end and 4 inches of flank on the sirloin end. Intermediate is 4 x 3. Short cut is 3 x 2.

3. **Top Sirloin, Boneless.** After separation from the bottom sirloin, no trimming is necessary or is done on the top sirloin so the terms "regular" or "trimmed" are unnecessary when referring to this cut.

4. **Bottom Sirloin, Boneless, Regular.** Most bottom sirloins are sold as "regular" with the flank meat attached (see arrow). Removing the flank meat changes the name to bottom sirloin, boneless, trimmed.

Test 4

CUTTING TEST — FOUR FABRICATED CUTS FROM TRIMMED FULL LOINS		
Item	Description	Yield Per 100 lbs.
1. Tenderloin, Special Trim	As pictured. Fat & membrane removed	7.5
2. Strip Loin, Boneless	As pictured. 4″ x 3″, intermediate	25.5
3. Top Sirloin, Boneless	As pictured.	19.5
4. Bottom Sirloin, Boneless, Regular	As pictured, with flank attached.	12.0
Grinding Beef	Approximately 80% lean.	12.5
Usable Cuts		77.0
Fat	———————	11.5
Bone, Shrink, Cutting Loss	———————	11.5
Fat, Bone, Shrink		23.0
Total		100.0

*For computer and manual pricing, conduct your own production line cutting tests.

From "*Merchandising Beef Loins*," *National Live Stock and Meat Board, Chicago, Illinois, p. 14. Reproduced by permission.*

FIGURE 6-2 (*continued*)

PORTION CONTROL BONELESS LOIN STEAKS*

Similarities in NAMP-USDA specifications of the steaks at the right are: The cut surface of both steaks at the large end must be at least 1½ inches wide at the narrowest diameter. Elsewhere, the narrowest diameter must be no less than 1 inch, exclusive of surface fat.

Differences in specifications are: Close trim steaks may have no more than an average of ¼ inch surface fat (½ inch maximum at any point). Special trim steaks must have all surface fat removed, together with the "side strap" and the "silver skin."

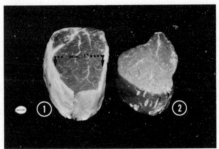

1. Tenderloin Steak, Close Trim (1189)
2. Tenderloin Steak, Special Trim (1190)

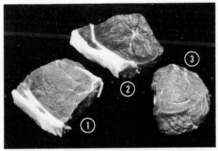

Pages 16, 17 and 18 contain step by step instructions for making the three top sirloin steaks shown at the left. Table 6 on the opposite page "Comparative Tests — Top Sirloin Steaks" provides an opportunity to compare the yields of the three steaks when they are made from top sirloins, boneless.

1. Top Sirloin Steak, Boneless, Regular (1184)
2. Top Sirloin Steak, Boneless, Semicenter Cut (1184A)
3. Top Sirloin Steak, Boneless, Center Cut (1184B)

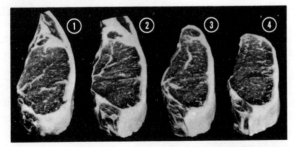

The four beef strip loin steaks, boneless, identified at the right, are pictured above.

1. Strip Loin Steak, Boneless, 3″ Tail (1178)
2. Strip Loin Steak, Boneless, 2″ Tail (1180)
3. Strip Loin Steak, Boneless, 1″ Tail (1180A)
4. Strip Loin Steak, Boneless, No Tail (1180B)

Fixed Price Contracts. In some situations either a formal or informal contract (written or oral) may be negotiated by the buyer and the purveyor. This type of contract is normally used with items such as milk, bread, ice cream, and linen products. There may or may not be a closing date for the contract. The purveyor agrees to furnish to the establishment merchandise at a specified price for a period of time.

Normally all products of a like nature are purchased from one company. For example, all dairy products used would be purchased from the same company. Should there be a change in price, the buyer has the opportunity either to accept the new price or cancel the contract.

Futures Contracts. Futures contracts take two slightly different forms. In one form, the buyer is not exactly sure as to the exact amount of merchandise, nor does he wish delivery until some future date. At the same time he wishes to assure himself of a price so that he in turn may make contracts (as in industrial feeding) or price his own menus.

In the second form, the buyer again wishes to maintain a fixed price, for the same reasons, but a fixed amount of merchandise is guaranteed in the contract.

The advantage of the futures contract is that it allows the food service establishment to fix its own costs for that period of time. An example would be a contract feeder who must supply a college for a full year. Unless it can reasonably be assured of most of its costs, the contract may turn out of be a losing one.

The disadvantage of futures contracts is that should costs go down the buyer may be paying in excess of going market prices.

QUOTATION SHEETS

Every purchasing agent should utilize a quotation sheet, and management should insist that all the records of quotations be kept for at least six months. The use of quotations protects the establishment as well as the purveyor and buyer, since misunderstandings regarding prices can easily be corrected by referring to the quotation sheet. The reputable buyer protects himself by being able to prove at any time that not only is he performing his tasks, but, in addition, as the quotation sheet will show, he is purchasing at the lowest possible price. (There are some exceptions to this rule.)

A quotation sheet may be combined with other forms, depending upon the needs and the policies of the organization. Two examples of quotation sheets are given below. Figure 6-3 is a quotation sheet that is used exclusively to determine which purveyor has the lowest prices (presuming that all purveyors have specifications and are quoting on the same products). Figure 6-4 shows a quotation sheet that is used in conjunction with an inventory sheet. Either of the two forms may be used as an order sheet, or a separate

FIGURE 6-3 *Sample Quotation Sheet*

AAA RESTAURANT
Quote Sheet

By _____ Date _____

Amt.	Item	V Sales Co.	W Sales Co.	Z Sales Co.
2	Lettuce-Ice	6.25	6.35	6.10
12	Tomatoes 5 x 6	4.25	4.00	4.50
3	" 6 x 7	4.00	4.10	3.75

purchase order form may be used. Each establishment should design its own forms based on its needs and its own procedures and organization.

Some organizations have sufficient volume so that the purveyors may deliver specific items without having to worry whether minimum orders need to be given. In these cases, obviously the purveyor quoting lowest on each item would receive the order for that item. In other cases, it may be necessary to split the order and give to each purveyor several items. The total cost of the order is important. In the examples given (Figures 6-3 and 6-4) although the "Z" Sales Company quoted a lower price on two of the items, the total cost of the order, should the establishment purchase from Z Sales, would be higher, since the bulk of the order is in 5 x 6 tomatoes, on which they quoted the highest price.

For the smaller operation, a simple method of combining ordering with the quotation sheet would be to circle the price quotation of the company that the buyer is giving the order to (see Figure 6-4). For the larger company and with larger orders it may be necessary to make up a separate purchase order.

The forms shown in Figure 6-3 and 6-4 are used when orders and quotations are given by telephone.

FIGURE 6-4 *Sample Combined Quotation and Inventory Sheet*

AAA RESTAURANT
Inventory & Quote Sheet

Inventory By _____   Date _____

Quote By _____

Item	On Hand	Order	V Sales	W Sales	Z Sales
Lettuce-Ice	2	2	6.25	6.35	(6.10)
Tomatoes 5 x 6	6	12	4.25	(4.00)	4.50
Tomatoes 6 x 7	2	3	4.00	4.10	(3.75)

FACTORS INFLUENCING AMOUNTS AND FREQUENCY OF ORDERS

As can be noted in Figure 6-4 (and under normal operating conditions in any food service establishment) amounts to be ordered are determined by the buyer based on a forecast of needs and amounts on hand (inventories). A number of other factors may also influence the amounts to be ordered:

1. Type of merchandise (perishability)
2. Storing facilities (size of freezers, storerooms)
3. Shipping costs
4. Discounts for quantity buying
5. Credit
6. Turnover desired
7. Location of establishment (in the country or near a convenient market)
8. Delivery schedule of purveyors

9. Convenience and cost of ordering
10. Availability of products (long or short supplies)
11. Weather predictions and forecasts
12. External factors (strikes, interest rates)
13. Production schedules and skill of employees

The knowledgeable buyer, by working with one or several of the above factors, may be able to improve the quality of the products he purchases while at the same time lowering the cost. For example, the agent may take advantage of low freight rates by slightly enlarging his storage facilities, particularly for products that have a long shelf life. In other instances orders may be given to several purveyors having different delivery schedules, to purchase products (produce, in particular) that have a rapid rate of deterioration. Fresher products may mean higher yields.

Note that the controls required and the skill level of the purchasing agent for food products are at a much higher level than those required in liquor purchasing. The degree of control should also be greater, since prices are not of a constant nature and vary from dealer to dealer. With liquor, a given product can normally be obtained from only one or two dealers. In food purchasing the same products are sold by any number of vendors.

Liquor quality will not vary (i.e., a brand of liquor is the same at all times). Most food products, however, are purchased by item, not by brand. Prices in some cases are not published, but rather quotations are given, so that a written record must be retained to verify that indeed the purchasing agent has taken advantage of the lowest quotation.

Finally, the instability of markets and the latitude that a food purchasing agent has in selecting purveyors necessitates that tighter controls be utilized so that management can at any time verify that "the best quality for a given purpose has been purchased at the lowest possible price."

OTHER FORMS AND CONTROLS

In large organizations, purchase requisitions, purchase orders, and the procedures utilized in the purchasing of liquor products should be applied equally to the purchasing of food products. Normally, however, items purchased on a day-to-day basis, such as bread and dairy products and some meats and produce, may be excluded from this requirement.

Chapter 6

I. *Class Exercise*

Gather a list of purchasing reference publications, as well as the information published by local purveyors and other agencies.

II. *Study Questions*

1. What is meant by the term "quality"?
2. Why is purchasing food today more complex than it was 25 or 50 years ago?
3. What are the basic objectives in purchasing food?
4. Discuss the external factors that influence the decisions of the food purchasing agent.
5. Define the terms: rebate, discount, and kickback.
6. Discuss "timing" of purchases.
7. Draw up specifications for one food item.
8. List the 4 basic methods of buying.
9. What factors influence the amount purchased or frequency of ordering?
10. Discuss differences between beverage purchasing and food purchasing.

7

Simplified Mathematics for Food Cost Control

When partially and fully processed products were introduced into the food service industry ten to fifteen years ago, changes should have been made in purchasing, accounting, and control systems. The old rules and techniques applied by most operators, purchasing agents, and chefs were no longer valid.

Yet, personnel in the field continue to use archaic mathematical formulas and computations to determine food cost operating data. While improved information could be obtained today from computers, the use of computers thus far in food service control has been minimal. So the daily food cost percentages, the quantities to buy, and the determination of which product to buy are still largely performed on a rule-of-thumb basis that permits the operator to "guesstimate" within 5% of actual performance.

But profits today are normally no higher than 5%. Thus, using this rule-of-thumb basis, the operator may be working with a loss even before commencing to process food service products. Unless closer attention is paid to food purchasing and control systems so that better techniques are applied, the entire food service industry may be jeopardized.

The primary calculations with which every purchasing agent, chef, or food service supervisor is daily confronted are the same. The calculations are repetitive, involving both fixed and variable data. The variables usually are changes in wholesale prices and in the number of persons to be served.

THE BASIC FORMULAS

This chapter is concerned with the basic formulas needed for reaching correct answers and decisions. It will also present easy ways to make calculations once the variables are known.

Terminology

As Purchased (A.P.) Weight—Amount purchased, including bones, fat, unusable trim, outer layers, excess moisture, etc.

Edible Portion (E.P.) Weight—The actual net amount that must be obtained after processing has been performed.

Portion Size—Normally in ounces, the amount served to each individual.

Waste—The amount of unusable food that is lost due to processing, cooking and portioning. To determine the waste %, the weight of the total loss is divided by the A.P. weight of the product.

Waste or weight of loss ÷ A.P. Weight = Waste %

Yield—The amount of usable product remaining after all processing, cooking, and portioning is done. The figure is the reciprocal of the waste % (waste % + yield % = 100 %). The yield % can be obtained independently by dividing the A.P. weight into the net weight of the final usable product. The net usable weight is also called the yield:

Yield ÷ A.P. Weight = Yield %

Food Cost Control Problems

Daily Problems. Although all food supervisors are confronted with innumerable other decisions on a daily basis, there are three basic costing problems that must be solved every day. These are outlined below:

1. The amount to buy, based on predictable counts (paid lunches, bed counts, minimum guarantee on parties, or forecasts).
2. The portion cost.
3. Which product to buy based on lowest market price.

1. *Amount to buy*—For every function served, or every guest in a restaurant, or every menu item served, some determination must be made as to the quantity that must be purchased of every specific item.

Information as to the predicted number of persons to be served is sometimes obtained from the sales department or from forecasts made by managerial personnel. In turn, the portion size for each item must be combined with the expected number of persons. An adjustment must be made for the losses in cooking and processing. Finally, a fudge factor must be added or subtracted, due to the efficiency or inefficiency of either the kitchen or other departments. These calculations yield an amount that hopefully is within tolerable limits. (See Figure 7-1.)

2. *Portion cost*—A determination of the actual portion cost for every menu item must be made. Although this may only be done at infrequent intervals, the fluctuating market costs of the raw products that the industry uses frequently require updating of menu prices. All too often this updating information is omitted because the food and beverage controller is unable to calculate these costs readily. Yet the information needed to perform these

tasks efficiently can be available within moments once the initial data are calculated. (See Figure 7-2.)

3. *Most economical purchase*—To complicate matters still further, there may have been changes in the market price of these items during the interim. Certain products may have gone up in price, others down, and some may no longer be available. These complicating factors are often ignored for several reasons. By changing products, the easy routine and computations

FIGURE 7-1 *How Much to Buy—Old Method**

No. of Persons x Portion Size = E.P. Weight in Ounces

E.P. Weight Oz. ÷ 16 = E.P. Weight in Pounds

E.P. Weight ÷ Yield % = A.P. Weight

Example: 100 Persons—Portion Size 4 oz.—Yield 50%

100 x 4 = 400 ÷ 16 = 25 lbs.

25 lbs. ÷ .50 = 50 lbs. A.P. Weight

FIGURE 7-2 *Portion Cost—Old Method*

Amount Purchased x Price = Total Cost

Total Cost ÷ Portions Served = Portion Cost

Example: Yield 50%—Price $1.00 lb.

50 lbs. x $1.00 = $50.00

$50.00 ÷ 100 portions = $.50 Portion Cost

*A common mathematical error made by personnel charged with purchasing is to utilize the waste % figure rather than the yield %. In doing so, the E.P. Weight is utilized as follows:

E.P. Wt. = 25 lbs.   E.P. Wt. + (Waste % x E.P. Wt) = A.P. Wt.

For example: 25 lbs. + (.50 x 25) = 37.5 lbs. A.P. Wt. (Incorrect figure)

This basic mathematical error presumes that if 25 lbs. are required and it is known that there is a 50% loss, then by multiplying the E.P. Weight by the waste % and adding these figures, the A.P. Weight is obtained: 25 + 25 (.50) = 37 1/2 lbs. A.P. Weight. After utilizing this technique several times and not having enough to serve, the purchasing agent or chef adds a fudge factor to allow for "inefficiency" and eventually ends up by guessing at how much to buy.

with which the controller or purchasing agent is familiar will have to be adjusted or changed. Also, how exactly does one compare the price of beef chuck with that of round? The yields are different, products may be different, and even the quality may vary. But for many menu items, these can be used interchangeably. Thus, the buyer can compare beef ribs at different stages of processing and select which product to buy based on lowest portion cost. In fact, decisions such as this must be made almost every day by purchasing agents.

For example, even in selecting hamburger, should one purchase regular ground beef at 65 cents per pound or extra lean ground beef at 99 cents per pound? If these items are to be used in meat loaf, for which the net amount of the cooked product is the primary factor, then determining the true cost can save hundreds of dollars even for a small operation.

Thus, each week due to fluctuations in predicted sales, or every time a new function is booked, the same type of information is pumped into the system. The numbers game is again played, calculations are again performed, and once again an answer is obtained.

Variable and Fixed Data. The variable and fixed data with which we must operate are outlined below:

Variable
1. Market price of raw goods.
2. Number of persons expected.

Fixed
1. Portion sizes.
2. Yield percentages of products utilized.

Variable data generally involve the following:

1. *Market prices* are constantly changing. The differences between the costs of similiar items also fluctuate. For example (although today most operators do not purchase entire carcasses of beef), the prices of choice carcasses do change—a U.S.D.A. Yield 1 (see p. 151) may be 60 cents per pound whereas a U.S.D.A. Yield 2 may be 57 cents. Tomorrow the prices may be Yield 1 for 63 cents per pound and Yield 2 for 61 cents. Should the purchasing agent switch or not?

On page 151 the table indicates that the amount of usable product obtainable from a Yield 1 carcass (using minimum amounts) is 52.3 percent, whereas that obtainable from Yield 2 carcass is 50 percent. One method of determining the true price utilizes the following procedure:

$$\text{A.P. Price} \div \text{Yield \%} = \text{E.P. price}$$

At 60 cents for Yield 1, the true price is:

$$\$.60 \div .523 = \$1.15/\text{E.P. lbs.}$$

At $.57 for Yield 2, the true price is:

$$\$.57 \div .50 = \$1.14/E.P.\ lb.$$

At 63 cents for Yield 1 the true amount is:

$$\$.63 \div .523 = \$1.20/E.P.\ lb.$$

For Yield 2 at 61 cents the true amount now is:

$$\$.61 \div .50 = \$1.22/E.P.\ lb.$$

Another case is the selection of portion-cut steaks, which might be purchased for $3.00 per pound as compared to whole strippers at $2.25 per pound. Certainly allowances must be made for labor costs, the use of equipment and space, and many other fringe areas such as heat, light, power, and payroll benefits. But the basic question still remains—which is the better buy?

2. The *number of persons expected* for any week or for any day of the week will vary. Exactly how much should be purchased for each day can swiftly be calculated with this new system.

These two figures—market prices and the number to be served—are the only ones that vary. Thus every food service operator should be able to respond to these variables on a day-to-day basis and not delay in effecting necessary changes within an organization.

Fixed data generally involve the following:

1. *Portion size*, once fixed for a menu item, rarely changes. Portions may be different however, for varying styles of food service within one organization. They may also change from meal to meal—lunch portions versus dinner portions, à la carte versus table d'hôte.

2. For every product that is purchased, the *yield percentage* obtained from the item should normally not vary, once calculated. Minor changes are normal, but if a peeled tenderloin yields 53% of usable meat, then this percentage will not vary. If an unpeeled tenderloin yields 42%, then again this percentage will not vary over the long run. (A 1% or 2% deviation may occur due to shape of the animal, sex, human error, etc.)

WHY A SIMPLIFIED SYSTEM IS NEEDED

For the three primary problems that confront the food service supervisor, two factors change on a day-to-day basis and two remain unchanging for extended periods of time, as has been discussed above.

With this in mind, let us now examine present practices and compare them with the simplified system.

Under the system presently being utilized by many operators, the food buyer determines the amount of purchase by the procedure illustrated below.

If, for example, 100 people are to be served and the item being served is corned beef, in 4-ounce portions, the buyer would multiply 4 ounces by 100 to get 400 ounces. Next, he divides by 16 to convert to pounds, arriving at 25 pounds. Then, allowing for the fact that much of the corned beef is waste (presuming about 50%), he would divide the yield % into the original figure and arrive at a final total—50 pounds.

Every time the number of persons to be served changes, the buyer performs the same calculations and wastes the same amount of time in determining the correct amount.

To determine portion costs, the buyer has any number of systems that may be used. The simplest one takes the total purchase price for any item and divides it by the number of persons that can be served. The resulting answer is the portion cost. The actual true cost is usually only available after the function, since the actual amount served cannot be determined until that time.

To determine which of two products to buy, the same type of calculation must be performed for each product. Every time the market price changes, the buyer must recalculate his costs by going through the same steps. In Figure 7-3 is the comparison of the cost of corned beef round (item 2) and corned brisket of beef (item 1). At what market price these two products are of equal value in relationship to each other is difficult to determine. Normally, as the market price of each changes, the purchasing agent recalculates both sets of figures to determine which then has the lowest portion cost.

In summary, under the methods generally used, each time the buyer purchases a varying amount of merchandise, he must go through all of the steps shown in Figure 7-1. Or if this takes too much time, a guess is made, and the excess amount is fed to the staff, or a run out may occur.

Portion costs are determined at infrequent intervals and are calculated normally after the food has already been served, far too late for money-saving decisions.

Finally, due to the complexity of the mathematics, the selection of which item to buy is too often based not on lowest cost but rather on the purchasing agent's friendliness with the purveyor, familiarity with the product, or a half dozen other reasons, none of which answer the major primary question—"which is the most economical buy?"

HOW THE SIMPLIFIED SYSTEM WORKS

The simplified system enables the food service operator to utilize a basic mathematical formula to calculate the solutions to all three of the primary problems in cost control: 1) amount to buy; 2) portion costs; and 3) most economical product, presuming the same quality. The formula can remain the same in operations for extended periods of time and the constant figures can be utilized for indefinite periods.

FIGURE 7-3 *Comparison of Best Buy—Old Method*

Item 1

Price $1.00 lb.
Yield 50%

Total Amount Required

50 lbs. A.P. Weight
(previously determined)

50 x $1.00 = $50.00

$50.00 ÷ 100 portions = $.50 portion cost

Item 2

Price $1.30 lb
Yield 75%

Total Amount Required

25 lbs. E.P. Weight
(known)

Step 1.
25 lbs. ÷ 75% = 33 lbs. A.P. Weight

Step 2.
33 x 1.30 = $42.90

Step 3.
$42.90 ÷ 100 = $.429 portion cost

    An additional step is required when a second product is tested. The EP weight of 25 lbs. is known: For Product 1, the A.P. weight has been previously determined; for Product 2, you must first determine the A.P. Wt. Add steps 1, 2, and 3 to clarify this procedure. Then check to see if it is clear.

SIMPLIFIED MATHEMATICAL FORMULA

New Terms
Portion divider
Portion factor

Information Given or Available
A.P. price (varying market prices)
Portion size
Yield %

Information Desired
1. Portion factor—calculated only once
2. Portion divider—calculated only once
3. Amount to buy
4. Portion cost
5. Most ecomonical purchase

Two new terms are introduced at this point. *Portion divider* is a mathematical figure or constant that can be used for indefinite periods. For those who have access to computers, the constant can be fed into the computer and all the information desired can be obtained with it.*

The second, *portion factor*, is not really a new term. All food operators use it, but perhaps call it by another name. It is the actual number of portions served per pound for any given product. The portion factor may differ for each menu item, but normally it does not change.

Information available to the buyer that also seldom changes is the *portion size* and the *yield percentage* for any product. Yield-percentage information may be available to the controller or buyer from data supplied by various associations and purveyors. Preferably, however, it should be obtained by performing yield tests in the establishment. Information available to the buyer that does change frequently is the *market price* and the *forecast of sales*.

In order to set up a simplified system, several calculations must be performed initially. Once these are done the numbers will remain the same. For every menu item, a portion factor and portion divider must be ascertained. Once established, the system is ready for operation, so that the buyer or controller can quickly perform his duties.

Portion Factor.

To determine the portion factor, simply divide the portion size of the menu item into 16 (ounces per pound); the result is the portion factor. (See Figure 7-4.) Note that several different portion factors for the same kind of products may be used in the same establishment. A 12-ounce strip steak and a 14-ounce strip steak may be served in the same hotel in different dining rooms. Each menu item has its own portion factor.

FIGURE 7-4 *Determining Portion Factor*

$$16 \div \text{Portion Size} = \text{P.F.}$$

Example:
Calculated only once.

$$16 \div 4 \, \text{oz.} = 4$$

Portion Divider.

To ascertain the portion divider for each menu item, multiply the portion factor by the yield % of the product used. The answer is the portion divider.

*A simple Cobol or Fortran program can be written by using the formulas given in the summary.

FIGURE 7-5 *Determining Portion Divider*

Yield % x P.F. = P.D.

Examples: *Item 1—Corned Brisket*

.50 x 4 = 2.0

Item 2—Corned Round

.75 x 4 = 3.0

Calculated only once.

When different products are used for one menu item, each product will have a different portion divider. In the example shown (Figure 7-5), the portion divider is calculated for a 4-ounce portion. In Item 1, when this product (corned brisket of beef) is used with a normal yield of 50%, the portion divider would be 2. If corned rounds are used and a 75% yield were obtainable, the portion divider for the rounds would be 3. (Although other products may be used for this menu item, such as prepared or cooked meats, only these two examples will be demonstrated in the following calculations.)

All future calculations concerning this menu item are now simple to do.

Amount to Buy.

Using the new method, the expected number of covers, or persons, is simply divided by the portion divider, and the answer is the amount that must be purchased. (See Figure 7-6.) Note that the answer is the true A.P. Weight. Allowance need not be made for shrinkage or losses.

FIGURE 7-6 *Determining Amount to Buy*

No. of people ÷ P.D. = A.P. Weight

Item 1

100 ÷ 2.0 = 50 lbs.

Item 2

100 ÷ 3.0 = 33.3 lbs.

Other daily information can also be obtained by utilizing the portion divider.

Portion Costs.

Determining portion costs, even with fluctuating prices, is an easy process. Simply divide the portion divider into the current market price. The resulting answer will be the new portion cost for the menu item. If rounds were selling at $1.80, the procedure would be to divide the $1.80 by the portion divider for that product, which in this case would be 3. The new portion cost would be $.60.

In the examples shown in Figure 7-7, the portion cost for Item 1 is $.50 and for Item 2, $.43. In the systems now commonly used for obtaining this information, the calculations would be more difficult and probably less accurate.

FIGURE 7-7 *Determining Portion Cost*

A.P. Price ÷ P.D. = P.C.

Item 1

$1.00 ÷ 2.0 = $.50

Item 2

$1.30 ÷ 3.0 = $.43

The Best Buy.

The market price of one item in relation to a similar product often increases or decreases. At some stage of this fluctuation, it may become desirable for the purchasing agent to switch from one product to another to save money. Using the portion divider this point of change can readily be determined by the process shown in Figure 7-8.

FIGURE 7-8 *Determing Product to Buy, Based on Fluctuating Market Prices*

Item 1

A.P. Price ÷ P.D. = P.C. $1.00 ÷ 2 = $.50

Item 2

P.C. Item 1 x P.D. Item 2 = Equal Market Price $.50 x 3 = $1.50

The price of Item 1 in Figure 7-8 is $1.00 per pound. The portion cost is obtained by dividing the portion divider (2) into this purchase price. To determine at what price to switch products, the portion cost for the product presently being used (Item 1) is multiplied by the portion divider of the other product (Item 2). The resulting answer is the price at which both products are of equal value. If the purchase price of Item 2 is below that value, then it is a better buy. When the price of Item 2 is higher than the equivalent value, Item 1 is the better buy.

The simplified system presented in this chapter can be readily utilized in any operation having a computer. More importantly, for the majority of operators without computers, vital day-to-day information can be obtained by utilizing the portion divider. Exact quantities to purchase can be quickly calculated with only one mathematical computation simply by dividing the portion divider into the expected number of persons. (See Figure 7-6.)

New portion costs can be obtained even with fluctuating prices, again by the simple process of dividing the portion divider into the new market price of the item. (See Figure 7-7.)

Finally, the point at which the purchasing agent should switch from one product to the next can quickly be obtained by merely multiplying the portion cost of any item by the portion divider of the alternate. (See Figure 7-8.)

The simplified system may be utilized in all types of food service operations, whether profit-oriented or not, including hospitals and schools. It may be utilized by wholesalers and purveyors. It may be used for purchasing and comparing convenience products. It may also be adapted to obtain other data, or modified, depending on the products that are purchased. It is not the only method that can be used. It is, however, in the long run, the simplest.

ESTABLISHING A SIMPLIFIED PROGRAM

1. Determine portion sizes for each menu item.
2. Determine yield percentages for each product that may be used for any menu item.
3. Determine portion divider for all possible products that may be purchased for each menu item.
4. System is now ready. If a computer is available formulas may be programmed into computer. If not, either a desk calculator or tables may be used, so that information is immediately obtainable.

Example: Hot corned beef sandwich, portion size 4 oz.

Products that may be purchased;

1. Raw corned rounds of beef	75% yield
2. Raw corned briskets of beef	50% yield
3. Cooked corned rounds of beef	95% yield
4. Cooked corned briskets of beef	90% yield
Portion Factor $= 4$	

Portion Divider

1. Raw rounds of beef   .75 x 4 = 3.0
2. Raw briskets of beef   .50 x 4 = 2.0
3. Cooked rounds of beef   .95 x 4 = 3.8
4. Cooked briskets of beef   .90 x 4 = 3.6

The program is now ready to be fed into a computer, or a simple chart may be made up with the information obtained above. As market prices change or the number of covers to be served changes, the new information (variable) is fed into a computer or a simple computation may be made by using a desk calculator or slide rule, or even by a hand calculation. Figure 7-9 illustrates the portion factor for the most common portion sizes. The portion factor in this table may be multiplied by the yield percentage of a product to obtain the portion divider for the product.

FIGURE 7-9 *Portion Factors for Common Portion Sizes*

Portion Size	Portion Factor	Portion Size	Portion Factor
1 oz.	16.0	5 oz.	3.2
1 1/2 oz.	10.6	6 oz.	2.7
2 oz.	8.0	7 oz.	2.3
2 1/2 oz.	6.4	8 oz.	2.0
3 oz.	5.3	10 oz.	1.6
3 1/2 oz.	4.6	12 oz.	1.3
4 oz.	4.0	16 oz.	1.0

First determine which product is most economical to purchase:

1. Raw rounds @ $1.45/lb. ÷ 3 = $.48
2. Raw briskets @ $1.05/lb. ÷ 2 = $.53
3. Cooked rounds @ $1.95/lb. ÷ 3.8 = $.51
4. Cooked briskets @ $1.85/lb. ÷ 3.6 = $.51

Raw rounds would be most ecomonical, but an additional cost should be added for labor and utility costs incurred when cooking the meat. Initially, the lowest portion cost can be the determining factor. If at a later time prices fluctuate, the switch point method may be used.

If management decided to purchase cooked briskets, then the final step would be to divide the portion divider (P.D.) of the briskets (3.6) into the expected number of persons to determine the amount to purchase:

700 persons ÷ 3.6 = 195 lbs. A.P. Weight

Chapter 7
I. Class Exercises

1. As purchasing agent for Sweet Sal's Sandwich Shoppe, you serve the following items:

Cold Turkey Sandwich	2-oz. portion	82% yield—uncooked breasts
Hot Turkey Sandwich	3-oz. portion	90% yield—cooked turkey roll
Turkey Dinner	5-oz. portion	77% yield—uncooked turkey roll

If you expect to serve 100 cold turkey sandwiches, 200 hot turkey sandwiches, and 375 turkey dinners, how much turkey will you have to buy for each item?

2. You are catering a banquet for a group of 1,250 people. The menu consists of:

Shrimp cocktail—5 per person—avg. 18/lb.—A.P. price $5.00/lb.
Roast Round of Beef—6-oz. portion—yield 85%—A.P. price $1.39/lb.
Baked Potatoes—count 120—cost $12.00 box
Fresh green beans—87% yield—4-oz. portion—A.P. price $.49/lb.
Rolls & Butter—90 pats/lb.—A.P. prices $1.02/lb—Rolls $.05 each
    Total portion cost for both equals $.13
Individual ice cream slices—2 oz. sauce
    Slices cost $.12—Sauce costs $12.00 for a 5 lb. jar.

a. Determine how much to buy
   i. Shrimp
   ii. Round of Beef
   iii. Fresh green beans
   iv. Dessert

b. Determine *total* cost for each dinner (per cover per plate).

3. As the purchasing agent for the Super X Sandwich Shoppe, you expect 625 people to eat dinner over the weekend. Of these, 300 will order mashed potatoes, 200 will order french fried potatoes, and 125 will order baked. You use the same type of potato for all menu items. If a baked potato (6-oz. portion) has a 100% yield, if french fried potatoes (4-oz. portion) have an 80% yield, and mashed potatoes (4-oz. portion) have a 90% yield—how many pounds of potatoes will you have to buy?

4. You are serving the following menu to a group of 750 persons:

Clams on the 1/2 shell—4 per order—$2.00/doz.
Roast Turkey—52% yield—A.P. price $.49—6-oz. portion
Sweet Potatoes (candied)—91% yield—5-oz. portion—portion cost $.12
Frozen Peas—3-oz. portion—90% yield—A.P. price $.27/lb
Rolls & Butter—72 pats/lb.—$.69/Doz.—portion cost $.12
Apple Pie—1/8 pie portion—A.P. price $1.20/pie

    a. Determine how much to buy

        i. Clams

       ii. Turkey

      iii. Peas

      iv. Pies

    b. Determine *total* cost for each dinner (per cover or per plate).

II. Study Questions

    1. Discuss 3 daily problems of food service operators.

    2. What are "variable data"?

    3. What are "fixed data"?

    4. Explain "portion factor."

    5. Explain "portion divider."

    6. How do you determine portion cost?

    7. What is a switch point?

8

Yields

Buying for the food service industry differs greatly from buying for other types of industries in that with many of the food items that the buyer purchases the net usable amount of the product varies. For example, the buyer for an electrical manufacturing company purchases wire for lamp cords. He knows that each of his lamps may use 5 feet of cord and that to manufacture twenty lamps he needs to purchase 100 feet of cord. No cord is normally wasted nor will it spoil even if held for long periods of time. The buyer for the food service establishment, however, may be faced with the problem of purchasing enough potatoes for twenty portions of a half pound each. If only ten pounds are purchased, however, there may be a shortage of potatoes since in the processing of the potatoes some of the product is lost in the peeling, some in the cooking, and some of the potatoes may have spoiled.

The amount of a product that remains after the processing performed within an establishment is called the *yield* or *yield percentage.* Yields vary with each type of food. Yields may also vary from establishment to establishment, and even within an establishment. In order to more fully understand the many ramifications of yields, it becomes necessary to understand why they are important and what they are used for, and to determine why they vary within any one establishment.

With each type of product, such as produce or meats, the method of purchasing the product (its market forms) and the degree of processing that has been performed on the product prior to delivery may vary. A buyer for an establishment may have the option of purchasing the item in several different forms, each having a different yield.

For example, in Chapter 6, four different types of strip steaks were listed under the specifications section (see Figure 6-2). In addition to purchasing any of the portion-controlled items, the purchasing agent may decide to buy this item from a purveyor either as a short loin, with or without the bone, or as an entire loin and utilize some of the remaining areas of the loin for other menu items.

In some cases he may choose to buy the item partially or fully prepared or cooked (e.g., shrimp and other seafoods). Although the cost of the food may be of primary interest to the purchasing agent, the cost of labor, equipment, and energy, and the quality of the final product must all be considered in the final analysis.

MEATS

In the restaurants and hotels of yesteryear, the chef or the purchasing agent normally bought an entire carcass of an animal. The animal was then butchered into the various cuts of meat needed for the establishment. In some cases this method was inefficient, if the establishment was unable to fully utilize all the cuts available from a carcass. Perhaps it found that additional supplies of certain cuts were required due to the demands and preferences of its customers. With changing technology and improved methods of marketing, this system has completely (or almost completely) vanished from the food service industry. Now the buyer need only purchase those items that he specifically knows his customers prefer.

Meats are purchased in varying forms, since any given establishment may differ in the method in which it serves the product or even in the method in which it prepares the product. A roast, for example, may be purchased with varying degress of trim, with or without a bone, with varying amounts of muscle or fat, with different degrees of aging, of different quality, and from different classes or breeds of animals (heifers, steers, black angus, etc.). The purchasing agent's function is to determine which method of purchasing a product will be the most economical, presuming the end product will be of the same quality.

Basic Formula for Determining Yields for Price Comparisons

In order to determine the yield of a given product for an establishment, the product must be weighed at the onset of the yield test, and then the net remaining product must be weighed. The yield percentage is then calculated:

Remaining weight ÷ Original weight = Total yield percentage

Any one product may normally be tested from the original state of purchase until the final cooked and served product. This is a *total yield* test.

It may not be necessary or desirable, however, to perform a full yield test on products. In some cases, the causes of higher or lower yields on a product are attributable to conditions outside the food service establishment. To determine true food costs, the final edible amount of the product is compared to the as purchased (A.P.) weight—the original weight. Other types of tests, however, may determine the efficiency of a department or the efficiency and honesty of a purveyor.

This yield test may be performed at any stage of the processing. If an attempt is being made to compare the products of two purveyors, however, the yield test must be performed at the same stage of processing. It is impossible, for example, to compare the boneless product of one purveyor to the bone-in product of another. Both products must be at the same stage of processing (boneless) and then comparison tests may be run.

The types of tests that are necessary in meat products are discussed below.

Trim Tests

A trim test determines the amount of the excess fat or unusable meat that has been left on by a purveyor (or your own butcher). For example, fully defatted tenderloins of beef should have no outside fat remaining on the tenderloin. Partially trimmed or defatted tenderloin may also be purchased. The weight of the tenderloin prior to being fully trimmed as compared to its completely defatted weight is the yield percentage.

$$\text{Fully trimmed tenderloin} \div \text{Partially defatted tenderloin}$$
$$= \text{Trimming yield percentage}$$

The degree or thickness of interior and exterior fat that cannot be used in serving will naturally reduce the amount of the usable edible portion that can be served. Each establishment must establish standards and specifications. For roasts, a maximum of one-half inch of exterior fat is recommended, for steaks and chops no more than 1/4 inch. Items such as hamburger or steaks must be handled in a slightly different manner, depending upon how the meat is to be utilized.

Aging

With certain cuts of meat it is desirable to age them for varying lengths of time, depending upon the tastes and pocketbooks of the customers. Aging, however, causes meat to lose weight (due to the loss of moisture). Normally a 5%-10% shrinkage occurs during the first two weeks of aging, with lesser shrinkage upon further aging. There is no convenient or accurate method for determining how long a purchased product has been aged. One has to rely upon the taste and tenderness of the end product and the reliability of the purveyor. An aged product, since it has lost some moisture in the aging process, may shrink less during cooking. One method for determining how much the product has been aged is to place it in your own aging refrigerators for finishing to the final degree of aging that you prefer, and determining how much the product shrinks during the aging process in your own coolers. Shrinkage will be affected by the moisture or humidity in the refrigerators as well as by the condition of the animal. Normally, for many establishments, two weeks of aging is sufficient to satisfy the palates of most customers. In some cases clientele may prefer no aging at all.

Boning Yields

A product may be partially or fully deboned. To accurately compare products, the end product must be exactly equal in the length or amount of bone. With some items, the weight of the remaining bone may also have to be determined at some future stage of processing.

Boneless weight ÷ Bone-in weight = Boning yield

Yield by Carcass Weights

The yield grades for beef as established by the federal government normally result in a yield of 52.4% or more for a carcass that has been graded *Yield 1* down to a yield of 45% or less for those carcasses graded *Yield 5*. These figures are based on the *live carcass weight of the animal*. (See Figure 8-1.)

Usable cuts of meat ÷ Live carcass weight = Yield percentage

Since there will be a difference in market price, the astute buyer purchasing whole carcasses can easily determine what the difference in market price for each grade should be by simply dividing the expected yield percentage of the yield grade into the purchase price. For example, with *live cattle* graded Yield 1, the expected yield % is 52.4. If the market price was $.59 per pound, the actual cost for usable meat would be:

$$\$.59 \div 52.4 = \$1.13/lb.$$

A *dressed carcass* of graded Yield 5 selling at $.80 per pound would have a maximum yield of 65.9. (See Figure 8-2.) The actual formula would be:

$$\$.80 \div 65.9 = \$1.21/lb.$$

Price/lb. ÷ Yield % = Actual cost/lb.

Thus, at this market price it may be feasible for the buyer to purchase a live animal graded Yield 1 and save about $.08 per pound. Any increase in price above $.59 for Yield 1 would mean that the buyer might have to switch to another yield grade. The net price for other yield grades would be calculated in the same fashion. In the above example the comparison can be made at different stages of processing, since the expected yield % for each stage is known.

Normally, purchasing agents for food service establishments do not buy whole carcasses, so it is necessary to establish yield percentages for the primal cuts that may be purchased. This may be accomplished by the following calculations:

Usable meat ÷ Primal cut wt. = Yield %

FIGURE 8-1 *Live to Usable Cuts of Meat*

Yield or cutability grade: *Corresponding predicted percentage*
                                   yield of boneless major cuts trimmed
                                   of excess fat:

Yield 1	54.6 to 52.3
Yield 2	52.3 to 50.0
Yield 3	50.0 to 47.7
Yield 4	47.7 to 45.4
Yield 5	45.4 and lower

From "A Demonstration of Beef Carcass Yield and Cut-Out Values," G.H. Wellington and J.R. Stouffer, New York State College of Agriculture, Cornell Misc. Bulletin 73, 1966, page 4.

FIGURE 8-2 *Dressed to Usable Cuts of Meat*

Dressed Carcass   *Yield Percentages are:*

Yield 1	79.8% or more
Yield 2	75.2 to 79.7
Yield 3	70.6 to 75.1
Yield 4	66 to 70.5
Yield 5	65.9 or less

"How to Buy Meat for Your Freezer," Consumer and Marketing Service, Home and Garden, U.S.D.A. Bulletin No. 166, Rev. Dec. 1969.

True cost therefore is equal to:

A.P. price ÷ Yield % = E.P. price

Pork, beef, and lamb all have yield grades that may be used to determine the most economical method of buying. (See Figures 8-3, 8-4, and 8-5.) The grade for pork carcasses is based upon a combination of quality and the expected yield from the carcass of the four lean cuts (ham, loin, picnic, and the Boston butt). The yields for pork are given in Figure 8-6.

Lamb yield grades are numbered 1 thru 5, and average 3.5% difference in expected usable cuts between each yield grade. Yield grades for lamb are comparable to yield grades for beef (dressed carcass yield percentages).

Steaks

If portion-controlled steaks or chops are purchased, they again may be bought in varying sizes and with varying specifications. Portion sizes vary depending upon the cut of meat, the amount of trim allowed (length of tail for example, as shown in Chapter 6), and whether the steak is bone-in or

FIGURE 8-3 *Yield Grades for Pork*

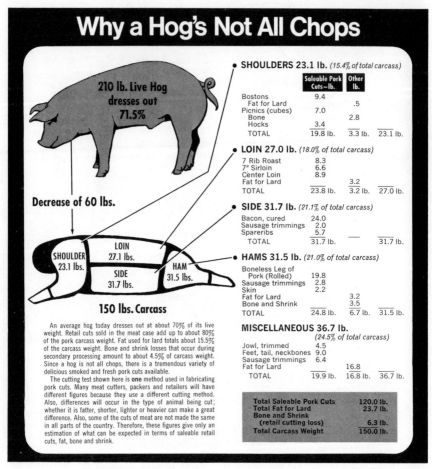

Why a Hog's Not All Chops

210 lb. Live Hog dresses out 71.5%

Decrease of 60 lbs.

SHOULDER 23.1 lbs.

LOIN 27.1 lbs.

SIDE 31.7 lbs.

HAM 31.5 lbs.

150 lbs. Carcass

An average hog today dresses out at about 70% of its live weight. Retail cuts sold in the meat case add up to about 80% of the pork carcass weight. Fat used for lard totals about 15.5% of the carcass weight. Bone and shrink losses that occur during secondary processing amount to about 4.5% of carcass weight. Since a hog is not all chops, there is a tremendous variety of delicious smoked and fresh pork cuts available.

The cutting test shown here is **one** method used in fabricating pork cuts. Many meat cutters, packers and retailers will have different figures because they use a different cutting method. Also, differences will occur in the type of animal being cut; whether it is fatter, shorter, lighter or heavier can make a great difference. Also, some of the cuts of meat are not made the same in all parts of the country. Therefore, these figures give only an estimation of what can be expected in terms of saleable retail cuts, fat, bone and shrink.

SHOULDERS 23.1 lb. *(15.4% of total carcass)*

	Saleable Pork Cuts—lb.	Other lb.	
Bostons	9.4		
Fat for Lard		.5	
Picnics (cubes)	7.0		
Bone		2.8	
Hocks	3.4		
TOTAL	19.8 lb.	3.3 lb.	23.1 lb.

LOIN 27.0 lb. *(18.0% of total carcass)*

7 Rib Roast	8.3		
7" Sirloin	6.6		
Center Loin	8.9		
Fat for Lard		3.2	
TOTAL	23.8 lb.	3.2 lb.	27.0 lb.

SIDE 31.7 lb. *(21.1% of total carcass)*

Bacon, cured	24.0		
Sausage trimmings	2.0		
Spareribs	5.7		
TOTAL	31.7 lb.	—	31.7 lb.

HAMS 31.5 lb. *(21.0% of total carcass)*

Boneless Leg of Pork (Rolled)	19.8		
Sausage trimmings	2.8		
Skin	2.2		
Fat for Lard		3.2	
Bone and Shrink		3.5	
TOTAL	24.8 lb.	6.7 lb.	31.5 lb.

MISCELLANEOUS 36.7 lb.
(24.5% of total carcass)

Jowl, trimmed	4.5		
Feet, tail, neckbones	9.0		
Sausage trimmings	6.4		
Fat for Lard		16.8	
TOTAL	19.9 lb.	16.8 lb.	36.7 lb.

Total Saleable Pork Cuts	120.0 lb.
Total Fat for Lard	23.7 lb.
Bone and Shrink (retail cutting loss)	6.3 lb.
Total Carcass Weight	150.0 lb.

Reproduced by permission of the Pork Industry Committee, Chicago, Illinois

boneless. Planning the appropriate portion size for an operation will be governed by menu prices, the "class" of the operation, and the food cost percentage desired, as well as by other pertinent considerations such as what type of meal is being served (lunch or dinner) and even the size of the china.

If, for example, small tables and small china are being used, it may be desirable to serve a boneless steak that has the same net amount of edible meat but takes up less space on a plate. A restaurant designed to serve gourmands, however, may prefer to serve a larger steak with the bone in, which will require larger plates or platters and may even require larger tables.

FIGURE 8-4 *Yield Grades for Beef*

A STEER'S NOT ALL STEAK...
an important factor in the price you pay for beef

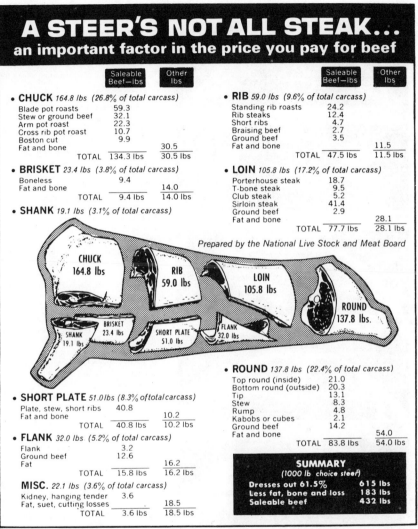

	Saleable Beef—lbs	Other lbs
CHUCK 164.8 lbs (26.8% of total carcass)		
Blade pot roasts	59.3	
Stew or ground beef	32.1	
Arm pot roast	22.3	
Cross rib pot roast	10.7	
Boston cut	9.9	
Fat and bone		30.5
TOTAL	134.3 lbs	30.5 lbs
BRISKET 23.4 lbs (3.8% of total carcass)		
Boneless	9.4	
Fat and bone		14.0
TOTAL	9.4 lbs	14.0 lbs
SHANK 19.1 lbs (3.1% of total carcass)		

	Saleable Beef—lbs	Other lbs
RIB 59.0 lbs (9.6% of total carcass)		
Standing rib roasts	24.2	
Rib steaks	12.4	
Short ribs	4.7	
Braising beef	2.7	
Ground beef	3.5	
Fat and bone		11.5
TOTAL	47.5 lbs	11.5 lbs
LOIN 105.8 lbs (17.2% of total carcass)		
Porterhouse steak	18.7	
T-bone steak	9.5	
Club steak	5.2	
Sirloin steak	41.4	
Ground beef	2.9	
Fat and bone		28.1
TOTAL	77.7 lbs	28.1 lbs

Prepared by the National Live Stock and Meat Board

	Saleable Beef—lbs	Other lbs
SHORT PLATE 51.0 lbs (8.3% of total carcass)		
Plate, stew, short ribs	40.8	
Fat and bone		10.2
TOTAL	40.8 lbs	10.2 lbs
FLANK 32.0 lbs (5.2% of total carcass)		
Flank	3.2	
Ground beef	12.6	
Fat		16.2
TOTAL	15.8 lbs	16.2 lbs
MISC. 22.1 lbs (3.6% of total carcass)		
Kidney, hanging tender	3.6	
Fat, suet, cutting losses		18.5
TOTAL	3.6 lbs	18.5 lbs

	Saleable Beef—lbs	Other lbs
ROUND 137.8 lbs (22.4% of total carcass)		
Top round (inside)	21.0	
Bottom round (outside)	20.3	
Tip	13.1	
Stew	8.3	
Rump	4.8	
Kabobs or cubes	2.1	
Ground beef	14.2	
Fat and bone		54.0
TOTAL	83.8 lbs	54.0 lbs

SUMMARY
(1000 lb choice steer)

Dresses out 61.5%	615 lbs
Less fat, bone and loss	183 lbs
Saleable beef	432 lbs

Supply and Demand are not the only factors in the price you pay for beef. For instance, today's modern-type 1,000 lb choice steer produces an approximate 615 lb carcass which the packer sells to a retailer who trims away 183 lbs of fat, bone and waste . . . ending up with only 432 lbs of beef that he cuts, wraps and sells to customers.

Of that a surprisingly small amount is steak and a much larger quantity is roasts as shown in the chart above. Retail stores put a higher price on steak and a lower price on pot-roasts and ground beef so that they sell it all . . . not end up with only less-in-demand cuts like pot-roasts and short ribs left in the cooler.

Reproduced by permission of The National Live Stock and Meat Board, Chicago, Illinois

FIGURE 8-5 *Yield Grades for Lamb*

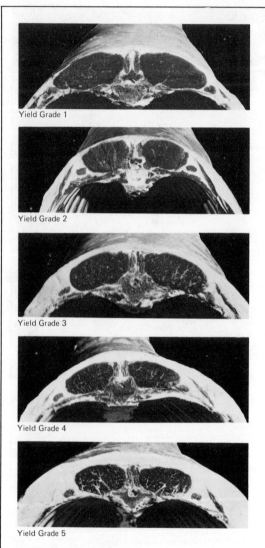

Yield Grade 1

Yield Grade 2

Yield Grade 3

Yield Grade 4

Yield Grade 5

2. Cutability

The USDA initiated work in developing standards for livestock and meat in 1918. The primary aim of the department was to develop a market news reporting service for livestock.

The boundary lines between grades (quality) were not based on giving either retailers or consumers value for their money. They were based on what was needed to classify meats for price reporting.

Presently, lamb carcasses are quality graded on a voluntary basis using the following standards: conformation (overall thickness in relation to the length of the carcass), finish and feathering.

In March of 1969, yield grade or cutability standards for lamb carcasses were adopted. These yield grade/cutability standards are also voluntary and do not change the present quality grades. They can be used with or without the quality grade, or not at all.

Yield grade standards are based on: fat thickness measured over the center of the rib-eye muscle between the 12th and 13th ribs, the amount of kidney and pelvic fat and conformation grade of the leg.

Yield grades are based on five standards (1 through 5) within a quality grade. Grades 1 and 5 represent only 10% (or less) of total lamb kill; grades 2 and 3 are the viable grades.

Steaks, unlike some cuts of meat such as roast prime ribs of beef, are almost invariably portioned by the raw ounce weight. Portion sizes may be reduced to as little as 8 ounces. Portions smaller than that are difficult to cook to the desired degree of doneness—it may be impossible to cook a thinner steak rare. Steaks having bones (T-bone, Porterhouse, etc.) must be proportionately larger (by weight) in order to cook properly.

FIGURE 8-6 *Expected Yields of the Four Lean Cuts
Based on Chilled Carcass Weight, by Grade*

Grade	Yield
U.S. Number 1	53 percent and over
U.S. Number 2	50 to 52.9 percent
U.S. Number 3	47 to 49.9 percent
U.S. Number 4	Less than 47 percent

From "U.S.D.A. Grades for Pork Carcasses," U.S.D.A. Consumer and Marketing Service, Marketing Bulletin No. 49, April 1970.

Cooked yield percentages of steak are not normally considered, once the raw portion size is determined, since adulteration is impossible and shrinkage is determined primarily by the degree of doneness. The high cost of steaks and chops and other meat items is attributable in part to the demand for these items, as well as the exceptional waste that occurs in all animals. Figures 8-4 and 8-5 demonstrate these facts.

Chopped Meat

This section has purposely been entitled chopped meat, since without chemical analysis it is impossible to determine exactly what has been placed into ground meat by various purveyors. For the majority of food service establishments, desirable ground meat specifications may have a variation of fat content from 15% to 25% (30% being allowed under federal and most state laws). It should be made entirely from striated muscles, without including organs, cheek meat, or cartilage.

Unfortunately, there is no way for anyone to measure exactly what has been included in the ground meat merely by looking at it. Purveyors have been known to add excessive amounts of fat, by-products of beef, pork, veal, chicken parts, water, milk, vegetable proteins, and cereals. Even if one had the equipment to determine the amount of fat in the product, this would not verify whether or not the fat was actually beef fat or some other type of fat. Nor would it in any way determine what other ingredients might be in the mixture.

For this reason, many food service establishments prefer to purchase whole sections of meat and grind or chop it themselves. (Chopping is preferable to grinding.) Even with this method it is difficult to assure that a homogenous mixture with the proper ratio of lean to fat will be maintained at all times.

Price Comparisons

For the purchasing agent interested only in the savings of a few cents per pound, it is possible to purchase chopped meat that will be lower in price. If the meat is to be used for hamburgers or like menu items in which the cooked portion size is unimportant (presuming of course, that an adequate portion is served) then perhaps the apparent savings of a few cents per pound in the raw product may be a wise decision.

Closer examination however, may reveal that this approach may be foolhardy. For example, a buyer is able to obtain chopped meat at 59¢ per pound and utilizes it for 4-ounce hamburger patties that upon cooking shrink to 3 1/2 ounces, which is considered the proper size for his establishment. Each hamburger (excluding other costs) costs slightly less than 15¢. Suppose, however, that by purchasing a finer grade of meat he was able to purchase patties weighing 3 3/4 ounces that upon cooking shrunk to the same 3 1/2-ounce cooked portion size. By utilizing the yield formulas developed earlier, one is able to calculate that with the first product a yield of 87.5% is obtained. With the second product a yield of 93% is obtained.

Cooked weight ÷ Original weight = Yield %

Product 1	*Product 2*
3.50 ÷ 4 = 87.5%	3.50 ÷ 3.75 = 93%

The formula to determine true E.P. price is again used.

A.P. price ÷ Yield % = E.P. price

Thus the true cost of the first product is $.674 per pound. If the second product is purchased for 61¢ per pound the true cost of each item would be:

Product 1	*Product 2*
$.59 ÷ .875 = $.674/lb.	$.61 ÷ .933 = $.653/lb.

The buyer could also determine how much of an increased price could be paid for the better chopped beef by the following formula:

E.P. price of present product x yield percentage (prod. 2) = A.P. price (prod. 2).

This amounts to:

$.674 x 93% = $.629/lb.

Thus if the second product could be purchased for less than $.629/lb., a savings would be effected.

In comparing products it is first necessary to determine the yield percentage for each product. This is done by the original formula:

Remaining weight ÷ Original weight = Yield percentage

The second stage of the comparison is performed by comparing the true (E.P. price) of one product with that of the other. E.P. prices are determined by the formula:

$$A.P. \text{ price} \div \text{Yield } \% = E.P. \text{ price}$$

The E.P. price is the real cost to an establishment for any given product.

Finally, if an establishment uses a particular product and wishes to determine at what point it would be more economical (again presuming equal quality) to switch to another product, the formula is:

$$E.P. \text{ price (prod. 1) x Yield } \% \text{ (prod. 2)} = \text{Price of product 2.}$$

When product 2 is sold for less than that amount, it would be more economical to purchase the second product.

Cooking Yields

All meats will shrink to some extent during the cooking process, due to the loss of moisture and the melting of fat. The amount of shrinkage depends to a great extent upon the final temperature of the cooked product, as well as on the temperature at which the product was cooked. The method of cooking may also affect shrinkage, since moist heat cookery may result in less moisture being lost from the product.

It is generally recommended that meats be cooked at low temperatures (250°F.—300°F.) as this type of cookery results in less shrinkage from both the loss of moisture and the loss of fat. Roasts cooked under these conditions will also be cooked more evenly throughout. However, since a great deal of the flavor in meats comes from the browning of fat, care must be taken to insure that these flavors are not sacrificed to insure a higher yield.

In addition, although the roast may weigh more at the end of the cooking cycle (heavier than roasts cooked at high temperature), some of this weight may be in the form of a layer of uncooked exterior fat that must be trimmed prior to service. Yield tests that attempt to prove that low-temperature cooking results in higher yields are not reliable unless they also take into account serving yields.

In addition to the temperature at which roasts are cooked, the final internal temperature will to a great extent influence the yield percentage of cooking. In yield tests comparing roasts cooked at different temperatures, care must be taken to insure that the internal temperature of the tested products are the same at the end. Unless this is done, the test will not be valid.

Consideration must also be given to how the meat was handled prior to cooking. Meat that has been frozen may or may not be thawed before cooking. In a study conducted in 1969* meats that were cooked from the frozen state gave a slightly better yield (2%) than those thawed prior to cooking.

Serving Yields

In finer establishments, only lean slices may be used. In lower-priced operations, ends, shreds, and even unappetizing-looking pieces may be served. The actual number of portions that can be served from a roast multiplied by the portion size determines the net serving weight. Again, the yield percentage is determined by dividing the original weight prior to serving into the serving weight.

$$\text{Serving weight} \div \text{Original weight} = \text{Serving yield \%}$$

Summary of Yield Formulas

As can be noted from the various types of yields that must be determined, the formulation or testing for roasts (or steaks or other cuts of meat) may be done in stages, although the total yield of a cut of meat can be tested by performing only one test. The operator is mainly concerned with the amount of servings that he is able to obtain from any given cut of meat. The primary test, therefore, is to use the purchase weight as the base figure and the serving weight as the final figure to obtain a total yield percentage for the cut of meat. The various other yield tests that may be performed and the formulas for each test are listed below:

Total test:

$$\text{Serving weight} \div \text{Purchase weight} = \text{Total yield \%}$$

(Serving weight is equal to actual number of portions times portion size.)

Aging yield:

$$\text{Weight after aging} \div \text{Weight prior to aging} = \text{Aging yield \%}$$

Cutting yields (may be just trimming or may be boning yield):

$$\text{Weight after trimming} \div \text{Weight prior to cutting, boning, trimming}$$
$$= \text{Boning or Cutting Yield \%}$$

(Weight after trimming is weight of product ready to go into the cooking process.)

Cooking yield:

$$\text{Weight after cooking} \div \text{Weight prior to cooking} = \text{Cooking yield \%}$$

---

* "The Study of the Different Handling Methods for Frozen Roasts in Institutional Food Service," B.E. Shoemaker, B.C. Breidenstein, and D. S. Garrigan, National Live Stock and Meat Board and the National Association of Meat Purveyors, October 1, 1969.

Serving yield:

Serving weight ÷ Weight after cooking = Serving yield %

Although the total test percentage is the most important, it may be necessary for the food and beverage buyer or controller to perform any or all of the yield tests. In any operation, undue losses may be caused by one department or by inefficiencies in one step of the operation.

For example, the controller may determine by the total test that he is not obtaining as many servings as expected, and thus has a lower total yield percentage than is normal for a particular cut of meat. However, until further tests are performed, he may not know why these losses are occurring. Perhaps the cook is using too high a temperature or overcooking the roast. Or it may be that the losses are occurring due to the carelessness of the server in not accurately portioning each serving. Each yield test, therefore, is performed, to determine whether a specific function in the operation is being carried out according to the standards established by management.

Aging tests determine whether the meat has been aged by the purveyor. They may also be used to determine whether the establishment is, in fact, aging under the proper conditions. Excess losses at this stage indicate that meat purchased was too fresh or that adjustments in humidity, temperature, and aging times are required.

Cutting yields are necessary to determine whether butchers in the operation are careless, but they may also indicate the cutting quality of the meat purchased. Heifers will generally yield slightly fewer steaks per carcass than steers.* Grades of meat may have different amounts of interior and exterior fat even in the same grade. Thus, it may be necessary for the buyer to buy yield grades as well as quality grades. The purveyors may not be meeting the specifications of the establishment.

In some cases, the meat may not be handled properly within the establishment, so that there are excessive losses due to unnecessary trimming or cutting. An example of this may be the practice of some operators to purchase whole ribs of beef, let them age, and after aging trim out certain parts that are not normally served in the establishment. These parts, however, had they been trimmed out prior to aging could have been used for ground beef. After aging they are almost useless and must be discarded. The alert controller must be aware of these practices and effect changes either in purchasing or handling procedures that will eliminate this unnecessary waste.

Yield tests must be performed in such a manner that they truly represent actual handling procedures within the establishment. When a cutting test is performed, it must be done by the butcher who normally

---

* "Effect of Weight Grade and Sex of Beef Carcasses on Yield of Packaged Beef for the Freezer," J.W. Cole, C.B. Ramsey, and A.R. Cavander, Univ. of Tennessee, Agriculture Experiment Station, Bulletin #345, July 1962, page 24.

handles the meat, not by the head butcher, who may be more careful in his procedures. Cooking and serving tests must be done in the same manner. Since there are variations in the structures of animals and since procedures for handling may change from time to time, yield tests must be performed several times and must be repeated at intervals so that any deviation from established procedures may be quickly remedied.

The discussion above has been primarily concerned with meat roasts. The same types of tests and procedures, however, must be established for all kinds of meats, poultry, and fish.

POULTRY

When purchased in varying weights poultry will differ in yields. The smaller bird generally has a lower yield in edible meat (see Figure 8-7). Extra-large birds may yield less, in that there may be an overdevelopment of bone structure and excessive fat in proportion to lean meat. With both poultry and fish no aging is allowed to occur. Thus the buyer or controller would be concerned primarily with the yields obtainable due to the varying stages of processing in which the item may be purchased and the yields obtained due to handling (cutting, boning, and cooking) within the establishment. Information on the dressing percentages of turkeys is available from the National Turkey Federation, "Turkey Handbook," 1950.

It may also be advantageous for the purchasing agent to purchase parts of the bird or animal, since only certain sections may be used. As can be noted from the table in Figure 8-7, if only the breast and legs are used, this amounts to a mere 58% of the carcass. If the operator has no other use for the remaining parts, he may find it more economical to pay substantially more for these selected parts rather than buying the whole bird. (Figure 8-8.) The formula would be:

A.P. cost of whole bird ÷ .58 = Equal price for breasts and legs

Note that no factor has been included for the labor cost involved with the cutting or breaking down of the whole poultry.

An operator has the option to change menu prices or to change portion sizes. To facilitate mathematical computation, it is convenient when working with portion sizes that are computed in ounces to determine and refer to the number of portions obtainable from one pound. (See Figure 8-9.) This is primarily done because many of the poultry and other products are purchased on a per-pound basis. Thus, if a 4-ounce portion is to be served, the chef or the buyer may state "we get 4 portions per pound," or simply "4 to 1."

FIGURE 8-7

COMPARATIVE YIELDS OF LARGE AND SMALL BROAD BREASTED MEAT-TYPE TURKEYS

The late L. E. Cline of the University of Nevada made some studies for the Norbest Turkey Growers Association on the comparative yields of broad breasted meat-type turkeys of various sizes.

TABLE 1   (Toms)

Size of Individual Birds N. Y. Dressed Weight Basis	Total Pounds of N. Y. Dressed Weight Toms	Drawn-Weight	Whole Roasted Weight	Total Yield of Edible Meat	Yield of Breast Meat
32 lbs.	100 lbs.	90.6 lbs.	63.1 lbs.	52.2 lbs.	21.6 lbs.
30 lbs.	100 lbs.	90.0 lbs.	63.0 lbs.	51.3 lbs.	20.6 lbs.
28 lbs.	100 lbs.	89.6 lbs.	62.5 lbs.	50.3 lbs.	20.3 lbs.
26 lbs.	100 lbs.	88.2 lbs.	62.3 lbs.	49.6 lbs.	19.6 lbs.
24 lbs.	100 lbs.	88.3 lbs.	61.7 lbs.	48.3 lbs.	18.8 lbs.
22 lbs.	100 lbs.	87.7 lbs.	60.8 lbs.	47.3 lbs.	18.2 lbs.
20 lbs.	100 lbs.	87.0 lbs.	60.5 lbs.	45.5 lbs.	18.5 lbs.
18 lbs.	100 lbs.	85.5 lbs.	59.4 lbs.	43.3 lbs.	15.6 lbs.
16 lbs.	100 lbs.	84.4 lbs.	58.8 lbs.	41.2 lbs.	13.8 lbs.

TABLE 2   (Hens)

22 lbs.	100 lbs.	87.3 lbs.	62.7 lbs.	47.7 lbs.	15.5 lbs.
20 lbs.	100 lbs.	87.0 lbs.	62.0 lbs.	47.0 lbs.	15.5 lbs.
18 lbs.	100 lbs.	86.6 lbs.	61.1 lbs.	46.7 lbs.	16.1 lbs.
16 lbs.	100 lbs.	86.3 lbs.	60.0 lbs.	45.6 lbs.	16.3 lbs.
14 lbs.	100 lbs.	85.7 lbs.	58.6 lbs.	42.9 lbs.	17.1 lbs.
12 lbs.	100 lbs.	85.0 lbs.	57.5 lbs.	43.3 lbs.	17.5 lbs.
10 lbs.	100 lbs.	84.0 lbs.	55.0 lbs.	41.0 lbs.	19.0 lbs.
8 lbs.	100 lbs.	82.5 lbs.	51.3 lbs.	37.5 lbs.	20.0 lbs.

All figures in Tables 1 and 2 are based on the dressed weights of broad breasted meat-type individual birds shown in dressed-weight columns. Table courtesy of Norbest Turkey Growers Association.

From "Turkey Handbook," National Turkey Federation, 1950, p. 32.

FIGURE 8-8 *Percentage of Each Part in*
Ready-to-Cook Poultry

Breast	26%
Legs	32%
Back & Neck	23%
Wings	11%
Gizzard	5%
Liver	2 1/2 %
Heart	1/2 %

FIGURE 8-9 *Yield of Poultry*

	Ready-to-Cook Carcass (*lb*)	Cooked	*White Meat*	*Dark Meat*	*Skin*	*Neck Meat*
Chicken						
broiler	2.8	2.1	0.6	0.5	0.2	0.04
Capons	6.2	4.1	1.5	1.3	0.3	0.00
Turkey (Male)	9.4	6.8	2.7	1.7	0.4	0.16
(Female)	6.1	4.6	1.8	1.2	0.3	0.10

	Total Edible Meat	*Total Bone*	*Loss*
Chicken broiler	1.5	0.5	0.1
Capons	3.1	0.7	0.3
Turkey (Male)	5.0	1.4	0.3
(Female)	3.3	0.9	0.3

Source: Unpublished data, Dr. J.R. Stouffer, College of Agriculture, Cornell University, Ithaca, N.Y.

SUMMARY OF PURCHASING OF MEATS, YIELD TESTS, CALCULATION OF COMPARABLE PRICES

Obviously, any buyer has the option to purchase cuts of meat in different forms. He may purchase a roast that is oven ready and merely has to be placed in the oven and cooked, or he may elect to purchase the item fully cooked and processed. The purveyor will charge different prices at each stage of the processing. The buyer, therefore, must be able to formulate an equation that will enable him to compare cuts of meat at comparable stages and at different prices. A typical situation is discussed below:

The XYZ Hotel is presently purchasing prime ribs of beef "as they fall." This is to say that the ribs weigh about 35 pounds each, from U.S.D.A. choice meat, cut between the 5th and 6th rib of the animal, and between the 12th rib and 13th rib. The length of the rib bones is 10 inches from the bottom of the chine bone. No trimming or additional cutting has been performed. The price for these ribs is $.89 per pound.

The buyer for the XYZ Hotel is now considering purchasing the same quality ribs in a boneless cut as specified by the National Live Stock and Meat Board Numbers 108 and 1108 R. For this item his purveyor is asking $1.45.

Normally, in order to compare prices, the purchasing agent would first have to perform cutting tests within his own establishment. He would thus determine the actual yield that he was able to obtain from the product he was buying ("as they fall" ribs), and then compare the total costs of the two products.

For example, if 100 pounds of ribs were tested, he may find:

Yield Test Results *

Weight of Ribs—boneless, tied, and short cut	56.5 lbs.
Cap meat, no fat	1.5
Short ribs, ribs 6, 7 and 8 cap off	7.0
Ground beef, 50% lean	10.5
Waste, fat, bones, and shrink	24.5

At this point one method for comparing values is to equate the total cost of the two products. If the buyer purchased 100 pounds of ribs "as they fall," his total cost would be $89.00. If he purchased 56.5 pounds of ribs prepared, his cost would be 56.5 x $1.45, or $81.92. To this he would add the value of the short ribs (determined by market price at time) at an estimated cost of 49¢ per pound, the value of the grinding beef at an estimated cost of 30¢ per pound, the value of the cap meat at an estimated cost of 89¢ per pound, and the estimated scrap value of the bones, etc., at a cost of 2¢ per pound, for a total of $8.41.

Sample Value Comparison

1) As they fall

$.89 x 100 lbs. = $89.00

2) Oven Ready

$1.45 x 56.5 lbs. = $81.92

Other Items
Short Ribs

$.49 x 7 lbs. = $3.43

Grinding Beef

$.30 x 10.5 lbs. = $3.15

* "Merchandising Beef Ribs," National Live Stock and Meat Board, p. 7.

Cap Meat

$.89 x 1.5 lbs. = $1.335 or $1.34

Bones, etc.

24.5 lbs. x $.02 = $.49

Total = $81.92 + 3.43 + 3.15 + 1.34 + .49 = $90.33

The total value for the ribs based on what it would cost the buyer to purchase the item on a comparable basis is thus $90.33. However, the buyer must add to this figure the cost of his labor required to cut up the rib, the cost of the equipment necessary for this, and incidental costs. Thus, although in effect the savings were about $1.33, the total cost for the "as they fall" rib was higher when all other costs were included.

Sometimes operators may consider that the value of the cap meat, the short ribs, ground beef, and scrap value for the bones and fat are almost equal to the incidental costs and the labor costs, although in this case the high value of $8.41 would probably exceed those costs.

In the case above it would probably be wiser for the buyer to purchase the prepared items, since no labor and incidental costs would be added.

In cases where there is no scrap value for any of the incidental cuts obtained, the yield percentage may be divided into the as-purchased price of the original item to determine what should be paid for a product that would have no further butchering losses.

Suppose, for example, that the 56.5 pounds obtained from the 100 pounds in the original form was the only item obtainable from this cut of meat. (This happens particularly in some boning, trimming, aging, and cooking yields tests.) In that case, if 56.5 was divided into 89¢, the total price paid for the cooked roast would be:

A.P. price ÷ Yield % = E.P. price

$.89 ÷ 56.5 = $1.57

In cases where the establishment cannot use the by-products or in cases where there are no by-products (as in a boning process), the minimum price one would expect to pay for a cooked and prepared cut would be $1.57. To this, of course, must be added the labor charge that would be incurred by the processer. At the same time, the processer may be able to reduce the price somewhat in that he may be able to utilize the by-products.

Another example of this type of processing and decision making is analyzed below.

In this case the buyer would be purchasing 67 pounds of beef porterhouse steaks at a price of $1.47/lb., for a total price of $98.49. If he wished to purchase a short loin that would give him the same amount of steaks, he would have to purchase 100 pounds, for which he would expect to pay about the same total price. This means that:

Yield % prod. 2 x E.P. price prod. 1 = A.P. price prod. 2/lb

67% x $1.47 = $.985 /lb.

By using the yield percentages obtained either from testing or from data obtained from sources such as the National Live Stock and Meat Board, the buyer may simplify his mathematical computation, as is discussed below.

If purchasing a product that has a yield percentage, divide the yield percentage into the purchase price to obtain the price that should be paid for a ready product.

A.P. price, unprocessed ÷ Yield % = Price for ready product

If a ready product is available and the buyer wishes to know what to pay for a product for which the establishment will do the processing, multiply the purchase price of the ready product by the yield percentage of the unprocessed product to determine the market price that should be paid for an unprocessed item.

Ready product price x Yield %, unprocessed item
= Price for unprocessed item

Naturally an adjustment must be made for the cost of labor to process the product and the cost of the by-products available. As can be noted in this cutting test, the cost of the by-products and the cost (estimated) for labor to process the item appear to be very close (presuming a butcher or skilled chef would be paid $5.00 per hour and the loin would be fully processed in about 15-20 minutes).

The purchasing agent and the chef sometimes are hesitant to purchase processed meat items, since it may be more difficult to fully evaluate the quality of the cut. Quality and grading are based on a number of factors, such as the degree of marbling, the color of the meat, the finish (exterior fat), bone structure, texture, etc. When meat is processed, some of the quality indicators are removed, so that judging the quality is more difficult.

Those characteristics that cannot be judged in processed meats (depending upon the degree of processing) are the overall conformation of the carcass, the thickness of the muscle structure of the animal, the porosity of the bones, the amount of cartilage at the ends of the thoracic vertebrae and at the ends of the lumbar vertebrae, and the general ossification of the vertebrae themselves. Realistically then, it is possible for the buyer to get "stuck" or to purchase processed items which do not meet the standards that have been set by management. In these cases reliance upon reputable dealers as well as physically inspecting their processing plants will be necessary to insure high quality at all times.

FISH AND SEAFOOD

These products have yield price tags comparable to those of meats and poultry and may be considered in a similar manner.

PRODUCE

Determining yields for fresh produce is just as necessary as calculating yields for meats and other high-value items. The technique is the same. However, the buyer should be conscious that fresh produce has a higher perishability rate than other items and yields may vary considerably should older items be received. Yield percentages for various fresh produce products (and many other foods) are available from the Food Purchasing Guide for Group Feeding in Agriculture Handbook No. 284, published by the U.S.D.A. The first page of the information for fresh vegetables is shown in Figure 8-10.

CANNED VEGETABLES

Yield percentages for canned vegetables are also available in Agriculture Handbook No. 284, (see Figure 8-11).

Variances from those figures listed in the tables will occur in fresh produce and even in canned goods. These variances occur due to the age of the product (even with canned goods, products will deteriorate and break down) and the quality standards of the packer. Figures listed are for average or minimum yields. Some packers will can products with much higher drained-weight yields.

FROZEN PRODUCTS

Most frozen items will yield close to 100%. However, with certain items care must be taken to determine whether the weight indicated on the package is the true weight of the product or the glazed weight. Many fish products (particularly shrimp) are dipped in water to coat the item with a protective ice glaze. In some cases the weight listed on the package is the weight prior to glazing. In other cases the weight is after glazing. Buyers should be conscious of this fact and also be aware that no regulations exist that govern the amount of glaze that may be placed on the product.

FIGURE 8-10 *Yield Percentages for Fresh Vegetables*

Fresh vegetables as purchased	Unit of purchase	Weight per unit [1]	Yield, as served	Portion as served	Portions per purchase unit	Approximate purchase units for— 25 portions	100 portions
		Pounds	*Percent*		*Number*	*Number*	*Number*
Asparagus	Pound	1.00	---	4 medium spears, cooked	3.38	7½	29¾
	do	1.00	49	3 ounces cut spears, cooked	2.61	9¾	38½
	Crate	28.00	49	do	73.17	[2]	1½
Beans, lima, green:							
In pod	Pound	1.00	40	3 ounces cooked	2.13	11¾	47
	Bushel	32.00	40	do	68.27	[2]	1½
Shelled	Pound	1.00	102	do	5.44	4¾	18½
Beans, snap, green or wax	do	1.00	84	do	4.48	5¾	22½
	Bushel	30.00	84	do	134.40	[2]	[2]
Beet greens, untrimmed	Pound	1.00	44	do	2.35	10¾	42¾
	Bushel	20.00	44	do	46.93	[2]	2¼
Beets:							
With tops	Pound	1.00	43	3 ounces sliced or diced, cooked	2.29	11	43¾
Without tops	do	1.00	76	do	4.05	6¼	24¾
	Burlap bag	50.00	76	do	202.67	[2]	[2]
Blackeye peas, shelled	Pound	1.00	93	3 ounces cooked	4.96	5¼	20¼
Broccoli	do	1.00	---	2 medium spears, cooked	4.57	5½	22
	do	1.00	62	3 ounces cut spears, cooked	3.31	7¾	30¼
	Crate	40.00	62	do	132.27	[2]	[2]
Brussels sprouts	Pound	1.00	77	3 ounces cooked	4.11	6¼	24½
Cabbage	Bulk	1.00	79	2 ounces coleslaw	6.32	4	16
	do	1.00	75	3 ounces sliced, cooked	4.00	6¼	25
	do	1.00	80	3-ounce wedge, cooked	4.27	6	23½
	Crate or sack	50.00	80	do	213.33	[2]	[2]
Cabbage, Chinese	Pound	1.00	88	2 ounces raw	7.04	3¾	14¼
Carrots, without tops	do	1.00	82	2 ounces shredded or grated, strips or diced, raw.	6.56	4	15¼
	do	1.00	75	3 ounces sliced or diced, cooked	4.00	6¼	25
	Bushel	50.00	75	do	200.00	[2]	[2]
Cauliflower	Pound	1.00	45	2 ounces sliced, raw	3.60	7	28
	do	1.00	44	3 ounces cooked	2.35	10¾	42¾
	Crate	37.00	44	do	86.83	[2]	1¼
	Crate, large	50.00	44	do	117.33	[2]	[2]
Celery	Pound	1.00	70	3 ounces chopped, cooked	3.73	6¾	27
	do	1.00	75	3 ounces sliced, raw	4.00	6¼	25
	do	1.00	75	2 ounces strips, raw	6.00	4¼	16¾
	Crate	60.00	75	3 ounces chopped, raw	240.00	[2]	[2]
Celery hearts (24 pack)	Crate or box	30.00	95	2 ounces strips, raw	228.00	[2]	[2]
Chard, untrimmed	Pound	1.00	56	3 ounces	2.99	8½	33½
Collards	do	1.00	81	3 ounces cooked	4.32	6	23¼
	Bushel	20.00	81	do	86.40	[2]	1¼
Corn, in husks	Dozen	8.00	37	3 ounces cooked kernels	15.79	1¾	6½
	do	8.00	---	1 ear, cooked	12.00	2¼	8½
	5-dozen crate or bag.	40.00		do	60.00	[2]	1¾

FIGURE 8-11 *Yield for Canned Vegetables*

Canned vegetables as purchased	Unit of purchase	Weight per unit	Yield, as served	Portion as served	Portions per purchase unit	Approximate purchase units for— 25 portions	Approximate purchase units for— 100 portions
		Pounds	*Percent*		*Number*	*Number*	*Number*
Asparagus:							
Cuts and tips	No. 300 can	0. 88	61	3 ounces	2. 86	8¾	35
	No. 10 can	6. 31	60	do	20. 19	1¼	5
Spears	No. 300 can	. 91		6 medium	2. 57	9¾	39
	No. 10 can	6. 44		do	18. 53	1½	5½
Beans, lima, green	No. 303 can	1. 00	69	3 ounces	3. 68	7	27¼
	No. 10 can	6. 56	69	do	24. 14	1¼	4¼
Beans, snap, green or wax	No. 303 can	. 97	59	do	3. 05	8¼	33
	No. 2½ can	1. 75	59	do	5. 51	4¾	18¼
	No. 10 can	6. 31	62	do	20. 87	1¼	5
Beans, dry—kidney, lima, or navy	No. 303 can	1. 00	80	6 ounces	2. 13	11¾	47
	No. 10 can	6. 75	80	do	14. 40	1¾	6¾
Bean sprouts	do	6. 62	52	3 ounces	18. 37	1½	5½
Beets:							
Diced	No. 303 can	1. 00	66	do	3. 52	7¼	28½
	No. 10 can	6. 50	69	do	23. 92	1¼	4¼
Sliced	No. 303 can	1. 00	61	do	3. 25	7¾	31
	No. 10 can	6. 50	65	do	22. 53	1¼	4½
Whole baby beets	No. 303 can	1. 00	62	do	3. 31	7¾	30¼
	No. 10 can	6. 50	66	do	22. 88	1¼	4½
Carrots:							
Diced	No. 303 can	1. 00	62	do	3. 31	7¾	30¼
	No. 10 can	6. 50	69	do	23. 92	1¼	4¼
Sliced	No. 303 can	1. 00	62	do	3. 31	7¾	30¼
	No. 10 can	6. 50	66	do	22. 88	1¼	4½
Chop suey vegetables	do	6. 38	100	do	34. 00	[1]	3
Collards	No. 303 can	. 94	72	4 ounces	2. 71	9¼	37
	No. 2½ can	1. 69	70	do	4. 73	5½	21¼
	No. 10 can	6. 12	61	do	14. 93	1¾	6¾
Corn:							
Cream style	No. 303 can	1. 00	100	do	4. 00	6¼	25
	No. 10 can	6. 62	100	do	26. 48	1	4
Whole kernel	No. 303 can	1. 00	66	3 ounces	3. 52	7¼	28½
	No. 10 can	6. 62	66	do	23. 30	1¼	4½
Kale	No. 303 can	. 94	72	4 ounces	2. 71	9¼	37
	No. 2½ can	1. 69	70	do	4. 73	5½	21¼
	No. 10 can	6. 12	61	do	14. 93	1¾	6¾
Mushrooms	No. 8 Z	. 78	64	3 ounces	2. 66	9½	37¾
	No. 10 can	6. 44	66	do	22. 67	1¼	4½
Mustard greens	No. 303 can	. 94	72	4 ounces	2. 71	9¼	37
	No. 2½ can	1. 69	70	do	4. 73	5½	21¼
	No. 10 can	6. 12	61	do	14. 93	1¾	6¾
Okra	No. 303 can	. 97	68	3 ounces	3. 51	7¼	28½
	No. 10 can	6. 19	61	do	20. 14	1¼	5
Okra and tomatoes	No. 303 can	. 94	100	do	5. 01	5	20
	No. 10 can	6. 31	100	do	33. 65	[1]	3

Chapter 8

I. *Class Exercises*

1. Determine the yield % for the following:

A.P. weight rump roast—172 lbs.
Weight of trimmed fat—5 lbs.
Weight of boneless meat—152 lbs.
Oven ready roasts—129 lbs.
Miscellaneous ground beef—23 lbs.
Cooked weight of roasts—119 lbs.
Number of 5-oz. servings of roast beef—325

Determine:
a. Trimmed yield %
b. Trimmed yield % from boneless weight to roasted weight
c. Cooking yield %
d. Serving yield %
e. Total yield % for roast beef

2. Determine the yield % for the following:

Live weight of turkeys—375 lbs.
Dressed weight of turkeys—300 lbs.
Weight of gizzards—15 lbs.
Oven ready turkey—275 lbs.
Weight of livers—10 lbs.
Weight of cooked turkey—225 lbs.
Number of 5-oz. servings of roast turkey—625

Determine:

a. Dressing yield %
b. Dressed to oven ready yield %
c. Cooking yield % from dressed weight
d. Serving yield %
e. Total yield % for roast turkey

II. *Study Questions*

1. What is a yield percentage?
2. List and discuss the varying types of yield tests that may be necessary for meat, fish, or poultry products.
3. What are government yield grades?
4. What are the expected yield percentages for yields 1-5 for "dressed to usable cuts of meats" for beef?
5. How are pork carcasses graded for yield percentages?
6. Discuss the difference between A.P. and E.P. price.
7. How do you compare yield percentages of products?
8. What methods can you use to determine yields in fresh products versus canned products? What equipment may be required?

9

Receiving, Storage, and Inventory Control of Foods

The principles that were applied in the beverage department will also be relevant to food control. There are, however, some outstanding differences in the controls and their actual implementation. Beverages primarily disappear or shrink due to theft. Food products can spoil and will normally lose weight due to dehydration. Often they are purchased in forms that bear no direct relationship to the final product for which they are utilized. Tomatoes, for example, may appear whole, sliced or quartered, chopped, in sandwiches or salads, as garnishes, or may be processed in some fashion to make soups or sauces.

The purchase unit for food is either by the box (lug, basket, etc.) or by the pound. There is no practical method yet devised that will determine the exact revenue that this type of product will produce. With liquor, on the other hand, it is relatively simple to determine potential sales value of purchase units, and in all cases the purchase units are limited to volume measurements (fifths, quarts, etc.). Foods may be purchased in so many forms (units, piece, ounce, pound, crate, basket, till, etc.), used in such a variety of finished products, and have such variable yields that without the assistance of computers, and unless some form of ranking is used to measure relative values, no system can be devised to adequately control all food items.

Fortunately, the value of many of the food items is so low in relationship to weight or volume that unwarranted shrinkage due to theft is not a problem. Good management techniques are required, however, to prevent natural shrinkage due to spoilage and other inefficiencies.

The dollar value of food merchandise governs the amount of controls that must be placed upon the system to guarantee the security of the merchandise. Liquor varies slightly in dollar amount from a low of about $3.00 per quart to a high of $15.00 to $20.00—the vast majority of the bottles (quarts) and brands falling into a range of $5.00 to $7.00. Foods, however, fluctuate in price from potatoes, which cost about $5.00 per hundred pounds, to caviar, which may run as high as $80.00 per pound.

Most foods do not have high values in relationship to weight or volume—with the exception of meats and some seafoods. Few employees will bother to steal low dollar value items, since the risk of being caught far outweighs the value of the product. Of the several thousand items kept in stock in many restaurants only about 10% of them have high dollar values. Management's efforts to secure items from theft or pilferage should concentrate primarily on these items.

This does not mean that normal security should be ignored but rather that, just as with liquors, special locked areas should be assigned to key items, with a limited number of personnel allowed access to these areas. Since most of the items of high dollar value require similar types of storage conditions (refrigerated or frozen) or perhaps occupy limited space (as with jars of caviar), it becomes fairly simple to give priority ratings to this merchandise and to set up accurate control systems to account for all items.

PRIORITY RATINGS, DOLLAR VALUES, AND INVENTORY TURNOVER

Unlike inventories for other types of industries, the size of inventories that are maintained in food service relate not only to "keeping quality" but also to the amounts required to be "in-process," and the level of usage (sales). Ideally, inventories should be reduced to a minimum, or in fact, no inventories should be maintained, since an inventory merely ties up capital. If optimum conditions were maintained, as goods arrived on premises they would be processed and sold. Since this would be impossible to achieve, inventories allow for the fact that some time is needed to process goods (cooking, preparation, etc.) and that there will be a lapse of time between delivery and sale. With highly perishable goods, this lapse is kept to a minimum. Deliveries of this type of merchandise are more frequent, and often deliveries are made daily, or even several times a day. In some cases, the size of the storeroom facilities dictates that this frequency be maintained. In other cases, a larger storeroom plus the non-perishability of the product permit larger inventories to be stocked.

In-Process Inventories

In-process inventories in food service establishments normally are negligible. No maturing process is required, and once processed the food may immediately be served. (Compare this with the liquor or wine industry, in which the products must be held for periods of months or years before they are ready to be sold.) The larger the in-process inventory becomes in relationship to sales, the greater the chance for loss due to spoilage. *The value of in-process inventories should amount to no more than one and one-half of one day's food cost.*

Batch Inventories

Most food items are purchased in batch lots. The size of the lot is determined by perishability, storage facilities, frequency of use, transportation charges, sales forecasts, and perhaps credit policies and discount allowances given for quantity purchases. A minimum or par stock is normally maintained at all times. Reorders are given when stocks are in danger of falling below the minimum levels.

The size of the minimum stock to be maintained should allow for unusual sales. At no time should the establishment be "out of stock" of any item, except in those cases where the item is not regularly served or where the cost of maintaining the stock outweighs the loss of potential sales from being out of stock.

An example of this may be the case of maintaining a sufficient inventory of live lobsters, so that there are always live lobsters available. Lobsters, however, being highly perishable and very costly, should be maintained at minimum levels so that little if any are lost due to spoilage. If normal sales are thirty-six lobsters per day, and lobsters will only keep for two or three days, a daily delivery of this item will prevent losses, and perhaps it is possible to have on hand as many as fifty-four. In this case, should lobster sales fall or rise by 50%, adequate inventories will always be maintained and yet no losses should occur due to spoilage. If deliveries are made every other day, however, consideration should be given to the relative value of the safety factor in having a sufficient amount to cover all contingencies. If sales fall 50 percent, then only 18 would be sold each day. If 72 are kept on hand (two normal days' supply), then by the third day only 54 would have been used and 18 would have spoiled. If less are kept on hand, the operator is in fact purchasing safety at the expense of losing sales.

The value of these lost sales as compared to the value of the lost inventory must be weighed and evaluated. Then a decision will be made based on the possibilities of running out, compared to the possibilities of spoilage. If 100% stock is maintained (72 for two days), then there may be a 1% chance that the establishment will run out, but the chances of spoilage may be 70%. If only 54 are kept on hand, then there may be a 20% chance of running out but only a 10% chance of spoilage. The potential costs of running out must be compared with the actual costs of carrying the merchandise in stock and the costs of spoilage.

In most cases, a customer, when told a menu item is no longer being served, will select another item from the menu, so that no sales are lost. Should this occur frequently or should too many items on the menu be sold out, the chances of losing the customer increase. On the other hand, once an item has spoiled, it is the same as a lost customer, since it never can be sold.

If one uses a normal food cost percentage (approximately 40%) and normal food cost profit percentage (approximately 5%), then every item that spoils necessitates eight other sales to make up the loss plus one more to get back the original 5% profit. The operator that never runs out of any item (with the exception of those operations that may have types of menus that tend to prevent this) may, in fact, have high unnecessary food spoilage losses that could be prevented by simply reducing inventories.

INVENTORY CONTROL METHODS

1. Open Storerooms	4. Perpetual
2. Bin Cards	5. Issues
3. Dual Bin	6. Min-Max

Full-service operations normally have over 1000 items to account for. The need for an accurate method of inventory control is imperative. The method selected, however, will differ considerably in various types of food service establishments, due to the type of service as well as the volume of business.

Open Storerooms

For the small operator, in most cases an open storeroom is maintained. No one individual is responsible for recording merchandise issued or received daily, although one person is held accountable for ordering and taking inventory. The problems that arise with this method are shortages due to theft and running out of merchandise, either due to abnormal use of a product or the fact that in ordering, the item was overlooked. Two methods may be used to prevent these occurrences, either by the installation of written bin cards indicating par stocks or by the use of the dual bin system.

Bin Cards

A bin card with minimum stock levels posted should alleviate the problem of running out somewhat, since the person taking inventory prior to ordering can check visually if the stock has fallen below the par required. Hopefully other employees, when removing stock from the storeroom, will notify management whenever they note that the level has fallen below the desired par. Often however, when employees are in a rush, they will fail to note the shortage or forget to notify management. Since no one individual can be held accountable, this system often breaks down. It should only be used where a limited number of persons have access to the storeroom and all are alerted to the system.

Dual Bin

Under this method, two inventories of crucial items may be kept. One is available to all employees (those having normal access to supplies), while the other is used as the emergency amount to be held on hand at all times.

With this method, management is automatically notified whenever the regular stock runs out, so that no emergency will exist.

In practice, the employees will go to the storeroom to replenish supplies, note that none are available, and notify management that the stock has run out. Management has a small reserve that is then placed into service. Since it is not practical to keep dual inventories for all items, it is customary to select those that are used by many persons (an example would be catsup, which in small operations may be replenished by the busboys or waitresses directly from the storeroom) and do not occupy much space. Extra condiments, small reserve supplies of napkins, straws, stirrers, etc. may be kept in a locked cabinet, with the persons in charge of any shift being the only ones with access to the keys.

Perpetual Inventories

Perpetual inventories are used primarily in those operations having a full-time storekeeper who is responsible for the issuing of stock as well as maintaining records, and who assists in insuring that there is an adequate supply of merchandise. The recordkeeping may be by either a master inventory list or bin cards, which must be posted as merchandise is received or issued. Minimum stocks (pars) are indicated on the records, so that the storekeeper is automatically alerted whenever reordering is necessary. Inventory control systems that are incorporated into a computer system greatly simplify recordkeeping, purchasing, issuing, and reordering. Most large purveyors have found that by switching to a computer, sizes of inventories have been kept at minimal dollar values and the labor required for recordkeeping has been greatly reduced. Computer hardware and software have been developed to the point that almost any size food and beverage operation can now obtain the necessary equipment at a reasonable cost.

The min-max system was explained in Chapter 3. The issue system is discussed later in this chapter.

ABC ANALYSIS

The determination of inventory policy requires that management make a series of trade-offs between conflicting sets of costs, i.e. between the costs of ordering and the costs of holding inventory, between the costs of holding safety stocks and the possible cost of running out of stock.*

In food service, the cost of ordering merchandise (processing purchase orders, paying bills, receiving and checking merchandise, and verifying all

---

*"Practical Techniques and Policies for Inventory Control," Management Services Technical Study No. 6, p. 20. Published by the American Institute of Certified Public Accountants, Inc., 666 Fifth Avenue, New York, New York 10019.

control systems) is often overlooked, although in some establishments some forms of control have been implemented to reduce these costs. Allowing deliveries to be made during limited periods of time reduces the cost of having a full-time employee as a receiving clerk, and may allow him to also double as the storeroom clerk.

Certainly, the combining of forms used for quotations and for purchasing will reduce processing costs. Generally speaking, however, processing costs cannot be reduced to the same extent as in other industries, since the number of deliveries that must be made is dictated primarily by the perishability of the products rather than by the incidental costs. With low-value non-perishable items, however, larger inventories may be kept on hand to reduce the possibility of running out as well as to reduce the handling charges involved.

Typical items that may fall into this category would be catsup, salt, pepper, etc., which occupy little space and have low value. Thus they may be stocked in larger quantities. If ten cases of catsup are used per week, and weekly deliveries of dry goods are received, the catsup may be ordered on a biweekly or even monthly basis. By grouping foods into several categories some inventory-taking may be reduced from a weekly count to a once-a-month basis.

This first group may be entitled "Group A." Into it should be placed all items that are non-perishable, of low value, and are used constantly.

Most food operators accomplish this to some extent. Dry, frozen, and canned goods items may be ordered on a weekly basis; meats and poultry several times per week; and produce, dairy, and bread products daily. Purchasing agents and food controllers should further modify this practice by breaking down each major food category into A, B, and C items, and thus take into consideration the value of these items as well as their perishability. Further examination of dry goods and canned products should reveal that B and C items do exist.

B items may be classified as those that are non-perishable, are used on a consistent basis, and are moderate in cost. Examples of this might be frozen or canned goods falling into a price range of $5 to $10 per case. Fruits, vegetables, and juices are often in this category.

C items may be categorized as those that are non-perishable and used consistently, but are more costly. Thus large amounts would not be kept on hand. Canned and frozen meats, fish, and poultry might be placed into this category.

Lastly, a category might be established for those items that are only used occasionally, either for special events or for menus that might occur during a specified period of time. Specialty items such as smoked clams or oysters, quail, game hens, pre-prepared hors d'oeuvres, and like items might be listed in this category. The food and beverage controller or chef would verify these items as being in stock should a special function be planned for the given calendar period.

Perishable items must be placed into several categories as well. Here the breakdown is dictated by the degree of perishability and the frequency of delivery. If produce is delivered daily, inventories may be physically checked every day. If deliveries are made semiweekly, then the count would be made just prior to ordering.

Inventory verification (the physical count of merchandise) takes time and thus costs money. Whenever it is possible to reduce the number of items that must be counted without adding too much to the cost of inventory on hand, total handling costs may be reduced. Since hundreds of items, or even thousands, may be kept in stock (consider the number of paper goods, items that are low in cost but non-perishable), the ABC Analysis system will give management adequate control while at the same time reducing handling costs.

RECEIVING

As with liquors, it is imperative that all merchandise that has been ordered and sold to the food service establishment be delivered. The suggestion was made previously that it usually is unprofitable to remove from an establishment low-value merchandise. Employee theft of low-value items is normally not a problem. Many food items, however, are high-value items. Security measures still must be enforced to control these items.

The principal area that is of concern to management is that it is easier not to deliver an item than to deliver it. In addition, this kind of theft requires no trucking or surreptitiousness. Large amounts may "disappear" by the signature of the receiving clerk when, in fact, no merchandise has been received. This type of theft is normally accomplished by collusion between the clerk and the deliveryman.

Another possibility is that the deliveryman may remove other merchandise while delivering his own—a relatively common practice. Since a truck is already at the door, the actual physical removal is a simple chore. In those cases where the deliveryman is attempting to remove merchandise on his own without the consent of the receiving clerk, constant vigilance and prohibiting deliverymen in areas other than the receiving dock should prevent excess losses from this type of theft.

When routemen and receiving clerks conspire together to defraud an establishment, additional controls must be used, which should eliminate any practices of this type. In large operations, most deliveries are forwarded either directly to the kitchen or to storage areas where another individual has the responsibility for the merchandise. When receiving work sheets are used, possibly an additional column for the signature of the storeroom clerk or chef will transfer the goods from the care of the receiving agent to either of the other departments. The storeroom clerk or the chef will have to verify that he is receiving all the merchandise that he has signed for. If receiving sheets are not used and all the products of a particular purveyor are transferred to one area, then it is possible to merely have the storeroom man or chef sign the invoice.

If, however, the order is split, with some of the merchandise being transferred to the storeroom and some going directly to the kitchen, it becomes necessary to institute some other type of control. In large operations, the normal procedure is for the receiving clerk to split an order according to prior instructions and enter the appropriate dollar amounts on his receiving sheet. (See Figure 9-1).

As can be noted, the actual dollar amounts from the invoices should be entered in the appropriate column. In practice, however, although the dollar amounts are accurate (since they have been taken directly from the invoices), the amounts of merchandise shipped to each area are not closely controlled. This can lead to gross errors in accounting for actual food costs, since the receiving sheet is often used as one of the original sources for calculating daily food costs.

The normal procedure is for the receiving sheet to be forwarded to the accounting or auditing department. The dollar amounts from "direct shipments" are used and added to daily requisitions to determine daily food costs. For control, another form should be required, since there is no verification that the entry of direct shipments actually is the amount received in the kitchen or other working areas. Just as with requisitions, the party receiving the merchandise should sign for the amounts received. In turn, this form should be compared with the amounts entered in the direct shipments column.

Another simple method for verification is for all direct shipments to be accompanied by a requisition form, which must be signed by the department receiving the merchandise. The requisition would be turned in with the receiving sheet. It may be necessary for a separate requisition to be used, since the receiving sheet does not normally leave the receiving dock. This receiving requisition form should be made out in triplicate. One copy should remain with the department receiving the merchandise, one with the receiving clerk, and one forwarded to the accounting office.

Goods on an invoice from a purveyor may be shipped to several departments, besides some of the merchandise being shipped directly to the storeroom. Accounting must verify that the total amount of the invoice has been accounted for by either requisitions or a signed invoice (as in the case of the full amount being shipped directly to the storeroom and the storeroom clerk signing the invoice).

In small operations, the cost of the bookkeeping may not warrant the use of this or other forms. It may be more feasible for spot checks to be made

FIGURE 9-1 *Receiving Sheet*

XYZ COMPANY _____ DATE _____ CLERK _____

Purveyor	Invoice Number	Total Amount	Storeroom	Liquor	Direct to Department		
					Department	Amount	Received By

by the manager or purchasing agent. These checks, performed at random times, may serve to verify the quality received as well as the amounts. Another possibility is to have the receiving clerk date stamp all the merchandise (a practice that should be performed anyway on highly perishable merchandise). Then a physical count may be taken within a short period of time after the delivery, since the merchandise should not have been consumed or utilized in that brief span of time.

The function of the receiving clerk in food operations is much more complex than the task of the receiving clerk who only accepts liquor. As noted earlier, liquor does not vary in quality but food does. Not only must the food receiving clerk inspect all merchandise to make certain that the correct quantities have been received, but a careful scrutinization must be made to insure that the quality of the goods is in accordance with the prescribed specifications as laid down by management.

Since much of the merchandise is perishable, this inspection must include an examination to detect signs of deterioration and concurrently an inspection to determine freshness. This freshness may be determined by a visual examination or in some cases from the date stamps used by purveyors (as in the case of dairy and bread products). After acceptance it may be advisable for the receiving clerk to date stamp (and perhaps note the weights on the items), so that in the processing of products within the operation the earliest dated items will be used first. Some operations may find that color coding merchandise is advisable and more convenient.

Certain items are more difficult to examine (either in relationship to quality or quantity) than others. For example, fresh chickens are normally crated in cartons that contain ice. To accurately weigh the chickens, they must be removed from the crates and then placed on a scale. Frozen items, particularly those packed in rigid containers (cans of juice or food in aluminum packages), may have been thawed and then refrozen while in transit, but no determination of quality can be made at the receiving dock. Fresh fruits and vegetables can be weighed to determine if they meet the standards (normally a weight range), but should small amounts of merchandise be removed by an unscrupulous purveyor it would be extremely difficult for the receiving clerk to detect this deception. Three or four oranges or lemons may be removed from a carton without noticeably affecting the total weight of the carton. The amount of time that the clerk would have to spend to count each crate of lemons or oranges, however, certainly would not warrant this type of examination.

Finally, with the great amounts of food that are received by establishments, it is easier for receiving clerks merely to accept the figures presented by the purveyor, since verification of weights, quality, and quantities may involve much work and time. Obviously, the only method to insure that the job is performed is for management to spot check and insist that every item received be inspected.

Unless an establishment has a full-time receiving clerk (which normally is warranted only with those establishments grossing over $1 million a year), the job of the receiving clerk is often relegated to the chef, cook, or in many cases the dishwashers. Unless the individual is trained for the receiving of merchandise, is aware of the importance of careful receiving, and has the authority to reject merchandise if it does not meet the standards of the establishment, receiving becomes meaningless. Although management may have authorized and instructed the chef to perform this task, he may become tied up with his own work. Food may be in a critical stage in the cooking process, and thus he delegates the task to the nearest person at hand. Although it is not always possible, the establishment not having a full-time receiving clerk should request deliveries at certain times of the day. Thus the chef or other authorized and trained person would be able to schedule his work to allow for the arrival of shipments.

FOOD STORAGE AND INVENTORY CONTROL

In the storage of food, most operations confine the duties of the storeroom keeper to the control of items on a non-perishable nature. Food items such as produce, meats, dairy products, fish, and poultry are normally shipped directly to a kitchen or to butcher shops in which processing may be initiated. Thus, although the problem of spoilage must still be considered, the storeroom keeper is primarily concerned with the maintenance of adequate supplies of merchandise and the recordkeeping involved with the allocating or the charging of food to various segments of an operation.

For the vast majority of food service establishments, the storeroom keeper is not even concerned with the allocation of food to different outlets. With the exception of large operations, only one actual restaurant or food service establishment is involved, and only one source of income must be compared with cost figures. Again, in most operations it is not feasible to hire a full-time storeroom keeper, since the wages for this individual may exceed any savings effected and, in fact, other methods of control are available.

Operations grossing less than $1 million per year normally do not require a full-time storeroom keeper unless the individual is capable of performing other duties, as the issuing of merchandise for this volume is not a full-time job. With proper training of the staff, it may be feasible to keep a locked storeroom and issue merchandise only at certain hours. This duty may be performed by the chef or other responsible individual. It is not advisable to keep an open storeroom to which all employees have access. Extra precautions should be taken when the storage area is removed from the mainstream of the normal operation. Storerooms in basements or outside the main buildings must be locked.

If a full-time storeroom keeper is employed, then it should be his function to account for all the merchandise issued to the various function rooms. Just as with beverage operations in which there is more than one bar, the requisition forms and issue forms that are used by the food service outlets must indicate to which segment of the operation the costs are allocated. Again, only authorized individuals should be allowed to requisition and sign for stores.

Earlier in this chapter it was mentioned that unless a business is grossing over $1 million a year it may not be feasible or economical to hire either a full-time receiving clerk or a full-time storeroom keeper. Yet the control of merchandise at this stage of the operation is essential. One possibility is to combine the tasks of the receiving and storeroom clerks so that they are performed by one person. Normally, in operations with larger volumes this is feasible, and the combined jobs will provide sufficient work to employ a full-time individual.

In smaller operations the problem arises as to the value of employing a full-time individual, since in most cases shipments occur five or six times a week (excluding dairy and bread) and issuing can be done within a short period of time. Again one must look to the possibility of combining jobs. Often, relatively low skill tasks are performed by highly paid personnel. These tasks might be transferred to the storeroom and receiving clerk. For example, the menu for a given day may call for beef stew. If the task of requisitioning and combining the original ingredients is performed by the chef, this is a waste of talent and money. instead, the chef should merely inform the storeroom clerk that beef stew is featured on the menu. In turn, the storeroom clerk would have a recipe card listing the ingredients. He could weigh out and measure the ingredients, thus simplifying the task of the chef. This preportioning system permits the higher-paid personnel to perform more highly skilled jobs and lessens their work load. It also provides for a built-in training program, so that a storeroom clerk can either further his career by advancing to a position in the kitchen or perhaps with record-keeping experience advance to an accounting position.

PERISHABLE MERCHANDISE

Dairy, meat, and other perishable products are more difficult to control. Extra precautions must be taken to insure that excessive stocks are not maintained and that the oldest merchandise is always issued first. It is recommended that the storage of perishable merchandise be centralized (that is, all merchandise of the same type be stored in one location). Often this is not feasible, however, since several departments may need the same type of item.

For example, each food outlet in a hotel may need fresh milk, and certain minimum stocks must be maintained at each outlet. Occasionally, one outlet may suddenly find itself with a surplus of milk or another may find itself short of the item. Just as in bar service, the recommended procedure is to maintain minimum par stocks at each outlet and to store the major supply of the item in one central location. Issues made from this central area must be accounted for in the same manner as issues from the storeroom.

ISSUES TO DETERMINE AMOUNTS TO ORDER

Another method of controlling inventories and determining orders is by the utilization of totals that are determined from issue and requisition slips. Under this method, all stocks are kept at a par. Whatever is consumed is simply reordered. Verification of these amounts should be determined periodically (particularly with perishables) by physical counts.

The advantage of this system is that not every item need be physically counted or each bin card examined. A simple method is to have a master inventory card for each item for each week or other period of time, depending upon the reorder period. Any card that has been used is placed into an active bin categorized by type of food. The storekeeper therefore need only look at those cards in the active bin to determine which foods need to be reordered. If not enough of a particular product has been issued to warrant a reorder, the card remains in the active bin until such time as an order is necessary. Only then is the card returned to the master file. (See Figure 9-2.)

FIGURE 9-2 *Procedure for Par Stock Reordering*

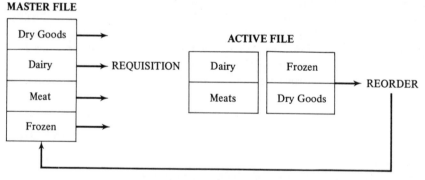

RE-ISSUING OF MERCHANDISE

One of the most difficult allocation of costs occurs when merchandise is taken from one food outlet and transferred to another. Almost every operation has food left over that is transferred to an employees' dining room or eaten at the end of the serving period. Often, in some hotels, one dining room will close at a certain hour, and leftovers may be turned over to another restaurant that continues to operate.

Unless this merchandise is accounted for, no control system exists, since, in fact, no one in the establishment actually knows how much food was or should have been used and in turn how much cash should be received. Few food service operators accurately account for these transfers, and many ignore them completely. All transfers of this nature should be accounted for in the same manner as liquor is when transferred from one bar to another. It is true that an exact determination often cannot be made (as in the case of transferring a half full pan of stew), but reasonably accurate estimates can and should be made.

GENERAL PROBLEMS IN INVENTORY CONTROL

Several types of problems exist that make the task of the food controller more difficult. Unfortunately, rather than attempt to exercise control of these areas, little effort has been expended by operators to resolve these issues.

Spoilage of Merchandise While in Storage

All operators will attempt to keep spoilage to a minimum by the proper rotation of goods, but natural spoilage and shrinkage does occur. In accounting for costs, food controllers should allocate a space on the storekeeper's report for shrinkage and spoilage. By ignoring the problem on reports, storekeepers in effect are forced to fudge figures to reflect actual physical inventories. The simplest method would be to authorize the storekeeper to report on a separate requisition form any item spoiled or damaged. This figure would be closely watched by the controller to insure that no excessive charges are made to this account, which should be set up as a separate expense item. (See Figure 9-3.) Note that this form generates a request for credit form that would be initiated by the accounting office and forwarded to the appropriate purveyor.

Estimating Value of Merchandise

Unlike liquor, in which a partially filled bottle may be accurately estimated, food items may combine many different ingredients of varying costs. Thus the value of a finished product may be difficult to estimate, particularly if some of the item has been sold or if leftovers from another menu item were used. Total recipe costs can be used to estimate values of menu items and leftovers.

The assignment of a dollar value to leftover merchandise and the utilization of leftovers is of major concern to food managers. Often, on high-value merchandise, chefs will store the food rather than serve it to employees or to use it in other items. In many cases this item is improperly stored or cannot be used on the menu for an extended period of time (particularly with cyclical menus), and the food spoils.

FIGURE 9-3

SPOILAGE REPORT

HOTEL WINDSORY   Date _____

                                                 Clerk _____

Item	Amount	Reason
1/3 case lemons	$ 4.00	Moldy – obtain credit
1 gal. vinegar	1.75	Dropped bottle
TOTAL		

Goods in Process

In any kitchen, hundreds of items are opened for the production of merchandise. For example, partially used spices, sauces, condiments, trimmed and washed produce, etc., are all kept in readiness so that menu items can rapidly be prepared. The value of these items may be considerable. In addition, food may be partially processed one day for service on another. Accounting for these items can be difficult as well as time consuming.

It is suggested that operators make a close examination of standard items in use at all times and establish a figure for these basic "goods in process" items. Adjustments can then be made rapidly should any special items be in the process of preparation. This "Par Goods in Process" figure normally will not vary greatly from one accounting period to another. However, special care should be taken, particularly if accounting periods end just prior to a busy weekend, when many kitchens will have large amounts of food in a partially prepared state.

In the cases where the item is used in the preparation of another food item (hamburgers or salisbury steaks chopped up to make a spaghetti sauce), the full dollar value of the item cannot be recovered. How much value should be assigned is a question of judgment. Again, accounting forms do not normally allow for readjustments of dollar values for leftovers.

Another situation of a similar nature is a menu item that is prepared for dinner, but the leftovers are sold the following day at a luncheon special at a lower price. Some type of reallocation of costs should be made. The exact amounts and methods, however, must be determined by the nature of the operation and the actual dollar value lost in the transfer. A system must, however, be set up so that monitoring of the amount of leftovers may be accomplished. Excessive amounts of leftovers indicate overpreparation, but unless a record is kept this type of determination cannot be made.

HIGH-VALUE MERCHANDISE

Meats, seafoods, and specialty items compare in value to liquors and must be secured in the same fashion. Too often, the systems for control in the butcher shop of food service establishments or the inventories of frozen meat products are handled in exactly the same manner as for the low-value items. No businessman or banker would leave several thousand dollars in cash unguarded. The typical food service establishment has meat, fish, and poultry on hand that in dollar value amounts to approximately the same sum, yet too often there are no safeguards to prevent unauthorized appropriation or requisitioning of the merchandise.

In most establishments, the number of these high-value items that must be accounted for are limited. Accurate records can be maintained without undue expense. In large full-service operations with a flexible menu, the total number of high-cost items should amount to less than 50, all of which can be inventoried or accounted for on one page. In specialized establishments, the number can be reduced to 10 or less. Strict accounting for these high cost items should, in fact, place controls on about 30%—40% of the merchandise purchased (dollar value). (See Figure 9-4.)

COST OF GOODS SOLD = PURCHASES = DOLLAR VALUE OF INVENTORY

General guidelines for inventory control may serve a useful function for a quick determination of the efficiency of the purchasing and inventory department. Food inventories are normally expected to turn over once per week, so that in effect the cost of goods sold, purchases, and the value of the inventory are all equal. Deviations from this standard indicate areas to be investigated.

For example, a good operation with a normal food cost of 40% and a dollar sales volume of $10,000 per week should expect that each week's purchases should amount to $4,000. Concurrently, the dollar value of the

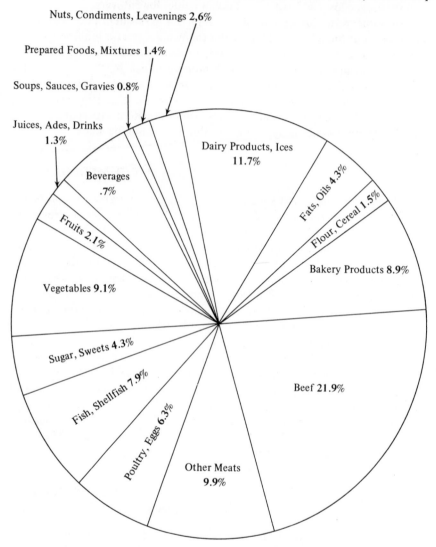

FIGURE 9-4 *Distribution of Estimated Value by Food Group*

Nuts, Condiments, Leavenings **2,6%**

Prepared Foods, Mixtures **1.4%**

Soups, Sauces, Gravies **0.8%**

Juices, Ades, Drinks **1.3%**

Beverages **.7%**

Fruits **2.1%**

Vegetables **9.1%**

Sugar, Sweets **4.3%**

Fish, Shellfish **7.9%**

Poultry, Eggs **6.3%**

Dairy Products, Ices **11.7%**

Fats, Oils **4.3%**

Flour, Cereal **1.5%**

Bakery Products **8.9%**

Beef **21.9%**

Other Meats **9.9%**

The Food Service Industry: Type, Quantity and Value of Foods Used,
Statistical Bulletin Number 476, Marketing Economics Division, Economics
Research Services, U.S.D.A., November 1971, Washington, D.C.

inventories should total $4,000. The controller may observe that inventory is at $5,000 and thus judge that an excessive amount of food is being stored and urge all concerned to reduce this amount. Purchases may vary slightly, particularly if a stocking up is done at the early part of the month (utilizing the principle of using purveyors' money as discussed in Chapter 6).

Although dollar amounts and turnover for all food items averages a turnover of once per week, highly perishable items such as dairy products and bakery items should turn over at least 4 times per week. Normal inventories for these items should be 1 1/2 days' supply. Variances again may occur, particularly in those areas where daily deliveries are not available.

Chapter 9

1. Discuss how large an inventory should be maintained. Explain why.
2. How does fraud occur in the receiving department? How can it be prevented?
3. Why are the receiving, storage, and inventory control functions for food more complex than for beverages?
4. Discuss "ABC Analysis."
5. Draw up a description of the duties of a food receiving clerk.
6. What duties would you assign to a storeroom clerk in an operation grossing $500,000/year?
7. Discuss the problems of issuing and reissuing food.
8. Set up a control system for low-value and high-value merchandise.

Food Checking
and Service

Food purchased in portion control form is comparatively simple to control. Issues from the storeroom (freezer, etc.) are in portion units, and a par stock similar to that used in beverage control can be set up for each station in the kitchen. The steak cook at the start of his shift will sign for the inventory in his refrigerator (locked), and he becomes responsible for that merchandise. The departing cook initials that same form, so that he is responsible for any merchandise that has "disappeared" during his shift. He must turn in the correct number of dupes (waitress requisitions) to account for the merchandise consumed.

If standard size pans and storage facilities are utilized, it becomes a simple matter to determine the exact number of steaks remaining at the close of each shift. Even with the press of business, it should only take three to five minutes for inventories to be counted. Since this inventory of high-value merchandise may amount to several hundred dollars, *it must be checked.* No cashier would consider taking over a register or starting her shift without first counting her bank, nor should cooks be allowed to transfer merchandise without this same type of check.

If portioned-control merchandise is not used (as in the case of roasts), then standard yields should be established for each food. Thus the number of portions for which each cook is held responsible can readily be determined. For example, from each prime ribs of beef, an establishment may determine that fifteen portions are obtainable. If the roast cook checking out from his shift has used two and one-half ribs, he should turn in dupes for 37 or 38 orders.

DUPES, PRECHECKING, AND FOOD CHECKER

Basically three different methods of control are utilized to account for the transfer of merchandise from the kitchen staff to service personnel. Each system, in addition to serving a control function, may also have an ancillary function, as explained below.

Duplicate System (Dupes). Under this type of control system the service personnel, in writing an order, make out a duplicate slip or carbon copy. In some cases when food is picked up from different stations in the kitchen, several slips must be made out. The slips are used to record the food leaving the kitchen. At the same time they may be used for ordering purposes—the cooks can look at the slips (on an order wheel or bar) and know what food should be in the process of cooking. At the close of the shift these slips should be compared with the checks and with the amount of food left to verify that all food removed from the kitchen has been charged on a check.

In order to compare duplicates with the customer checks, dupes are numbered and include the waiter's (waitress') initials, the check number, the number of guests, and often the table number. In some cases dupes are also numbered. (See Figure 10-1.)

Dupe systems are not recommended for operations in which there are a large number of customers. The process of cross checking each dupe with a guest check is extremely time-consuming and difficult. If more than one dupe is required in a kitchen (hot and cold stations) then the process is further complicated, and in addition the service personnel must spend valuable time in making out several dupes and writing the order several times. Dupes are most valuable when only one is required for each check, when the volume of customers is limited, and when carbons can be used so that service personnel do not waste valuable time (see low and high dollar check averages later in this chapter).

Modified dupe systems can be used for high-volume operations, however. This modified system can be utilized particularly if high-value merchandise is sold and many variations or types of dupes can be used. Dupes may be required by management in a coffee shop for steaks, chops, or other expensive items. Or perhaps special slips can be issued to each server to be turned over to a cook whenever a high-value item is picked up or ordered. The count of the special slips (or dupes) can be greatly reduced, and accurate comparisons can then be made with the charges on guest checks.

Prechecking. Prechecking systems are similar to dupe systems except that instead of a carbon copy or handwritten copy being turned in to the cook when ordering, the server goes to a cash register (modified) and rings up the order on the guest check. The register concurrently issues or validates a duplicate copy of the guest check. Cooks are only permitted (as with dupe systems) to issue food upon the receipt of this validated check. In theory, a comparison is not required, since the guest checks have been rung up and the total amount of sales is already recorded. Collusion can occur, however, between a cook and a server, and again a record of the food actually consumed must be made for comparison purposes.

FIGURE 10-1 *Duplicate Check*

12001

2 T stk/R

1 R B

Server	Check #	Table

To illustrate: Joan, a waitress, has two parties in one night who order the same items (steak). The cook issues four steaks but has only received one prechecked dupe. Unless management counts the steaks actually issued and consumed, Joan may reuse the one check and pocket the money received from the second party.

This fraud may also be discovered by counting the number of customers assigned to Joan's station and tallying this amount with the guest receipts. This comparison is reasonable in a food service operation in which a limited number of guests are handled by each server, but it may not be valid in coffee shops or fast food operations. The possibility of a guest being assigned to a waitress and not eating also exists (e.g. a party of six with one person not eating).

Food Checkers. Normally, food checkers are used in operations in which there is a large volume of business and a high customer count. As each server passes the food checker, the items on the tray are either rung up on the guest check or are compared with the guest check that has been previously rung up. The advantage of this system is that the process is simple and there is no need for comparison of dupes or checks. The food checker may also verify that the items are presented properly and look attractive.

The disadvantages are:

1. Since this check is made after the food is cooked there is a delay in service and food may get cold.
2. There is still the possibility of collusion between the checker and the server.
3. An additional person must be employed, which means another salary.
4. In rushed periods, the checker may simply verify the number of orders removed from the kitchen and not determine if they are the items listed on the check.
5. Physical space must be set up in the kitchen for the location of the checker's stand.

Ideally, the food checker should not be the same person that collects the cash, since this would preclude the comparison of the two figures. Often, however, due to the fact that the amount of business does not warrant the employment of two individuals, the two jobs are combined.

Although working exclusively for the food and beverage department, the food checker (as well as cashier) normally is directly under the control of and responsible to the accounting department.

The efficiency of any dupe or checking system relates directly to the amount of paperwork involved with the system, the increased delay in serving as a result of the checking system, and the actual net savings as a result of the system. These savings are, in effect, preventative, since the entire purpose of the system is to insure that management receives money for all the food it has sold to the customer. The expenses involved include the cost of printing numbered checks, the cost of the salaries of the food checkers, or other accounting personnel, and the invisible cost of slowing procedures and service, since cooks may have to handle dupes and thus be slower in actually serving the food.

For many types of food service, the amount and the value of the food items served precludes the use of certain types of checking systems. For example, a coffee shop may have a large percentage of their customers coming in only for coffee or perhaps a cold drink. Each person's check would be under 50¢. If stringent controls were established to account for these items, the accounting costs would be prohibitive. A dupe system would not be feasible, since the waitress may do much of the preparation herself (makes the coffee, serves the sodas, and she may also do some of the salad preparation).

During the course of an eight-hour shift, a waitress may serve a hundred or so customers. Each customer may purchase one or more items that have low value and are picked up from a number of different kitchen areas. The task of matching checks to dupes becomes impractical. On the other hand, management cannot afford the loss incurred due to waitresses purposely or inadvertently omitting items on the checks, or losses attributable to waitresses pocketing receipts by not turning in all monies received. Systems must be devised for each type of operation, and relevant accounting costs must relate directly to the customer and dollar volume of the operation.

LOW AVERAGE CHECK OPERATIONS

Coffee shop, fast food, and similar type operations probably have the most difficult problem in setting up a control system. They have a high number of customers, a correspondingly high number of checks, and a relatively low check average. The ideal situation would be one in which the customer pays a flat price (as with all-you-can-eat buffets) or pays at the end of the line, as with cafeterias. For other types of service, whether it be counter or table, the system must become more complicated, since food is not transferred directly to the customer and a single price is not charged. (See Figure 10-2.)

With buffet service, the only problem is to ascertain that each customer pays. A relatively simple system to check on the cashier may be used. Each customer's receipt should be given to a waiter, and for each receipt the waiter may be paid an additional amount of money. In some establishments, the amount of the waiter's share of tips may be based on the number of receipts. This receipt is turned in to the maitre d' or even the

FIGURE 10-2 *Routes of Cash and Food in Various Types of Food Service Establishments*

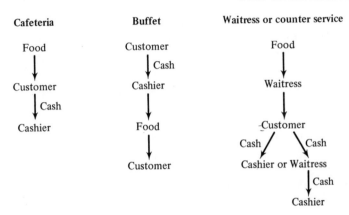

accounting department, but not to the cashier. Should a customer not have a receipt, the waiter would automatically notify management, since he would serve a customer without being paid. (Although a tip might prevent him from notifying his supervisor.) Should the total number of receipts not tally with the amount on the register, then a shortage has occurred somewhere. Another control method is to use two persons, one to take cash, the other to seat people. The tally from each must be equal.

With cafeteria service, the possibility that the cashier will not ring up all the food items still exists, but requiring her to total all items on the tray and present the customer with a receipt lessens the chances of this type of fraud or error. The newer type of registers that tally the various items sold as well as the total value of the check will also be of help in controlling losses, as exact amounts prepared for cafeteria lines are more readily determined. If some of the food items are prepared to order, the same type of checking problem that presents itself in full-service restaurants occurs. No exact total of the amounts prepared may be available, since the cook cannot keep track of totals while he is preparing the food.

With high-volume full-service restaurants, no exact record can be kept of the food issued to the waitresses. The speed of service and the fact that the waitresses help themselves to much of the food necessitates that other systems of control be set up to insure all monies are collected.

No system has yet been devised to guarantee collection nor to eliminate errors. Collection systems only reduce these possibilities. In many states, errors due to incorrect addition, omission of items on checks, or erroneous pricing cannot be collected from the server. Losses must be absorbed by management. Constant training of personnel, good supervision and continued alertness to variances in food costs and amounts consumed help to alleviate but not eliminate the problem. Definite action, however, can be taken to prevent the loss of high-cost items and to eliminate some of the careless errors:

Guide to Reduce Guest Check Losses

1. Require all personnel to use an adding machine when totaling checks.
2. Post all price changes and occasionally test personnel regarding prices.
3. Spot-check checks so that inconsistencies and consistent errors by individuals can be noted and corrected.
4. Use shopping services that will check to see that correct procedures for the handling of cash are followed.
5. Number checks and issue them to waitresses, and follow up so that missing ones can be accounted for within one day after the loss.
6. Print notices on the checks, the menu, and at the cashier's station that inform the customers as to how or whom to pay.
7. Train and remind personnel that the higher the check, the more they will receive (normally) in tips. Emphasize that each waiter or waitress is, in fact, making more than the house per customer (based on averages of 15% tip versus 5% profit), and thus stands to lose should checks not include all items. Train employees to take orders directly on the check, so that the billing of items is not forgotten. Should a waitress neglect to add a 50¢ dessert item on a $5.00 check, the net effect is a 50¢ loss in income, or 10% of the total revenue. Inasmuch as the normal profit for most food operations is approximately 5%, the house has lost money on this meal and must sell two other meals of equal value just to break even.
8. Direct traffic and customer flow in such a manner that cashiers are readily able to stop those who leave without paying.
9. Keep accurate records so that sales, costs, and variances can readily be determined.
10. Keep a record of head counts and check averages. This should be the responsibility of either the maitre d' or the cashier, or both.
11. Place special controls on high-value items so that exact records and inventories for these items are maintained.
12. Consider eliminating those high-priced items that are markedly different in price from the majority of your menu items. (Waitresses or waiters often order high-value items for favorite customers while only charging them for lower-priced items.)

    The house will not lose nearly as much when a bacon, lettuce, and tomato sandwich has been substituted for a hamburger as when a steak has been given away in place of the hamburger. Steps 11 or 12 will prevent this problem.

HIGH AVERAGE CHECK OPERATIONS

Since the average check is higher and the volume or number of customers reduced, accounting in high-priced restaurants may be and should be more detailed and involved than for fast food, and/or low-cost restaurants. Similar problems exist, since salads or other items may not be issued by the kitchen, desserts may be made and served directly by the waiter or waitress, and these items may be purposely or inadvertently omitted on the check. Primarily, however, the management is concerned with the higher-cost items, and the main thrust of the controls should be geared to account for these items. The same twelve suggestions given in the preceding paragraphs will help to alleviate shortages in the low-value items in high-priced establishments. The additional controls for high-value items should include:

1. A dupe (or a prechecking system) for every main dish and for all items issued from the kitchen.
2. A strict inventory procedure to be used for each menu item (main dishes, high-value appetizers, etc.).
3. Enforcement and tallying of dupes.
4. Comparative analysis of head counts, main dishes served, waiter check numbers, and cashier's count.
5. Separate control for each area (maitre d', accounting, cashier, chef) and verification and comparison of tallies from all areas.
6. Utilization of food checkers if size of operation warrants it.

Chapter 10
1. Discuss the 3 basic methods used for food checking.
2. Which system would you use for a low average check operation? Why?
3. Which system would you use for a high-volume medium check operation?
4. Which system would you use for a low-volume high check operation?
5. Establish a checking procedure for a medium-priced coffee shop open 18 hours each day. The operation seats 150 at tables plus 30 at counters.
6. Establish checking procedures for an 80-seat gourmet restaurant.

11

Menu Planning

CLASSIFICATION OF MARKETS

A determination of the type of menu that is to be offered is almost exclusively determined by the type of market that is being catered to. Markets may be broken down into various categories. Within a market there may be a number of conflicting factors that necessitate flexibility in the types of menus offered.

CAPTIVE VERSUS FREE MARKET

There are only a few situations in which there is actually a captive market. Obviously, prisons serve a captive market, but so do nursing homes and hospitals. To a large extent, school lunch feeding, from elementary school through college level, caters primarily to a captive audience, although in many cases the student may choose to bring lunch from home or even eat away from the school feeding facility. This market thus is both captive and non-captive. Menu planners must take into consideration both groups, which may, for a variety of reasons, either participate or not participate every day.

FACTORS AFFECTING MARKET

In establishing the type of market that an operation is catering to, the characteristics of the clientele determine not only the type of menu that will be most successful but also type of establishment. Clientele characteristics that must be considered are discussed below.

Age

For most restaurant operations, the age of the clientele is not a determining factor. For some, however, careful consideration must be given to the age of the guests. Certainly for nursing homes, school lunch feeding, and camps this is a primary concern.

Even within one type of operation (such as school lunch) there may be several breakdowns by age. Different menus must be written for each group. For children in the lower grades (kindergarten and first grade), finger foods are most popular. In college feeding and the secondary schools, knives and forks are not considered burdensome and a different menu may be designed.

Sex

Taste preferences among men and women and among boys and girls often differ (see Figure 11-1). Allowances must be made by menu planners should one sex predominate in the group. Salads and less starch may be desirable for a women's college. Larger portions and more bulk may be most effective for a men's college or sports training tables.

Economic Status

Menus are designed for the area in which the operation does its business. The ability of the people in that area to pay a given price for a given meal will determine the type of meal that will be served. A gourmet restaurant will normally not be successful in a low-income area, nor should a low-priced fast food hamburger restaurant attempt to establish its operation in a high-income area unless there is a high concentration of people, traffic, or unique eating or cultural patterns.

FIGURE 11-1 *Husbands' and Wives' Selections of Main Dishes by Type of Eating Place*

	Cafeteria		Diner		Drive In	
Main Dish	Husbands	Wives	Husbands	Wives	Husbands	Wives
Beef	47%	37%	44%	37%	26%	12%
Fowl	23	24	10	17	22	26
Pork	10	8	17	10	5	11
Seafood	3	5	7	6	11	15
Fish	8	15	6	9	8	6
Sandwiches	2	1	6	7	20	17
Pasta	1	2	1	1	*	2
Lamb	1	1	1	4	*	*
Salads	*	2	1	4	1	3
Cold Cuts	2	*	1	1	*	*
Other Meat	1	*	*	*	*	*
All others	2	8	6	4	7	8

Source: "Consumer Panel Report on Dining Out Habits and Attitudes," Standard Brands Inc., © 1965, p. 59.

Ethnic or Regional Preferences

Although several years ago it would have been foolhardy to establish ethnic food in an area that was not populated with a given ethnic group, this is not true today. American tastes have become more sophisticated. With the increased usage of convenience foods and the general increase in traveling for the American populace, most Americans today are familiar with many types of ethnic foods.

To cite one example, in 1960 a Mexican restaurant was opened in northern New Jersey. Within a short period of time the restaurant was out of business, primarily because it could not attract enough customers familiar with this type of cookery. Today, however, several Mexican restaurants have opened in the same area and are successful, as a result of the increased familiarity of the people with Mexican cuisine. Japanese, Chinese, and Middle Eastern restaurants are flourishing all over the country. There is even a restaurant which specializes not only in Mexican food but features kosher-style food (see Figure 11-2). Another operation is an Italian specialty shop that also specializes in kosher food.

American tastes have changed and will continue to change. Even in hospitals, instead of featuring primarily American food, a popular idea is to use a menu that highlights specialities from around the world. One night real French cuisine may be featured, another night Oriental, etc. (see Figure 11-3). This international theme is followed even on modified diets. College feeders are also carefully following the trend in tastes of youth today. Many offer health foods as well as having specialty nights that feature regional or international items.

Occupational Status

Just as there is a difference in the amounts of food consumed by members of different sexes, persons with different occupations will generally vary in the amounts and types of foods consumed. The businessman or woman who sits in an office all day will desire less food and usually a different type of food than the worker who is outdoors (particularly in winter) or doing physical labor. A businessman entertaining may need not only a different kind of menu but a different atmosphere from the individual who is merely going out on his lunch break. The factory worker who has only a half-hour for lunch needs different items from the office worker who has a full hour.

Meal Served

The meal served (lunch, dinner, snack) greatly affects the market. A restaurant serving dinner may perhaps expect to draw its clientele from the surrounding area, and the distance the patrons travel may be considerable.

On the other hand, few customers will travel more than five minutes or so for lunch, particularly if they have a limited lunch period.

Day of Week

For the majority of restaurants, the weekend business far outweighs the business achieved on weekdays. Thus, in many establishments, specialty foods (lobster or roast prime ribs of beef) may be placed on the menu only for these busy periods. The opposite is also true. Restaurants located in downtown areas, or who draw primarily from workers in the area, may choose to close on weekends or limit their menus to only a few items.

Although there are no statistics upon which to draw, higher-priced items generally will sell proportionately higher on weekends, as people are dining out more for entertainment purposes.

Menu planning is sometimes considered as a relatively unimportant tool of food managers. Actually, it is a major managerial tool for any food service establishment. It is used for three primary functions:

1. To satisfy the tastes of guests, patients, students, customers, etc.
2. To fulfill the dietary needs of the guests, should the situation demand this consideration.
3. As a tool to control food, labor, and equipment costs.

The type of menu is first determined by the particular market catered to by the establishments, or for which there may be a need as determined by market studies.

NON-COST-RELATED FACTORS

Types of Service

Contrary to common opinion, the type of service has no direct bearing on what particular menu is used by any given establishment. Often, because a menu is written in French the conclusion is drawn that the establishment has French service. The menu items also may cause this confusion. For example, if crepe suzettes are served, the diner (or reader) may conclude that this is a "high-class restaurant." However, crepe suzettes are often served in pancake houses, which may be classified as fast food establishments.

Any type of service may be used for any menu. There is no connection with the menu and the service utilized. French, Russian, American, and self-service could be used for almost any menu item. For example, prime ribs of beef-au-jus may be carved at your table (French), served at a banquet from a platter (Russian), served on an individual plate out of the kitchen (American), or even picked up by the customer from a steam table in a cafeteria line. Caesar salad may be tossed at the table (created by the captain

FIGURE 11-2 *Sample Menu Featuring Ethnic Food*

Mexican Combinations

SONORA
TWO SOUR CREAM GREEN ENCHILADAS
Rice and Beans
$4.25

MONTEREY
CHILE RELLENO, CHEESE ENCHILADA
and CRISP TACO
Side of Beans
$3.85

MEXICO
ENTOMATADA — TACO — CRISP TACO
and TOSTADA
$3.85

BAJA
RED CHILE or GREEN CHILE CON CARNE
Flour Tortilla, Rice and Beans
$2.95

LUIS SPECIAL
Albondiga Soup or Salad
Two of Any of the Following Items
CHEESE ENCHILADA — TACO — TAMALE
CHILE RELLENO
Rice and Beans
$3.95

BEEF COMBINATION
Albondiga Soup or Salad
TWO BEEF TACOS, TWO BEEF ENCHILADAS
or ONE BEEF TACO and
ONE BEEF ENCHILADA
Rice and Beans
$4.25

CHICKEN COMBINATION
Albondiga Soup or Salad
TWO CHICKEN TACOS, TWO CHICKEN
ENCHILADAS or
ONE CHICKEN TACO and
ONE CHICKEN ENCHILADA
Rice and Beans
$3.95

JALISCO
RED and GREEN CHILE BURRITO,
ENCHILADA STYLE
Side of Beans
$4.15

ACAPULCO
ACAPULCO MEAT and CHILE RELLENO
Dish of Rice and Beans
$4.75

OLD EL PASO
TACO, FLAUTA with GUACAMOLE
and ENTOMATADA
Rice and Beans
$4.25

YUCATAN
CRISP TACOS (3)
One Bean, One Beef and One Guacamole
$3.25

TIJUANA
TACO and ENCHILADA
Side of Beans
$2.85

a la Carte

Beef Taco	.95	Side of Beans	.75	Mexican Pizza	2.35
Chicken Taco	.95	Side of Rice	.75	Flautas (2)	1.95
Cheese Enchilada	.95	Side of Red Chile	1.45	Bean Burrito	.95
Chicken Enchilada	.95	Side of Green Chile	1.45	Beef Burrito	1.75
Beef Enchilada	1.20	Side of Taco Meat	1.25	Red or Green Burrito	1.75
Bean Tostada	.95	Guacamole, Small Dip	.95	Order of Corn Tortillas	.25
Guacamole Tostada	1.45	Guacamole, Large Dip	1.75	Flour Tortillas	.35
Green Enchilada	1.10	Soup	.75	Basket of Chips	.50
Enchilada (Sour Cream)	1.35	Crisp Taco	1.25		
Tamale with Sauce	1.15	Nachos (10)	1.65	Any Burrito served Enchilada	
Chile Relleno	1.35	Toasted Cheese Tortilla	1.45	Style 25¢ Extra	

FIGURE 11-2 *(continued)*

APPETIZERS

D-2	Chopped Liver 1.65	D-5	Greek Salad 1.40
D-3	Pickled Herring 1.55	D-6	Our Own Kishka .. 1.55
D-4	Creamed Herring .. 1.65	D-7	Smoked Salmon (Lox) 3.25

Combination Sandwiches

On Rye

D- 8	PASTRAMI and CORNED BEEF	2.75
D- 9	TURKEY and DANISH HAM	2.85
D-10	PASTRAMI and ROAST BEEF	2.75
D-11	CHOPPED LIVER and PASTRAMI	2.85
D-12	SALAMI and PASTRAMI	2.75

Served with Cole Slaw

DOUBLE DECKERS
Rye or White Toast with Dressing

D-13	BACON and EGG SALAD	2.65
	Tomato and Lettuce	
D-14	TURKEY, HAM and SWISS CHEESE	3.45
	Tomato and Lettuce	
D-15	PASTRAMI and CHOPPED LIVER	2.95
	Tomato and Lettuce	
D-16	HAM and SWISS CHEESE	2.75
	Tomato and Lettuce	
D-17	CLUB SANDWICH on Toast	2.65

SUBMARINE

D-18	CORNED BEEF .. 2.75	D-22	TUNAFISH
D-19	PASTRAMI 2.75		SALAD 2.35
D-20	DANISH HAM .. 2.75	D-23	EGG SALAD 1.65
D-21	ITALIAN 2.75	D-24	SALAMI 2.35

Served with Potato Salad

Sandwiches

On Rye or Kaiser

D-25	All White Turkey 1.95		
D-26	Pastrami 1.95	D-29	Brisket 1.95
D-27	Corned Beef 1.95	D-30	Danish Ham 1.95
D-28	Roast Beef 1.95	D-31	Salami 1.80
D-32	Liverwurst, Onion 1.65		
D-33	Chopped Liver .. 1.95	D-35	Tuna Fish Salad .. 1.65
D-34	Egg Salad 1.25	D-36	Swiss Cheese 1.65
D-37	American Cheese 1.25		
D-38	Cream Cheese .... .95		
D-39	Bacon, Tomato and Lettuce 1.75		
D-40	Sliced Egg, Tomato and Lettuce 1.45		

French Roll 25¢ Extra
Swiss Cheese 30¢ Extra

From our Grill

D-42	BONNIE BURGER	2.45
	Grilled Burger, Bacon, Tomato, Melted Cheese, Lettuce, Russian Dressing, on Kaiser Roll, French Fries ! ! ! All ¼ lb. Pure Beef	
D-43	BURGER	1.25
D-44	CHEESEBURGER	1.45
D-45	PATTY MELT with French Fries	1.95
D-46	REUBEN with Potato Salad	2.95
D-47	GRILLED CHEESE	1.15
D-48	GRILLED HAM, TOMATO and CHEESE, Potato Salad	1.95
D-49	HAM and EGG	1.65
D-50	BACON and EGG	1.65

HOT SANDWICHES

D-51	ROAST BEEF	2.65
D-52	TURKEY	2.65
D-53	BAR-B-Q BEEF	2.65

Served with French Fries

DAIRY

D-54	COTTAGE CHEESE with PEACHES	1.45
D-55	COTTAGE CHEESE with SOUR CREAM	1.25

Eggs and Omelettes served All Day on request
ANY ABOVE ORDERS CAN BE PREPARED TO TAKE OUT

"MOISHE'S DELIGHT" $1.90
D-56 PASTRAMI
Cole Slaw, Russian Dressing
with Swiss Cheese 25¢ Extra

D-57 WORLD FAMOUS VEGAS STEAK SANDWICH
$1.95

or

D-58 PIZZA STEAK $2.45
Green Pepper, Cheese, Potato Salad, Thin Slices
of Rib Steak Smothered with Onions on
French Rolls

"TREAT" $2.45
D-59 PASTRAMI and SWISS CHEESE
Cole Slaw, Russian Dressing

IRV'S NOSH
with Tomato, Lettuce and Onion

D-60	Cream Cheese and Lox on Bagel	3.75
D-61	Cream Cheese and Lox on Rye	3.75

HOT PLATTERS
Includes French Fries, Bread and Butter

D-62	VEAL CUTLET, Tomato Sauce	1.95
D-63	LIVER and ONIONS	2.25
D-64	CHICKEN in Basket	2.65
D-65	KISHKA	2.00
D-66	KNOCKWURSTS (2)	2.45
D-67	CONEY DOGS (2)	2.35
D-68	BRISKET OF BEEF	2.95
D-69	FRIED SHRIMPS	3.45

COLD PLATTERS

D-70	CHOPPED LIVER, SLICED EGG	2.65
	Tomato, Lettuce, Potato Salad, Cole Slaw	
D-71	TOMATO STUFFED with TUNA FISH SALAD	2.65
	Potato Salad, Cole Slaw	
D-72	EGG SALAD	1.95
	Tomato, Lettuce, Potato Salad, Cole Slaw	
D-73	OUR FAMOUS CHEESE BLINTZES	1.85
	Sour Cream	

D-74 CHEF'S SALAD
JAKE'S SPECIAL $2.65

D-75 Our Chili and Beans, Bowl 1.25		D-76 Coney Dog on a Roll with Sauerkraut 1.05
D-77	Knockwurst on a Roll with Sauerkraut	1.05

THINK THIN !

D-78	BURGER	1.95
	Jello and Cottage Cheese	
D-79	WHITE BREAST OF TURKEY	2.95
	Tomato, Lettuce and Cottage Cheese	
D-80	SALMON	3.45
	Tomato and Lettuce, Sliced Egg and Cottage Cheese	

SOUPS

D-81	Chicken Soup with Noodles and Matzo Balls	.85
D-82	Soup of the Day	.75
D-83	Beet Borscht, Sour Cream	.75

D-84	(3) Eggs, any style, Potatoes and Toast	1.45

Served Anytime

SIDE ORDERS

Baked Beans	.65
French Fries	.50
Onion Rings	.75
Small Dinner Salad	.65
Potato Salad	.50
Cole Slaw	.50
Cottage Cheese	.55
Small Side Cream Cheese ..	.35
Ham or Bacon 1.25	
Sausage 1.25	

DESSERTS

Jello	.50
Cheese Cake	.70
Chocolate Cake	.70

BEVERAGES

Coffee or Tea	.25
Iced Coffee or Iced Tea ..	.30
Hot Chocolate	.35
Sanka	.30
Buttermilk	.40
Milk ....small .35 large	.50
Egg Creme	.50
Soda	.30
Dr. Brown's	.45

TOAST and PASTRY

English Muffin	.40
Buttered Toast	.30
Bagel or Roll	.25

Extra Service Plate
25¢ per person

Beer .... Tap .40 - .50	
Pitchers	1.50

FIGURE 11-3 *Sample Menu Featuring International Specialties*

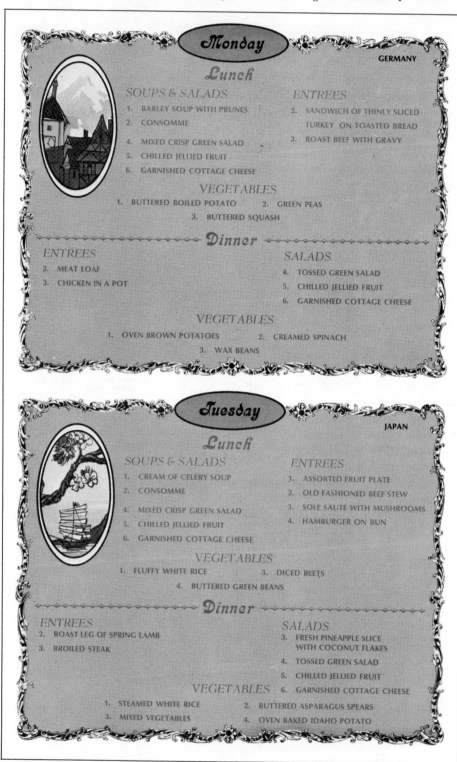

Monday

GERMANY

Lunch

SOUPS & SALADS

1. BARLEY SOUP WITH PRUNES
2. CONSOMME
4. MIXED CRISP GREEN SALAD
5. CHILLED JELLIED FRUIT
6. GARNISHED COTTAGE CHEESE

ENTREES

2. SANDWICH OF THINLY SLICED TURKEY ON TOASTED BREAD
3. ROAST BEEF WITH GRAVY

VEGETABLES

1. BUTTERED BOILED POTATO
2. GREEN PEAS
3. BUTTERED SQUASH

Dinner

ENTREES

2. MEAT LOAF
3. CHICKEN IN A POT

SALADS

4. TOSSED GREEN SALAD
5. CHILLED JELLIED FRUIT
6. GARNISHED COTTAGE CHEESE

VEGETABLES

1. OVEN BROWN POTATOES
2. CREAMED SPINACH
3. WAX BEANS

Tuesday

JAPAN

Lunch

SOUPS & SALADS

1. CREAM OF CELERY SOUP
2. CONSOMME
4. MIXED CRISP GREEN SALAD
5. CHILLED JELLIED FRUIT
6. GARNISHED COTTAGE CHEESE

ENTREES

1. ASSORTED FRUIT PLATE
2. OLD FASHIONED BEEF STEW
3. SOLE SAUTE WITH MUSHROOMS
4. HAMBURGER ON BUN

VEGETABLES

1. FLUFFY WHITE RICE
3. DICED BEETS
4. BUTTERED GREEN BEANS

Dinner

ENTREES

2. ROAST LEG OF SPRING LAMB
3. BROILED STEAK

SALADS

3. FRESH PINEAPPLE SLICE WITH COCONUT FLAKES
4. TOSSED GREEN SALAD
5. CHILLED JELLIED FRUIT
6. GARNISHED COTTAGE CHEESE

VEGETABLES

1. STEAMED WHITE RICE
2. BUTTERED ASPARAGUS SPEARS
3. MIXED VEGETABLES
4. OVEN BAKED IDAHO POTATO

FIGURE 11-3 (*continued*)

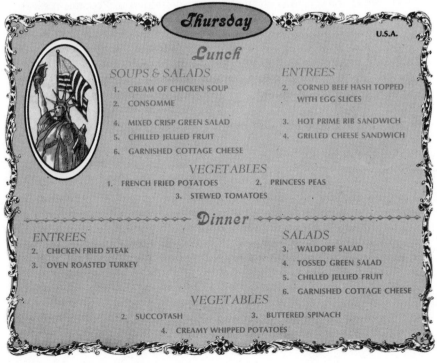

Wednesday
ITALY

Lunch

SOUPS & SALADS
1. MINESTRONE
2. CONSOMME

4. MIXED CRISP GREEN SALAD
5. CHILLED JELLIED FRUIT
6. GARNISHED COTTAGE CHEESE

ENTREES
2. GOLDEN BROWN BAKED CHICKEN

3. ITALIAN SPAGHETTI AND MEAT SAUCE

VEGETABLES
1. ZUCCHINI
2. CUT GREEN BEANS
3. AU GRATIN POTATOES

Dinner

ENTREES
2. COUNTRY STYLE LEAN PORK ROAST
3. ROAST VEAL
4. MACARONI & CHEESE

SALADS
4. TOSSED GREEN SALAD
5. CHILLED JELLIED FRUIT
6. GARNISHED COTTAGE CHEESE

VEGETABLES
1. BUTTERED PARSLEY POTATOES
2. ASPARAGUS SPEARS
3. BUTTERED CARROTS

Thursday
U.S.A.

Lunch

SOUPS & SALADS
1. CREAM OF CHICKEN SOUP
2. CONSOMME

4. MIXED CRISP GREEN SALAD
5. CHILLED JELLIED FRUIT
6. GARNISHED COTTAGE CHEESE

ENTREES
2. CORNED BEEF HASH TOPPED WITH EGG SLICES

3. HOT PRIME RIB SANDWICH
4. GRILLED CHEESE SANDWICH

VEGETABLES
1. FRENCH FRIED POTATOES
2. PRINCESS PEAS
3. STEWED TOMATOES

Dinner

ENTREES
2. CHICKEN FRIED STEAK
3. OVEN ROASTED TURKEY

SALADS
3. WALDORF SALAD
4. TOSSED GREEN SALAD
5. CHILLED JELLIED FRUIT
6. GARNISHED COTTAGE CHEESE

VEGETABLES
2. SUCCOTASH
3. BUTTERED SPINACH
4. CREAMY WHIPPED POTATOES

in an elegant restaurant), or at the other end of the spectrum, it may be from a "help yourself" salad bar in a low-priced restaurant.

Method of Pricing

The method of pricing again is not a determining factor in the major objectives of a menu, although it does influence food costs. By *method of pricing*, we mean whether the meal is à la carte, table d' hôte, or a combination of the two.

A la Carte. The true à la carte menu (at least in the United States) is seldom seen. Under the old guidelines that were used, every item that was served to a guest was priced separately. This included a separate charge for rolls and butter. Today, however, the term "à la carte" refers to those types of meals in which rolls and butter are included in the price of the entree, but all other food items are charged separately. Should the diner wish an appetizer, vegetable, potato, or dessert, a separate charge would be made.

Table d'hôte. Table d'hôte ("table of the host") menus formerly were used in establishments in which only one main entree was served, but the cost of the meal included all items from appetizer to dessert. The modern variation of this menu is the complete dinner menu. The guest has the choice of a number of entrees, but the price of the entree includes the complete meal. (Perhaps it should be noted here that the meaning of the word *entree* is the modern one, that is, "main dish.")

There is some confusion in the exact definition of "complete meal." Prior to World War II, a complete dinner normally consisted of an appetizer, soup, salad, entree, potato, vegetable, dessert, and beverage. The trend today is for people to eat less, and the complete meal in today's restaurants usually eliminates either the appetizer or the soup.

Combination Menus. As a result of the change in eating habits, as well as the need to simplify accounting procedures and variable costs, many

FIGURE 11-4 *Percentages of Total Market for Fixed and Cyclical Menus*

	Fixed with Changing Specials	Cycle or Rotating	Fixed— No Changes
Commercial	86.5%	12.6%	95.4%
Noncommercial	10.7%	86.8%	3.5%
Open Before 8 a.m.	58.4%	70.6%	21.5%
No Liquor	33.9%	75.6%	52.2%
Table/Booth	79.4%	14.6%	64.9%
Counter	9.4%	3.4%	8.4%
Carry Out/Drive-In	6.2%	2.1%	32.1%
School	3.9%	28.1%	.08%

Source: "Institutions Volume Feeding," April 1, 1974, p. 50.

restaurants today use a combination menu that is a compromise of the à la carte and the table d'hôte. There are no fixed guidelines for this menu. The exact items included in the price of the entree are normally spelled out on the menu itself.

The combination menu often consists of the entree, a potato (or other starch), a vegetable, rolls and butter. The beverage, appetizers, salads, vegetables, and desserts may or may not be included, depending upon the whims of managements (and of course, the desires of the clientele). In some cases the diner may have a choice of soup or a salad with the meal, in other cases the choice may be one of a vegetable or a salad. No fixed guidelines are laid down, but the variety of combinations normally is governed by the region of the country and the type of market that the establishment caters to.

A restaurant may also decide to have the complete dinner menu and also allow the customer to select the same items (or others) on an à la carte basis. Formerly, there were many establishments that followed the practice of having different portion sizes for complete dinner menu items and à la carte selections. The increased need to determine true food cost percentages as well as the confusion in ordering these items has all but eliminated this practice.

In those establishments in which both the à la carte menu and a complete dinner menu are served, it is difficult to determine true food cost percentages. The total selling price for the same items if priced on an à la carte basis would be higher than the charge for a complete dinner.

The obvious disadvantage of the complete dinners is that the food cost percentage is higher. The advantage of the complete dinner menu is that there is normally a greater profit per cover (customer) than with an à la carte menu, since the guest consumes more and has a higher check average. In these cases, the other relative costs (linen, labor, etc.) decrease percentagewise, since the check average is higher. With an à la carte menu, the diner may only choose one item, and the total charge may be low.

In addition to the variables of types of service and methods of pricing, the menu selection may be simple or extensive. A good rule is to have as few a number of selections as possible, since an increase in the number of selections will proportionately increase labor costs, equipment costs, and even food costs.

COST-RELATED FACTORS

Classification of Menus

Basically there are two types of menus, those that are unchanging (fixed) and those that vary in some way on a day-to-day basis (changing). Which basic type of menu to select is determined by the type of market that is being catered to by the establishment. In all cases, this determination should be made prior to the opening of an establishment. In fact, the menu should be designed and made up before the plans for the establishment are drawn up and any equipment is purchased.

Regardless of whether the establishment is a restaurant, a hospital, a school, or any other type of feeding institution, the type of market that is being served is the determining factor in the classification of the menu that is selected.

Fixed Menus

Fixed menus are primarily designed for those establishments in which the clientele are constantly changing and in which there are a large number of persons in the market itself.

Fixed menus generally have the following advantages:

1. Purchasing and inventory control are simplified. Since the items on the menu are continually used, the purchasing program may be rigidly controlled and done with little effort. Inventory amounts can be established and stock quickly rotated.

2. There are no leftovers. Items not normally consumed in one day may be carried over to be served the following day.

3. Staffing is simplified. Since the amount of time for the preparation of each item can be determined, the staffing for any volume of business can be readily determined.

4. With the same items being repeated on the menu, the staff is able to quickly develop the required skills in the preparation of the various items.

5. Miscellaneous costs are lowered. Costs of printing menus is reduced (and even can be eliminated in some establishments). Accounting controls, cash registers, etc., can be set up only for those items on the menu. This is particularly true in those establishments in which the fixed menu is a limited one (that is, with only a few items, as with McDonald's or Kentucky Fried Chicken).

6. Equipment requirements can be determined more easily and the types of equipment can be limited.

7. Personnel and equipment loads can be balanced and scheduled readily. Total overall costs can be reduced by careful programming of both.

8. If guests have a preference for a particular menu item that is served, they will often return to obtain it.

Fixed menus generally have the following disadvantages:

1. The market (customer, etc.) cannot be expected to frequent the establishment on a daily basis. The market, therefore, must be larger, and repeat business will be limited to the extent that the

menu "becomes boring." This will vary depending upon the type of establishment. McDonald's may expect its customers to dine at one of their establishments once or twice a week. On the other hand, a fine restaurant with a fixed menu may find that it can only expect its regular customers to visit once a month or even less.

2. The menu may become boring to personnel. This would occur not only in the sense of their preparation of the items but also if personnel are permitted to eat at the establishment. McDonald's personnel may tire of eating hamburgers. The employees of a finer restaurant may also tire of the food that is served and they are required to eat.

3. The operator of an establishment in which the menu is fixed is locked into costs. He must purchase those items regardless of market costs. If the price goes up, he still must buy those items.

4. The operator is unable to take advantage of market specials or seasonal changes. Should certain food items become available at a lower price, the operator is again unable to purchase them, since they do not appear on his menu.

5. Some items on a menu may not be servable if they are left over. As an example, prime ribs of beef in a better restaurant may be left over, but the operator may not wish to serve them rewarmed (particularly if they were well done to begin with) and thus they may have to be thrown out.

6. The operator is unable to change with the seasons or weather. The ice cream stand with a fixed menu is a typical example of this type of situation. Business may be at a peak during the warm months. When the colder months come or should there be rainy weather, business will decrease markedly.

7. There is an inflexibility for serving different meals. Often, the operator will design a menu that is primarily for one type of meal, that is, breakfast or lunch. Since the cost of the equipment does not change (nor in most cases the cost of the building or rental costs) it would be desirable to serve more than one or two meals. A fixed menu may make this difficult. Examples of this are the pancake houses that are attempting to serve dinners and the hamburger establishments that are trying to open early to serve breakfast.

Changing Menus

There are basically two types of changing menus, those that repeat themselves over a certain period of time (cyclical or rotating) and those that merely change on a day-to-day basis with no particular pattern (changing).

Changing and cyclical menus are designed for captive audiences or markets in which the clientele is limited (clubs, industrial feeding) and it is desirable for them not to become bored and perhaps to come back on a more frequent basis. With captive audiences, it should be noted that the second primary function of menus must be considered. That is, whenever a captive (or even partially captive) audience or clientele is served, care must be taken to make certain that a healthy, nutritionally sound, well-balanced menu is available.

In some cases (as hospitals, patient feeding) this becomes the primary function of the menu, and costs, and even patient's likes and dislikes, must take a secondary role. This does not mean that the patient's preferences are not considered. If possible, the patient should have his choice, providing the selection does not interfere with the primary role of adapting his likes to the dietary needs of his illness.

On the other hand, with student feeding (particularly with younger children) the menu selection must be designed with the children's preferences in mind. The balanced meal must be presented in a form in which the student will eat it. Ground meat (protein) would be least preferable in a meat loaf form but would be highly acceptable to children as a hamburger, a Sloppy Joe, or a meat sauce for spaghetti. Meat loaf may be the lowest-cost item to produce, considering labor costs, but the food service supervisor would be doing a disservice to his community by only considering this factor. His primary objective is to get the children to eat the item, not just to place the protein on the menu and keep costs down.

With some types of student feeding and with employee feeding, the audience or clientele no longer are captive. They have the option of selecting from a variety of items that may be placed on the menu. In many cases they may choose to bring their own meals. It no longer is mandatory for the operator to provide balanced meals. The emphasis in these cases is to present meals of a varied nature, so that the guest prefers to select from the menu. The type of menu items, the style of presentation, the method of cooking, and the quality of the product are all factors in the continued patronage of the guest.

Although the cyclical and changing menus are similar in nature, each has its own advantages and disadvantages.

Changing menus generally have the following disadvantages:

1. Supervisory time must be allocated for the planning of menus.
2. Continued changing of menus means that employees must be continually trained not only in the recipes but also in the presentation of plates, the portion sizes, and the entire procedure for the making of each new item.
3. There is a tendency for supervisors (or chefs) to place on the menu items that they prefer, often creating imbalances or repeating items.
4. Items on the menu may not be carefully balanced in variety, colors, textures, or tastes (too much pork, fish, etc.).

5. Records are difficult to maintain concerning the number of items that will actually be sold. Customers may or may not like an item one time, but in combination with other items it may sell more readily.

6. Larger inventories must be maintained to provide for variety.

7. It may be difficult to get rid of leftovers of an item in original form.

8. Scheduling of equipment and labor loads is much more difficult.

9. Labor costs will tend to be slightly higher, since maximum efficiency of personnel is difficult to achieve. Each time a new menu is listed the personnel must familiarize themselves with the items. This takes extra time.

10. Printing and miscellaneous costs may be higher.

There are also a number of advantages in the changing menu:

1. Neither the staff nor the clientele will become bored with the items listed.

2. Leftovers may be more easily used, since any item can be placed on the menu at any time.

3. Management may take immediate advantage of market specials.

4. Food costs may be lower due to advantages outlined in 2 and 3.

5. Creative personnel may utilize their talents to the fullest advantage.

6. Changes in seasons and weather can be adapted to without any special change in procedure.

7. Should there be either equipment failure or a shortage of personnel, the menu can be adapted to these changes readily.

8. If market prices of any items become high, these menu items can be eliminated from the menu.

9. It is possible to have small inventories and only those items listed on the next few menus need be stored.

Cyclical Menus

The cyclical (or rotating) menu is a compromise between the fixed and the changing menu. It takes from each some of the advantages and, unfortunately, some of the disadvantages.

Normally the cyclical menu is designed to be repeated over the period of time in which the market changes. It may also be designed in such a manner that with an unchanging market, the menu is of such an extended duration that the repetition does not become noticeable.

Examples of short-cycle menus would be those used in hospitals, in which the average patient remains only four or five days. With a weekly cycle menu, most patients will have left the hospital before the menu repeats itself. A summer resort might tend to use a three-week cycle, since many guests stay for two or slightly more weeks. Finally, in student feeding or employee feeding, menus may be of a six-week duration. Even within the six-week cycle, some items may be repeated due to their popularity, but the entire menu for that meal will be slightly different.

Cyclical menus generally have the following advantages:

1. Once a menu is planned, no additional supervision or planning is required.
2. Although the items change, after a period of time employees become familiar with each item and less time is needed for preparation, recipe study, etc.
3. Employees and clientele do not become bored.
4. Proper planning will allow for utilization of leftovers.
5. A well-balanced, colorful menu with a variety of tastes, textures, etc., can be achieved.
6. Although inventories will be larger than in a fixed menu, the inventory may be lower than in a changing menu.
7. After a period of time, a determination can be made of the volume of sales for each item. Items that do not sell readily can be dropped from the menu.
8. Equipment and personnel loads can be properly balanced to lower costs and increase efficiency.

The cyclical menu also incorporates some of the inefficiencies or disadvantages of the fixed menu and the changing menu:

1. Market specials cannot be fully taken advantage of.
2. Labor costs still tend to be higher than with a fixed menu, since each day new items must be prepared.
3. Should there be changes in the weather, the menu normally cannot be changed. If a main dish salad is planned for a given day, even if the weather turns cold, or it rains, the salad must still be listed on the menu.
4. Leftovers may be difficult to get rid of.
5. Large inventories may have to be maintained, since the next time it may be several weeks away before an item is on the menu again.
6. Printing and miscellaneous costs may be higher.

Obviously each type of menu has inherent advantages and disadvantages.

Combination Menus

For most restaurant operations and even for other types of institutional feeding, a combination of the cyclical and changing menu is used. The more popular items are on the menu every day, but a certain proportion of the menu changes each day to provide a variety for the clientele, to take advantage of the market specials, to utilize leftovers, and to balance out equipment and personnel loads. The ratio of these changing items to the fixed ones will depend on the particular operation, its clientele, and the desires of management.

Combination menus can be used for all types of markets. For limited markets in which a repeat clientele is an integral or substantial portion of the market, the addition of the changing menu, (either changing or rotating) prevents the customer from becoming bored. Those items that are popular can remain permanently on the menu, thus insuring the clientele that their favorite items will be available any time they frequent the establishment.

Careful planning can utilize leftovers and take advantage of market specials, thereby reducing food costs. With some of the fixed items, the operator still will be locked into costs, but the entire menu can be so constructed as to feature daily items. These daily items can be variable, to take advantage not only of the market specials but to fully use up any leftover items.

Labor costs can be reduced to some extent as compared to changing menus, since not every item need be prepared daily. With fixed menu items, some sauces, soups, etc., can be made in quantity and served over several days. Since a portion of their work changes all the time, employees need not become bored with their work tasks. At the same time, their meals can be served from the daily specials, so again the variety offered to them will not become tiresome.

INTERNAL FACTORS INFLUENCING MENU PLANNING

Menu planners must consider the market, the type of menu, and the specific meal being served. They must also realize that physical factors of the plant itself and the personnel involved in food preparation will influence and limit the type of menu items served.

Physical Equipment

The types of equipment available (fryers, broilers, etc.) may prohibit certain types of food from being prepared. At the same time, care must be exercised to determine that the individual pieces of equipment do not become overloaded. By this we mean that it would not be feasible in the average restaurant to have all broiled items on the menu, or all fried items. Even if a large broiler or fryer is available, if all items must be prepared in this manner, then at some time during peak periods of service a backup will occur, and undue delays in service will result.

Personnel Loads

In conjunction with overloading of equipment, care must be exercised to prevent one or two staff members from bearing the brunt of the preparation or service. If most items are broiled, the broiler man will be hard pressed and the fry cook may be standing around with nothing to do.

Number of People Served

The number of persons served at any given meal may tend to limit the type of menu items that may be served. Items that require individual preparation (eggs, crepe suzettes) may be eliminated from the menus at certain times due to the volume of business. The opposite is also true. Should there be a given meal or day in which a minimal amount of business is expected, a menu item such as roast prime ribs of beef may be eliminated, since the number of orders that would be sold would not warrant cooking the entire roast.

Hours of Service

It may be desirable from a fixed cost point of view to remain open for breakfast, lunch, and dinner. The variable costs for labor, however, may indicate that having a full menu is not justified, and thus a limited menu or selection may be used instead.

Examples of this situation may be the food service establishments in hospitals or employee feeding that switch to vending during evening or night hours. In commercial establishments, many operations serving liquor prefer to utilize a sandwich or supper menu after 10 or 11 P.M.

Skill Level of Employees

Although management may prefer to have a number of items on the menu that may be considered haute cuisine (see Glossary) or of a more complicated nature, the availability of labor and the skill level of employees in an area may preclude the selection of these items unless they are of a convenience nature.

SUMMARY

The decision to offer a mixed menu, a changing or cyclical menu, or a combination of the fixed and changing is based primarily upon the market to which an establishment caters. Increasing the number of items available on a menu will increase food, labor, and equipment costs.

Fixed menus normally can decrease labor costs as the employees become increasingly skilled in the tasks they perform. At the same time, the possibility of decreased food costs occurs, since the operator need only buy those items on the menu. No others must be on hand.

The changing menu requires additional supervision and greater skills on the part of the staff. Inventories are normally larger, but the establishment can take advantage of market specials to reduce food costs. The cyclical menu offers very much the same advantages and disadvantages, but the length of the cycle may adversely affect inventories and food costs.

FIGURE 11-5 *On What Day of the Week Do Families Eat Out?*
By Family Composition

	Mon.	Tue.	Wed.	Thu.	Fri.	Sat.	Sun.
Younger Couples— No Children	13%	13%	14%	12%	11%	14%	23%
Younger Couples— One Child	13	7	13	13	14	16	24
Two-Child Families	8	12	12	15	15	19	19
3-or-More- Child Families	8	10	14	13	15	19	21
Older Couples— One Child	8	10	19	15	13	16	19
Older Couples— No Children	8	10	19	15	13	16	19

by Community Size

2,000,000 or More	9%	9%	12%	11%	15%	20%	24%
450,000-2,000,000	7	10	14	11	20	16	22
50,000-450,000	10	11	12	15	13	16	23
2500-50,000	11	10	10	13	15	17	24
Rural	10	11	14	14	15	15	21

by Region

East	8%	9%	11%	11%	15%	20%	26%
Central	11	7	10	11	15	18	28
South	10	11	12	16	14	14	23
West	9	10	13	13	18	18	19

Source: "Consumer Panel Report on Dining Out Habits and Attitudes," Standard Brands Inc., © 1965, p. 41.

Finally, the combination menu is a compromise of the other types. It offers the advantages of both and also has some of the disadvantages.

The type of menu selected must be determined by the market being catered to. Management should be alert to changing markets. All menus, whether cyclical or fixed, whether breakfast or dinner, whether high or low priced, must contain certain ingredients that will attract the patronage of its clientele.

Colorful menus should be designed to include foods that are attractive in the presentation and varied in shapes, sizes, and textures. A poor selection would include a white fish with a white sauce, mashed potatoes, and cauliflower. Obviously, the repetition of the white color would be most unappetizing. Preferably, cut corn and peas should not be served concurrently, since the shape and texture of these vegetables are similar. In achieving a colorful menu selection, not only will the eye appeal be more pleasing to the customer but in most cases (with proper preparation) the nutritional value of the meal will be increased.

By selecting different types of preparation and different types of food (poultry, fish, meat), a more desirable menu selection will be presented that will appeal to a greater number of persons.

If care is used to insure that equipment is not overloaded with a variety of cooking methods, customers will have a greater opportunity to find items on the menu that are pleasing to their palates.

The selection of cooking methods also includes the presentation of items that are cold (salads, appetizers, desserts), which make for a better, well-balanced, and enjoyable meal.

Finally, the design of the menu itself should blend with the decor of the establishment and the theme of the restaurant. Items that are featured by an establishment should be highlighted in some manner on the menu (blocking out, color photos, large type). The style of print used should reflect the theme (e.g., Chinese-style printing). The colors of the menu should blend in with the decor.

Menus should be uncluttered, with an orderly progression of items. Thus the reader can find the appetizers or desserts without hunting through the entire menu to find a given item. Some description of items may be advisable, to enhance the appeal for the customer. "Iced Honeydew Melon" is preferable to "Honeydew Melon," but terms should be apt and not misleading, nor should excessive use of descriptive adjectives be employed.

Chapter 11

1. What type of operation would have a captive market? Free market?
2. List and briefly discuss factors affecting markets.
3. Demonstrate how the market for a restaurant might change for different meals (lunch, dinner) or days of the week.
4. What are the 3 primary functions of menu planning?
5. List and briefly discuss non-cost-related factors in menu planning.
6. List and briefly discuss cost-related factors.
7. What are the differences between fixed, cyclical, and changing menus?
8. Discuss the advantages and disadvantages of fixed, cyclical, and changing menus.
9. What is a combination menu?
10. What internal factors must be considered in menu planning?

12
Menu Pricing

Most restaurants and food service operations still utilize food cost percentages. It is becoming increasingly more difficult, however, for operators to determine what food cost percentages should be, particularly in light of the fact that more and more operators are switching to efficiency foods. Food cost percentages have for years been based on the premise that the food service establishment is a factory (a manufacturing plant in which raw materials are processed into finished goods) and that the labor involved in the processing of these goods accounted for a large percentage of operating costs.

Today, however, much of the labor cost can be eliminated. The manager of today is operating under an entirely new set of conditions, for which no standards have yet been established. Accounting procedures have not been refined, as yet, to the point where the operator is able to distinguish and differentiate between costs and percentages of processed goods and those of products still prepared on premises.

Most food service establishments of today are a mixture of efficiency products and in-plant produced items. For example, a typical party of four at a restaurant might order as follows:

2 Shrimp Cocktails—cooked and peeled on premises

2 Fruit Cocktails—purchased in gallon containers ready to serve

1 preportioned steak

2 boned and stuffed game hens (partially preprepared or oven ready)

1 prime rib of beef (cut, trimmed, and cooked on premises)

Although this order is abbreviated and does not include the number of variations that may occur with salads, desserts, breads, etc., it does illustrate the difficulty in determining what the food cost percentage for any item should be. Certainly, the labor involved with cooking and cleaning shrimp should result in the product being purchased at a relatively lower price, and thus a lower food cost, whereas the fruit cocktail merely has to be placed in the appropriate dishes and served to the guest. With the entrees, the steak may simply be put on the grill and the hens roasted, but the ribs of beef must be butchered. In reality, the food cost percentages for the fruit cocktail, the steak, and the hens should be much higher than for the shrimp and the rib of beef, since little, if any, processing for these items has to be done on premises. Yet in reality, few operators today fully consider these variables.

Managers are switching to convenience foods, which naturally must cost more since some of the labor cost has been removed from the operation itself and is included in the cost of the product. Yet few take this factor into account, and the same type of markup is expected on food costs as was realized when all processing was done on premises.

Literally hundreds of menu items may be produced in one food service operation. The items used to manufacture these products are now purchased in various stages of processing (raw, partially processed, or ready to serve). Thus, the task of determining the food cost percentage for any one item, as well as for the operation as a whole, becomes so complex that operators generally average all food cost percentages together.

When percentages change either up or down, management either tightens controls or pats itself on the back, whichever the case may be. In truth, there may be changes that are natural, due to the mix of sales and the weighted relationship of the cost of the items that are sold. Unless more accurate methods are devised for illuminating the variances and pinpointing the causes of these deviations, the food service operator will still be guessing as to what the true food cost percentages should be.

FOOD COST PERCENTAGES

After all other costs have been estimated (as discussed later in this chapter), a food service manager must determine within the predetermined price structure how much must remain, after deducting food costs, for the operation to run profitably. At that time, a percentage figure is selected, and the final fixing of menus prices is calculated based on:

1. The cost of the food, determined by calculating actual costs based on portion sizes. This cost should include some allowance for waste, human error, shrinkage, etc.
2. An allownace for short-term minor rises or drops in market prices.
3. An adjustment for high- and low-cost items (discussed later in this chapter).

For many years, operators of restaurants have calculated their menu prices by marking up costs 2, 2 1/2, 3, or 4 times. If a 40% food cost percentage was desired, in effect the operator would divide 40% into 100%, giving him 2 1/2. This figure would be used to multiply the actual food cost, to determine the menu price.

Food Cost x Cost Factor = Menu Price

A more accurate method, particularly when odd percentages are encountered (and few restaurants operate at convenient 40% or 33 1/3% percentages) is to simply divide the food cost percentage desired into the food cost to determine selling price.

Food cost ÷ Food cost % desired = Selling price

Procedures for Determining Menu Prices—Using Portion Divider

Information Given
A.P. price (purchase price)
Portion size
Yield percentage
Food cost percentage desired or menu price

Information Desired
Portion divider
Portion factor (portions per pound)
Selling price or food cost percentage
Portion cost

Five Steps To Solve Menu Pricing Problems

1. To determine portion factor, divide size of portion in ounces into sixteen.

16 ÷ Portion size = P.F.

2. To determine portion divider, multiply portion factor by yield percentage.

P.F. x Yield percentage = P.D.

3. To determine portion cost, divide portion divider into A.P. price.

A.P. price ÷ P.D. = P.C.

4. If food cost percentage is given to determine selling price, divide food cost percentage into portion cost.

Portion cost ÷ Food cost percentage = Selling price

5. If selling price is given, divide selling price into food cost.

Portion cost ÷ Sales price = Food cost %

Example: Shrimp Cocktail

4 shrimp—portion size
A.P. price is $4.10 per lb. (16—20 per lb.)
$2.10 selling price
$.06 cost of sauce per serving
Yield percentage is 100%

$$20 \div 4 = 5 \text{ portion factor @ 20 shrimp per lb.}$$

$$5 \times 100\% = 5 \text{ portion divider}$$

$$\begin{array}{r} \$4.10 \div 5 = \$.82 \text{ portion cost} \\ + \quad .06 \text{ sauce} \\ \hline \$.88 \text{ total portion cost} \end{array}$$

$$.88 \div 2.10 = .42$$

$$42\% = \text{Food cost percentage}$$

WEIGHTED SALES VALUES AND FOOD COST PERCENTAGES

In this chapter, a discussion of the variations in menu prices for high-and low-cost items (e.g., steak versus hamburger) and the resulting variance in food cost percentages for these items will be pointed out. Figure 12-1 illustrates how the mix of sales (the number of hamburgers versus steaks) varies from month to month, with resulting operating food cost percentage fluctuations.

Although the sales figure remains constant, there has been a fluctuation of up to 2.3% from month-to-month in the food cost percentage. In most situations, the manager or owner would be looking for the reasons for this variation, since only the total sales value figures and the total cost figures would have been calculated. At the end of February, the chef and the food

FIGURE 12-1 *Mix of Sales Variations—Month to Month*

Month	Total Sales	Steak Sales			Hamburger Sales			Totals	
		Dollar Sales	Food Cost %	Food Cost	Dollar Sales	Food Cost %	Food Cost	Food Cost %	Food Cost %
January	$7500	$4500	52%	$2340	$3000	35	$1050	$3390	45.2
February	7500	5000	52	2600	2500	35	875	3475	46.3
March	7500	4000	52	2080	3500	35	1225	3305	44.0

and beverage manager would have been called upon to tighten controls. At the end of March they would have been congratulated for being able to reduce the food cost percentages. Yet in all three months, the food cost percentages are normal, based on the weighted sales value of the items.

ESTABLISHING PRICES

Too often, menu prices in food service establishments, whether they be restaurants, cafeterias, snack bars, coffee shops, or gourmet rooms, are determined by what the traffic will bear rather than by what prices should be. The owner first determines what type or class of restaurant he wishes to run. He then looks at his competitors, sets his prices, and soon after, does some calculating to determine what his food cost should be. Whenever the "desired" food cost figure is not attained, remedial action is taken. Remedial action can be anything from firing the chef to cutting portions or lowering the standards of quality. Should, by any chance, a better than expected food cost percentage be attained, the operator congratulates himself on his fine management, pockets the extra profits, and continues blithely on his "predetermined" path.

Menu pricing is in fact the most difficult of tasks for an operator, since any number of variables will influence the final decision of what the price should be. A discussion of some of the major factors is given below.

Competition

Any operator must be aware of competition. He must not, however, allow himself to fall into the trap of setting his prices merely because others are at that particular price level. Competitive pricing must be done only in those cases where comparable products are served, in a comparable atmosphere, and with comparable service. One does not expect a discount house to furnish the same type of service as a regular department store. In turn, the department store offering services such as credit and delivery must charge a higher rate for including these additional services. Two restaurants offering the same steak may charge completely different amounts when the other factors are considered.

Service

Menu prices are influenced heavily by the types of services offered. This should be the case. Since labor is a major expense in food service operations, menu prices must relate to these services. When services are omitted or eliminated, as in the case of cafeteria lines or fast food operations in which the customer performs many of the normal duties of the waiters or waitresses, the prices of the menu items must be lowered to reflect the savings in these tasks.

Atmosphere

The cost of equipping a restaurant can be unbelievably expensive. As costlier decorations and furnishings are added, they must somehow be paid for. The customer will expect, when dining in a luxurious atmosphere, to pay an additional fee for the privilege of dining in this type of establishment. Since portion size, quality, service, and other factors all relate to each other, they in turn reflect the overall impression that management wishes to obtain by creating a particular atmosphere.

Waste

Often overlooked but always present, the various types of waste are very seldom reflected in menu pricing. Some types and percentages of waste are unavoidable, and thus should be included in the original pricing of the menu. Negligent waste caused by carelessness and poor management, however, should not be included.

Clientele

The type of clientele desired often dictates the approximate price structure for any restaurant. The restaurateur who focuses on an economic group in a particular income bracket does so by structuring his menu pricing to satisfy that group.

Quality

Quality is a nebulous term that cannot be defined strictly for products in which there may be disagreement as to what is good and what is bad. In New York City and some other metropolitan areas, a quality steak may be one that is aged for several weeks, U.S.D.A. Prime, cooked on the rare side. Other regional areas however, may feel that this kind of meat is too fatty, has a "rotten" taste, and must be cooked to a medium degree of doneness.

Quality must be related to price. The customer automatically sets some standard of his own as to what he expects for the price paid. The guest paying 29¢ for a hamburger is not expecting the same product that he would have had he paid 79¢. A guest ordering caviar for $7 per portion would certainly demand and expect a better quality than that served at a menu price of $2 per portion. What is meant in terms of quality with the hamburger is probably related to portion size. With the caviar the expectation would be primarily of the type of product served (imported beluga versus domestic or white fish roe).

Taste

No one can predict the tastes of a given customer, although there are general regional preferences that can readily be determined. The price of a beef stew can be $1 or $5. One would expect more meat of a higher grade in the $5 stew, but the taste of the $1 stew may be preferred by certain customers.

Portion Size

Menu prices are almost always based, in some part, on the size of the portion served. Whether or not the appropriate price for the portion size is actually being charged may be immaterial, since all the other factors listed will for the most part determine what is to be charged.

Portion sizes are determined by management and relate to the type of clientele (truckdrivers versus office workers), the price structure of the menu, and the type of meal being served (a lunch steak versus a dinner steak). Of course, portion size should fulfill the basic need of satisfying the customer, while appearing presentable and appetizing.

Portion sizes are not the primary factor for determining menu prices, but should be used as a tool for determining food cost percentages. At the same time, portion sizes may be adjusted within a narrow range so that minor adjustments may be made in the food cost percentage.

Location

Location in an area of the country, or even in a particular section of a city, may predispose a restaurant operator to a menu pricing structure that in turn will dictate the quality of the operation, the services offered, and even the portion sizes. As an example, the price structure for a small rural town would certainly differ from that in a large metropolitan area. Certainly, it is not just the location, but the needs of the clientele, the comparable levels paid in that area, and the other factors that all interrelate with one another.

Wage Rates

Wage rates for employees will to a large extent depend upon the economic conditions of the region. The laws of the state and the competition from other types of industries, however, often dictate the wages paid to the employees, which will be reflected in the charges made to the guests.

Other Costs

Other costs include major items that alter the amounts that normally would be charged. This is particularly true in such operations as nightclubs, which, due to the high cost of entertainment, must charge higher prices for similar types of foods and services. For example, a $15 dinner might actually be a $10 dinner and a $5 entertainment charge. In fact, it would be preferable for menu pricing and accounting controls to separate these additional charges, so they do not to reflect upon food cost percentages. In actual practice this is not feasible.

High-Low Items

No restaurant marks up every menu item by the same factor. Profit margins or food cost percentages are not the same for each menu item. A restaurant normally wishes to attain a certain gross profit percentage for its operation, but in doing so the percentage of profit obtained on menu items differs. This is especially true for those items that fall into either the highest- or lowest-priced cost category. An establishment may desire to operate at a food cost of 40%, but for items such as steak or lobsters that have a high cost, the price that would have to be charged to obtain the 40% cost might place the menu item beyond the desired price range of the operation. If a steak or lobster cost $3.50 to produce (including accompanying items), the price that would normally be charged would be:

$$\text{Food cost} \div \text{Food cost percentage} = \text{Selling price}$$

$$\$3.50 \div .40 = \$8.75 \text{ (selling price)}$$

On the other hand, a low-cost item such as chopped steak may cost only $1.15 to produce. (With the lobster or steak, the meat or fish cost about $2.75, plus $.75 for accompanying items. With the chopped steak, the meat alone costs $.40, plus the same $.75 for accompanying items.) Selling price should therefore be:

$$\$1.15 \div .40 = \$2.90$$

This disparity in prices would be of too great a magnitude for the average restaurant. Another consideration is that all menu items require the same expense for management and for incidental services (cost of the linen, waitress, services, and overhead). Thus, for practical purposes, the selling price for the chopped steak might be raised to $4.00, whereas the menu price for the steak and lobster might be lowered to $7.50. The profit per cover in reality is much more important than the food percentage. In some cases by slightly adjusting prices a greater overall profit can be achieved.

The following example illustrates how, by adjusting two menu items, the ratio of items sold can be altered, and in turn overall profits can be improved:

A large fast food operation specializing in hamburgers and steaks (low-priced with self-service) features the items shown in Figure 12-2. Their cost per portion and the number sold per day are listed.

The type of service for all items is the same. The cost of production for all items is the same, and the amount of time that each customer spends in the establishment remains the same no matter which menu item is selected.

FIGURE 12-2 *Fast Food Menu with Unadjusted Prices*

Menu Item	Menu Price	No. Sold	Cost	Profit
Hamburger	$ .59	5000	$ .47	$ .12
Rib eye steak	1.39	50	1.10	.29
Jumbo deluxe hamburger	.79	1000	.61	.18
Minute steak	1.49	25	1.12	.37
NY strip steak	2.19	60	1.60	.59

Overall Profits

	Profit per Item		Total Profit
Hamburger	5000 x $.12	=	$600.00
Rib Eye	50 x .29	=	14.50
Jumbo	1000 x .18	=	180.00
Minute	25 x .37	=	9.25
NY	60 x .59	=	35.40
		=	$839.15 Total

Menu prices could be adjusted as follows, with the idea of inducing the customer to purchase a higher-priced item, which would result in a greater overall profit. The results might be as follows:

FIGURE 12-3 *Fast Food Menu with Adjusted Prices*

Menu Item	New Menu Price	No. Sold	Cost	Profit
Hamburger	$ .59	4000	$ .47	$ .12
Rib eye steak	1.29	700	1.10	.19
Jumbo deluxe hamburger	.79	900	.61	.18
Minute steak	1.39	325	1.12	.27
NY strip steak	1.99	210	1.60	.39

Revised Over all Profits

	Profit per Item		Total Profit
Hamburger	4000 x $.12	=	$480.00
Rib Eye	700 x .19	=	133.00
Jumbo Deluxe	900 x .18	=	162.00
Minute	325 x .27	=	87.75
NY	210 x .39	=	81.90
			$934.65 Total

This 10% increase in overall profits could be accomplished without affecting anything but the overall net profit and the food cost percentage. Management would have to be aware that although the food cost percentage would increase, the net profits for the operation would also increase.

This same type of thinking can be used for establishments that are not even concerned with menu pricing—American Plan hotels, hospitals, college feeding operations, and the like. In these cases, the opposite type of planning is needed in order to attract the guest to items which cost less to produce.

A comparison of two menus may be used as an example:

Menu A	*Menu B*
Roast Prime Ribs of Beef	Roast Prime Ribs of Beef
Baked Filet of Halibut	Seafood Newburg
Broiled Half Chicken	Cornish Game Hen—Fruit Stuffing
Baked Virginia Ham	Broiled Pork Chops

Menu A has three items that are inexpensive to produce (chicken, halibut, and ham). But practically all guests will select the higher-priced item—the prime ribs of beef—and the overall cost to serve this meal will be high. Menu B, on the other hand, has several items (Newburg, hen, and pork chops) that may sway some of the guests away from the prime ribs of beef. Thus the overall cost of serving the guests will be reduced.

Management must seriously examine the popularity of various menu items. By exchanging these items they will be able to produce a menu that will reduce the total cost of service.

Another example of this type of situation occurred in a college feeding operation. Under the terms of the contract, steak had to appear on the menu at least once a week. Usually in conjunction with the steak, management served fried shrimp. The normal policy was to allow each student one portion of either shrimp or steak, and seconds were provided with other items (hamburgers, fried fish, etc.). The size of the steak portions were 8 ounces each. When a new manager took over the operation, one additional item was added to the menu. This was roast beef, cut from the same meat as the steaks. Substantial savings were effected since instead of an 8-ounce portion of steak, 6 ounces of roast beef were served. Even with the losses attributable to normal shrinkage, for each portion of roast beef served about a 15% savings was achieved.

An important factor in the alignment of menu prices is the gross profit per cover. The gross profit with the second price structure for the lobster or steak (as illustrated earlier in this chapter) would still be $4.00 per cover, and the gross profit for the chopped steak $2.85. If the first pricing system was used, the gross profit per cover for the more expensive items would be $4.25 and for the lower-cost items only $1.75. An unfavorable balance of sales (one in which there are greater sales in the lower-profit items) may result in lower profits, despite the fact that a better food cost percentage was attained.

Type of Cash Collection

Of growing importance in the food service industry today is the use of credit cards. Master Charge, BankAmericard, and others may be accepted by restaurants in lieu of cash. However, by agreeing to accept these cards the restaurant operator is automatically increasing his cost by about 6%. This 6% charge is the fee charged by the credit card companies to service the account, extend credit, and of course cover any uncollectible accounts.

Restaurants may find that a large portion of their business is accounted for by customers who prefer to charge their meals. Obviously, with profit margins in the neighborhood of 5%, an additional 6% charge would wipe out any profit. In order to cover this additional expense it is necessary for menu prices to be increased by an additional amount. The increase need not be the full 6% charge, since some customers will still pay in cash and an extra profit will be realized on these sales.

The percent of the increase should reflect the proportion of the business that is done in credit sales. If 50% of the sales are on credit, then a 3% increase would be justified. If 75% of sales were on credit, then a 4 1/2% raise would be valid. If only a small portion of sales are on credit, many operators choose to absorb the difference. Although this may be possible, the net profits will change, and the true value of extending credit should be closely examined to determine if an adjustment should be made.

DETERMINING PORTION SIZES— FORMULATION OF MENU PRICES

Every type of food has a range of "normal" portions, which will vary slightly. A brief list of these is as follows:

Dinner Size Portions

(Lunch may be 2-4 ounces less)

Meats, boneless, lean with traces of fat	4- 8 ounces
Meats, bone-in (steak or chops)	8-16 ounces
Meats, boneless (steaks or chops)	6-16 ounces
Stews, hashes, meat mixtures (pasta, rice)	6-12 ounces
Chicken, poultry, bone-in	8-16 ounces
Poultry, boneless	4- 8 ounces
Fish, whole	5-16 ounces
Fish, fillets	4-10 ounces
Shellfish, clams, oysters in shell (shrimp)	3-12 ounces
Shellfish, shucked	3- 8 ounces
Lobsters in shell	3/4-2 lbs
Vegetables	2- 5 ounces
Liquids (soups, juices, coffee)	3- 8 ounces
Fruits (net edible) excluding juice	2- 8 ounces
Rice, pasta (cooked), not as a main dish	4- 8 ounces

With the wide range of portion sizes for any given item, it is possible for the food cost of any operation to be controlled in such a manner that the operating food cost percentage can be adjusted or changed by adjusting portion sizes.

The variance in the quality of the raw produce purchased (i.e. U.S.D.A. choice versus U.S.D.A. commercial) and the purchase prices for these products will also allow an operator to adjust the food cost for any given menu item. These adjustments, however, are all made within the framework of the menu structure as originally determined by management.

Let us examine two types of food operations that may typify certain classes of restaurants, and determine how these adjustments may be made:

Restaurant A—Predetermined price structure—middle range—dinners from $3 to $7. All other incidental factors blending in with this price structure—linen service, waiters, maître d', etc. Menu item to be considered is a T-bone steak.

Purchase—U.S.D.A. Choice, bone-in, with three-inch tail, 1/4-inch fat trim—purchase price $1.75 per pound. Incidental costs for potatoes, bread and butter, salad, etc.—$.75 per person. If steak sold at $6.25 per portion, then it would be possible for management to utilize and serve a 16-ounce portion and still maintain a food cost percentage for this item of 40%.

$$\$2.50 \div \$6.25 = 40\%$$

Management has the option to vary the portion size (along with some changes in specifications), should they so desire, and still produce a product that would satisfy and fall into the range of acceptability for this type of operation and its clientele. Should a lower food cost percentage be desired, the portion size might be cut two ounces. Should a higher food cost for this item be acceptable to management, a better grade of meat might be chosen.

To lower food cost:

14-ounce steak (same quality)—$1.75/lb.—portion cost = $1.54. $1.54 + $.75 incidental cost = total new food cost $2.29. New food cost percentage:

$$\$2.29 \div \$6.25 = 36.7\%$$

By changing only the size of the steak, management is able to reduce food costs by 3.3%.

Restaurant B—a predetermined price structure of $5 to $10. To operate profitably, management wishes to attain a food cost percentage of 27% (other operating and fixed costs make it impossible to make a profit unless this figure is attained).

Steak is same 16-ounce size as in Restaurant A, but selling price is $7.75. At this selling price, the food cost percentage is:

$$\$2.50 \div \$7.75 = 32.2\%$$

Again management may reduce the portion size by two ounces:

$$\$2.29 \div \$7.75 = 29.6\%$$

In each case, management has reduced food costs (still not obtaining desired percentage in Restaurant B). Management also has the option to change the menu price, with or without a change in portion size.

If the presumption is made by management that portion sizes cannot be changed but that Restaurant A will change menu price to obtain the same food cost percentage (36%), then the menu price is adjusted as follows:

$$\text{Food cost} \div \text{Food cost percentage desired} = \text{Menu price}$$

$$\$2.50 \div 36\% = \$7.00 \text{ (rounded)}$$

In Restaurant B:

$$\$2.50 \div 27\% = \$9.25 \text{ (rounded)}$$

In both cases the menu items and portion sizes may be identical. But the food costs and percentages at which the establishments operate should differ. Before changing portion sizes or increasing prices, management should carefully examine other factors, such as those affecting efficiency and waste, to determine if improvements in these areas can first be made. In effect, a restaurant first establishes the price structure at which it will operate and then has a narrow range of variables capable of being changed that will enable the operation to achieve the desired standard food cost percentage.

Chapter 12

I. *Class Exercises*

1. Determine the following for each of the menu items listed below:
   a. Portion Factor (P.F.)
   b. Portion Cost Divider (P.C.D.)
   c. Portion Cost (P.C.)
   d. Selling Price

Turkey	**Round of Beef**
5-oz. portion	5-oz. portion
40% yield	72% yield
$.67 A.P. price	$1.78 A.P. price
42% cost	32% cost

Fish
7-oz. portion
74% yield
$.93 A.P. price
38% cost

Roast Beef
12-oz. portion
26% yield
$1.69 A.P. price
27% cost

2. Determine the following for each of the menu items listed below:

a. Portion Factor (P.F.)
b. Portion Cost Divider (P.C.D.)
c. Portion Cost (P.C.)
d. Food Cost Percentage

Chop meat
90% yield
$.99 A.P. price
4-oz. portion
$1.15 selling price

Swiss Steak
68% yield
$1.09 A.P. price
5-oz. portion
$2.75 selling price

Clams
6 clam portion
400/bu. = $20.00/bu. A.P. price
$1.90 selling price
Sauce - .08

3. Determine selling price @ 42% cost, for the dinner menu below.

4. Determine F.C. Percentage @ $7.25 serving, for the dinner menu below.

DINNER

Fruit Cup = $4.20/gal.   4-oz. portion (132 per gallon)
Vegetable and Potatoes   = $.22 cost
Salad   = .16 "
Relish   = .18 "
Bread and Butter   = .06 "

Entree—Leg of lamb
    A.P. price, $1.42/lb.
    Yield 48%
    5-oz. portion

Dessert—Apple pie—8 cuts/1 pie @ $1.14
Coffee @ $1.25/lb. (50 cups)
Cream and sugar = .02

II. *Study Questions*

1. Why is it difficult to use food cost percentages as a measure of efficiency?

2. What other factors (not food costs) should be used to determine a "good" operating food cost percentage for an operation?

3. What factors directly relating to food costs are used to determine menu prices?

4. What items nonrelated to food costs are used to determine menu prices?

5. What is the advantage of "balancing" menu prices?

6. Discuss the differences in objectives in menu planning popularity items for American Plan hotels and for regular restaurants.

13

Labor Cost Control

For the past few years, the rising cost of labor, the increase in minimum wages, the extended influence of the federal government in controlling wages and labor legislation in the restaurant and food service industry, and the general improvement in working conditions throughout the entire economy have been the dominating influences in the development of food service systems and the types of products used throughout the industry. No longer does the operator concern himself solely with food costs. Instead, the method or system under which the lowest combined food and labor costs can be obtained without lowering the quality will dictate the operating policy of the entrepreneur.

The importance of labor cost control cannot be overemphasized, particularly in view of the fact that, as a percentage of gross sales, labor costs will vary from about 15% to 65% of sales. Although chapters 13 and 14 are devoted to the control of labor costs, these chapters highlight only some of the considerations and problems of the industry. In effect, they only scratch the surface. Other books are available which more closely examine labor problems, and it is recommended that further studies be made by the reader to examine the problem in depth.

The continuing trend in the utilization of "convenience" foods and the forecast for increased usage reflects the industry's need to find ways to increase the productivity of the individual worker. Improvements in food technology, new types of equipment coupled with new types of food preservation (freeze drying, irradiation), lend hope to the operator who, over the past few years, has looked at statistics that indicate the true productivity per worker has in fact decreased rather than increased. In real dollars, the productivity of the food service worker has declined. The food service industry is on the low end of the totem pole regarding dollar output per worker. "On the average a worker in quantity food production produces 45% of the time, wasting or resting the remaining 55%. Your productivity should be 80 to 85%."*

In 1971, the School of Hotel Administration at Cornell University undertook a study concerning the outlook, practices, and personnel systems that were presently in force in the industry. They found that, with a few major exceptions, little has been done by members of the industry to promote career ladders for employees. The industry has created a series of dead-end jobs that offer little opportunity for promotion or advancement, particularly for minority groups. Although these minority group members are actively seeking work, the image the industry has had in the past—and has in the present—has caused members of these minority groups to shy away from employment within the industry. Despite a high percentage of unemployment in the nation, the industry is still unable to attract workers. This author, in private conferences with many educators in two-and four-year post-high-school institutions, has repeatedly been informed that many programs have stagnated due to the inability of the schools to recruit students.

FACTORS INFLUENCING LABOR COSTS

Labor costs are influenced by varying factors, some of a permanent nature, others temporary, and all to some degree able to be corrected so that costs may be lowered.

Permanent Factors

Very few factors that influence labor costs are truly permanent. Under the permanent category we must first place those over which the establishment has no control and which shall continue for an indefinite period of time. Such matters as labor legislation may be considered unchangeable except by long-range lobbying. The general trend is toward an increased number of regulations despite active efforts by business associations to stop this type of legislation. For the most part, union contracts must be considered permanent, although, of course, the operator may (and here we must emphasize *may*, since in some cases the courts have decided that they cannot) go out of business should they wish to eliminate the contract completely. A contract may also be voted out by the employees should they feel that the union is of no benefit to them.

The physical plant may be considered permanent, although remodeling and equipment changes may be made. For the most part, however, this is the last resort, since costs of remodeling and structural changes may be

---

*Lendal H. Kotschevar, *Quantity Food Production* (Boston: Cahners Books, 1974), p. 59.

prohibitive. Equipment is not permanent and may be changed readily, although with some cost.

Although the operator may wish to change the eating patterns of his clientele, the meal served (breakfast, lunch, or dinner) is unchangeable, and hours during which these meals are served cannot be changed.

One exception to this rule is Las Vegas, Nevada, which is a 24-hour town. Breakfast, lunch, and dinner are served any time of the day. The customers may be tourists who have been out on the town all night or they may be workers who have swing or graveyard shifts. It is not unusual to see a table of four in a restaurant with sandwiches being served to one individual, steaks to another, and pancakes to someone else. Lunch hours are not confined from noon to 2 P.M., since both workers and tourists are not on what may be considered "normal" schedules.

Weather generally is considered temporary, although summer, fall, spring, and winter are here every year, and general conditions can be predicted with reasonable certainty. What cannot be predicted and must be placed under temporary factors are daily weather conditions that may cause wide deviations in business volume.

Temporary Factors

Hours of operation, menu, type of service, and type of products used are all temporary and may be changed at any time should the circumstances warrant this change. For the most part, however, these conditions, once decided upon by management, will be in effect for long-range periods. If altered, they may change the entire sales patterns of the establishment.

Hours are easily altered. During time periods that prove unprofitable, the operator may choose to close, without greatly affecting the entire sales volume and probably with some savings.

Staffing for lunch and dinner hours differs. The same number of covers may be served, but since lunch "hour" may only be from 12:00 to 2:00 whereas dinner "hour" stretches over a much longer period of time, not as many personnel may be needed for the dinner rush period.

The lunch menu must also be designed so that the food can be placed before the customer within a reasonable period of time. The customer who has only 30-45 minutes for his lunch period cannot wait 20 minutes for an item to be cooked. For the establishment to be profitable, the maximum number of patrons must be accommodated within the lunch period. Thus, menu, preparation systems, and personnel must be geared to handle this type of business. For lunch, rather than serve one thickly cut chop that takes 15 minutes to cook, a partially cooked chop may be finished or two thinner ones may be served. Salads, pies or other dessert items may be precut and preportioned just prior to the start of service. Some items may be partially cooked and merely need to be finished when ordered. In dinner service an electronic oven may be ideal for reheating items (such as a slice of hot apple pie); during lunch periods the entire pie may be kept warm, since it will be consumed within a reasonable period of time and will not deteriorate in quality.

As can be noted then, each meal may require different types of services, equipment, and numbers of personnel. Management must examine menus and systems to determine whether the procedures being used do, in fact, meet the needs of that particular meal or whether they must be modified to allow for the variances in time periods and the needs of the clientele. Restaurants in New York City had to adjust the dinner hour service when theaters changed the curtain times from 8:30 to 7:30. Whereas formerly diners could have leisurely dinner, the urgency of getting to the theater on time now requires shorter prepartion and service times, as well as a condensation of the menu. Some restaurants advertised that the diner could return to the restaurant after the show for dessert, coffee, and after-dinner drinks.

Conversely, some restaurants must, by law or union contract, hire personnel for a period of time extending beyond the normal lunch hour or dinner period. During the regular periods of dining they may be filled to capacity. In the early dinner hours (4-7 P.M.), however, personnel must remain on duty but in reality have little to do. These restaurants have found it advantageous to advertise special prices for meals served during these slack periods. By discounting meals during these times, several operators have been able to attract additional customers who normally would not have patronized the establishment. Inasmuch as the only real cost for these meals is the food cost, since the labor has to be paid anyway, the meals could be sold at a profit even with the discount.

Employee Turnover

Although turnover expenses greatly increase the cost of labor, at an average cost of $232.18* per employee, food service operators often do not provide a separate account on profit and loss statements to allow for this expense. Instead, total payroll costs are lumped together. Management thus has no way to determine whether costs are high due to inefficiencies or the turnover.

These turnover expenses include hiring and firing or quit costs for interviews; record keeping, advertising, training and supervisory time to introduce employees to the job; waste and inefficiency till the employee is familiar with his job; losses due to the lowering of employee morale, particularly if they must "carry" the employee for a period of time; plus increased costs in unemployment insurance, etc., due to claims against the operator.

* John H. Freshwater and John C. Bouma, "Labor Utilization and Operating Practices In Commercial Cafeterias," U.S.D.A. Marketing Research Report No. 824 (Washington, D.C.: U.S. Govt. Printing Office, January 1, 1969), p. 29.

Minimum Staffing

The ideal situation for food service operators would be one in which at all times of the day, every station (broiler, dishwashing, waiters, etc.) must be fully manned. Obviously, this rarely if ever occurs. Thus, to maximize efficiency, the manager of the operation will schedule individual workers to utilize them at the proper times and eliminate unproductive periods or hours.

Here again, however, the operator faces a situation differing from most other industries. Fluctuations in volume must be handled within such a short period of time that additional reserve personnel are unable to be obtained in time to be of use to management. Scheduling is based upon management's most educated forecast, considering previous records, weather conditions, special events, etc.

In any operation, fluctuations will occur that may be as little as 5%, yet this fluctuation may cause a profitable operation to become unprofitable. For example, if normal sales are $1500 per day, a fluctuation of 5% will cause a decrease in sales by $75. This figure may represent the profit, since most food operations do not make a greater net profit than 5%. The operator is unable to determine how much volume will actually occur with much greater accuracy than 5%, and yet he is unable to decrease payroll costs at all, since employees cannot be laid off normally once they have been called in. A small savings may be achieved by letting some of the staff leave early. If that should occur too often, however, general employee relations will be impaired.

Should sales improve by 5%, a savings may be effected. However, service may be slow, with employees rushed to the point where the quality of products suffer and customer satisfaction declines. Although this also is unsatisfactory, it would be disastrous for the operator to overstaff. With those hourly employees not receiving gratuities, the cost would be prohibitive, and with employees who benefit from tips, an excessive number of employees means a lower total income for all, bringing employee dissatisfaction.

Within each department, careful guidelines and standards must be established that will dictate the normal work load for each employee. Just as an assembly line is run at a fixed rate of speed, the employee should be expected to produce a certain number of meals or to sanitize a certain number of dishes or to clean a certain area within a specified period of time.

Each operation or type of food service may have different standards. Although attempts have been made by authorities and experts to establish guidelines, food service operations differ in so many respects that a norm must be determined independently by every operator. These norms will vary from meal to meal. A waitress may be able to handle twenty customers during a lunch hour but only twelve during a dinner hour, despite the fact that the restaurant is the same one and the menu may not have changed.

These variations occur due to the work load placed on the kitchen and the rapidity with which orders are able to be cooked, the mood of the clientele (dinner customers may have more time to linger or prefer to have a cocktail before dinner and thus occupy a table for a longer period of time), or the customer may simply order a larger meal for dinner and thus need more time in which to consume it. There is also the possibility that one work area may be understaffed, or perhaps the busboy is inexperienced and unable to clear as efficiently as another employee. The list of variables is endless, but some sort of standard must be established for every position in each establishment.

A typical staffing chart might resemble the one in Figure 13-1.

FIGURE 13-1 *Staffing—By Type of Service*

Position	Gourmet Service	Standard	Buffet	Cafeteria
Cashier*	1	1	1	1
Maître d'*	1	1	1	0
Captain	4-8	0	0	0
Waitress (waiter)	8-10	5-7	4	0
Busboys	8-10	4	2-4	1
Porters (utility men)*	1	1	1	1
Chefs (or supervisor)*	1	1	1	1
Cooks (including baker & pantry)	4-5	2-4	2-4	2-3
Sanitation	3	1	1	1
Bartender**	2	1	1	0
Food Checker**	1	0-1	0	0

Note: For dinner service with 2 turnovers—number of employees per 100 seats.
* Fixed
** May not be required

Variations in staffing occur, since the state in which food is purchased and the number of items on the menu (cooked-to-order versus preprepared items) will affect the number of cooks required. The type of control system used may eliminate the need for a food checker. In addition, the length of the meal hour may allow fewer employees to be required if diners extend the eating period over a longer stretch of time.

A much greater number of sanitation personnel are required for gourmet service. In this type of operation, silver is used that must be polished, much greater care must be given to the handling of the more costly china, and normally many more pieces of china and silver are used per place setting.

Although the numbers in Figure 13-1 are based on two turnovers per evening, less than two turnovers will not greatly affect the number of personnel required. Those personnel marked with an asterisk (*) will not be decreased, since the positions cannot be eliminated. The other positions will not decrease by 50% even if sales should decline by that amount. If 100 seats need to be serviced, certainly a waiter cannot handle many more than 15-20 seats at one time in standard service. Thus the only possibility, should less than two turnovers be achieved, would be to utilize part-time personnel for the peak period and to stagger schedules so that the maximum number of personnel may leave as soon as the peak period has ended. Another alternative is to close a portion of the dining room and to allow some of the patrons to wait for a brief time.

For more than two turnovers, very few personnel would have to be added, these primarily being in the preparation and sanitation departments.

It becomes obvious that although labor cost percentages are used universally throughout the food service industry, these figures may not accurately represent standards. Many variations and differences must occur.

Figure 13-2 illustrates another possible staffing chart, based on number of patrons served. Management has an alternate method in determining the number of man-hours required to produce each meal, but even here variances will occur. Two operations serving the same number of persons may have differences in man-hours due to various states of preparation in which products are purchased, the level of skill of the employees, the efficiency of the equipment and layout, and perhaps even the eating habits of the clientele and the type of operation.

A private club, for example, because of the limited number of members and customers, cannot afford to gamble on the number of patrons that it will serve during a meal. It cannot cut down on its staff, as poor service in this type of operation would create a much greater threat to repeated patronage. Should there be poor service, many members will soon learn of the problem (even should it occur infrequently), since the patrons know each other.

On the other hand, a restaurant with a wider base of customers can occasionally gamble and reduce its staff. Should poor service occur on that occasion, other patrons will probably not hear of it. Even if some customers are lost, the percentage of business that the few customers that do get bad service represents is not nearly as much as that represented by the club member who does not return. A club may only have several hundred members and presuming each patronizes the club equally, one, two, or three hundredths of the business is lost. In a restaurant, the total clientele may number in the thousands. Thus the loss may represent only one thousandth of the total business. The manager of the restaurant can better afford to lower his payroll cost. The odds are in his favor, should an unusual increase

FIGURE 13-2 *Staffing—By Number of Patrons*

Staffing for Kitchen

Jobs to be Filled	For 0-49	For 50-99	For 100-175	For 175-plus
Chef	1	1	1	1
Cook	1	2	3	4
Salads—Pantry	1	2	2	3
Dishwasher	1	2	3	3
Potwasher	1	1	1	1
Cleaner	0	1	1	1
Storeroom Man	0	1	1	1
Baker	0	1	1	1

Staffing for Dining Room

Jobs to be Filled	For 0-37	For 38-58	For 59-75	For 76-95	For 96-112	For 113-129	For 130-145	For 146-166	For 167-plus
Hostess	1	1	1	1	1	1	1	1	1
Waiter—Waitress	2	3	4	5	6	7	8	9	10
Bus Boy	1	2	2	3	3	3	3	4	5
Bar Waitress	1	11/2	11/2	2	2	21/2	21/2	21/2	21/2

Source: John W. Stokes, *How to Manage a Restaurant of Institutional Food Service*, 2nd ed. (Dubuque, Iowa: William C. Brown Company, Publishers, 1973), p. 274.

in business occur, since it will not create the same type of problem that occurs in private clubs.

In determining how to measure the extent to which staffs may be increased or decreased, management must be meticulous in keeping records, which assist in predicting the volume of business that will take place. These records must include weather conditions, day of week, date, and special events (including those that take place in the nearby area).

Chapter 13

1. List and discuss the differences in temporary and permanent factors affecting labor costs.

2. Which of the factors discussed in 1 are controllable by management? Explain your answer.

3. What methods and factors need to be considered when determining staffing requirements?

4. Draw up a chart for staffing a 150-seat restaurant. Using this chart as a base, increase or decrease staffing based on the following conditions:
   a. Gourmet service
   b. Breakfast
   c. Exclusive use of convenience foods
   d. Union contracts requiring a minimum of 6-hour shifts
   e. 2 turnovers each hour for breakfast and lunch
   f. Country club dinner service

14

Labor Cost Analysis

APPROACH TO LABOR ANALYSIS

Innumerable methods have been used to determine the most efficient method of controlling labor costs. Basically, techniques have been developed as discussed below.

Productivity Per Man-Hour

In this method of control, each worker's position in a food service establishment is analyzed to determine the number of workers required to produce a certain number of meals. In most cases, the analysis is after the fact. Management determines how many meals have been served, and then compares this figure with the number of employees in each department. (That is, the number of hours worked).

Total meals served ÷ Employee man hours = Cover man-hour

FIGURE 14-1 *Productivity Per Man-Hour Analysis*

Labor Analysis	Dining Room			Week of ____
	# of Empl.	Hours	Total hours	Cover per man-hour
Hostess	1	8	48	29
Waitress—Full-Time	4	40	160	
Waitress—Part-Time	4	32	128	
Total Waitresses	9	——	288	9.7
Busboys	4	40	160	17.4
Total	13	——	496	5.6
Total Covers/Week	2792			

An analysis chart (Figure 14-1) of this kind is useful, since deviations in productivity (cover per man-hour) can be pinpointed by departments and adjustments to the payroll can be made. Obviously, for most efficient utilization of labor a forecast of expected sales must be used to schedule the labor. The analysis chart can only be made after the actual sales have taken place and the employees have worked.

Analysis charts cannot be compared from one operation to another unless the operations are either identical or so similar that only slight variations would occur. Variances in purchasing procedures (one operation using more convenience or ready foods) substantially affect the covers per man-hour in the preparation areas. Different types of dishwashing equipment can affect the covers per man-hour in the sanitation areas. Even the square footage of operations may influence the cover per man-hour figure in all departments, since the sanitation department will have to clean a larger or smaller area, the service personnel may have to travel greater distances, and the preparation areas may be laid out in more or less efficient style. The skill level of personnel also can dramatically affect this figure. An experienced waiter may be able to serve 16 people at one time, whereas a new employee may only be able to handle 10.

Labor Cost Percentage

Most common of all methods used is the straight percentage of sales. Labor costs may be taken as a whole or, preferably, by department, to determine actual costs as a percentage of total sales.

$$\text{Dollar cost of labor} \div \text{Food sales} = \text{Labor cost percentage}$$

This analysis may also be used for beverage sales. One difficulty that does occur is that waiters and waitresses often serve both food and beverages, so that a portion of the payroll for service personnel must be assigned to each department. This may be simply done by deducting a portion of the payroll from the food department and charging it to the beverage department. A simple analysis is demonstrated in Figure 14-2.

Again, an analysis of the payroll will indicate deviations from the established standards. These variations will show which departments are understaffed or overstaffed. Many operators will use the total payroll as the key indicator of normal labor percentages. This is not sufficiently accurate, however, since there is a tendency for departments to balance out (one being understaffed and the other overstaffed).

Sales Per Employee

The actual dollar revenue per employee is often used as an indicator of efficiency. However, the variance in menu prices from one establishment to another (fast food versus gourmet restaurant) often makes this figure meaningless. Comparisons of restaurants within the same price categories

FIGURE 14-2 *Payroll Analysis*

Total Food Sales   *$11,840.00*   *Week of* _____
Total Bus. Sales   *$24,000.00*

Dining Room	Salary or Wage	Total Wages	% of Food Sales
Hostess	$150.00	$ 150.00	1
Waitresses	H ($2.00)	576.00	5
Busboys	H ($1.85)	296.00	3
Total		$1022.00	9
Kitchen			
Total _____			

H = per hour

can be used to determine efficiencies of the staff as a whole, or a further analysis can be made by departments.

Again, care should be exercised in making judgments, since the variance in the use of efficiency foods may tend to distort these figures. An establishment using convenience foods would normally have fewer cooks, so that the dollar sales per cook would naturally be higher.

Productivity Analysis

Several methods are used with productivity analysis, depending upon the time and effort expended by management to accurately determine the efficiency of employees.

The simplest method is for a supervisor to observe at scheduled intervals the activities of each of the employees under his or her direction. (See Figure 14-3.) If all employees are working, the productivity rate is 100%. If only three out of five are actively engaged in production, then the rate is 60%. A further refinement of this type of chart (see Figure 14-4) may be accomplished by estimating the speed at which each worker is performing his duties.

As with the other methods of analysis, this examination must be done on a departmental basis. This is especially true since the hourly productivity requirements for each area will vary considerably.

The charts in either Figures 14-3 or 14-4 may be used for determining productivity and/or rescheduling of personnel. Figure 14-3 is more appropriate for job analysis to determine efficiency. An actual productivity factor may be arrived at by using the method in Figure 14-4. If normal

FIGURE 14-3 *Productivity Analysis*

Date _____

KITCHEN	8	9	10	11	*TIME* 12	1	2	3	4	5	6
Pantry											
1	P	P	T	L	P	P	I	I	I		
2	I	P	I	P	P	P	C	P	C		
3	P	I	B	P	P	I	C	I	I		
4	P	T	P	C	P	P	P	P	C		
Sanitation											
1		P	P	I	L	P	P	I	P	C	
2		P	P	I		P	L	P	T	C	P
3		I	I	I		P	I	L	P	I	I
4		C	C	P		P	P	L	I	I	C

Code: P - Production   C - Cleanup   B - Breaktime
        T - Transportation   I - Idle   L - Lunch

FIGURE 14-4 *Productivity Factor Analysis*

	8	9	10	11	12	1	2	3	4	5	6
KITCHEN											
Pantry											
1		1	2	3	3	2	1	0	1		
2			0	2	2	2	1	2	0	1	
3			2	3	3	3	2	0	1	2	
4			1	2	2	2	0	1	2	1	
Sanitation											
1		1	1	1	2	3	0	3	2		
2	1	2	1	2	3	2	2	1	1	1	
3	1	1	0	1	2	3	2	2			

Pace of Worker: Fast   = 3
                  Normal = 2
                  Slow   = 1
                  Idle   = 0

productivity is 2, then by totaling the amounts achieved by each worker and dividing by the number of observations, a productivity factor is arrived at.

For pantry worker 1, the total number of observations is eight and the total score is 13. Average productivity is;

$$13 \div 8 = 1.62.$$

Since productivity should be 2 to be 100%, then

$$1.62 \div 2 = 81\%.$$

For pantry worker 4, the total score is 11 with eight observations. Therefore,

$$11 \div 8 = 1.37 \text{ and } 1.37 \div 2 = 68.5\% \text{ productivity.}$$

These charts indicate a simplified means of measuring productivity. For more accurate measurements at least four observations per hour should be made.

Figure 14-3 may be used for reevaluating tasks and placement of equipment in conjunction with an estimate for productivity. Both, of course, may be indicators of the effort expended by individual workers. One note of caution: If workers know that they are being observed, there is a tendency to produce more than they would during normal periods. On the other hand, if workers are not informed that they are being observed, or of the purpose of the study, then there is a possibility that an unhealthy atmosphere might result and labor problems might arise.

PRODUCTIVITY SCHEDULING

The most effective method of controlling labor costs does not depend upon the scheduling of employees by determining their efficiency. Instead, it relies upon the established needs of the operation, which are determined by the schedule of sales. Normally, peak periods of operation can be forecast with reasonable accuracy, so that the number of employees needed for these peak periods can easily be determined. Production schedules and staffing then can be made up after the full staffing requirements for these peak periods are determined.

Ideally, if an employee can be used for more than one task (waitress making or dishing up salads, desserts, etc.), then during slack periods she can be employed to perform these other functions. If there is no work available, then it may be advisable to schedule part-timers or schedule lunch breaks, etc., during these slack periods.

There is a tendency for more and more food service operations to utilize convenience or ready foods. This may not be a wise decision, however, if no effective labor savings can be realized.

For example, a restaurant operation serves an average of 200 covers during the week (Tuesday thru Thursday), 250 on Friday, 350 on Saturday, and 300 on Sunday. The operation is open from 5 P.M. until midnight, with 85% of the sales between the hours of 6:30 and 10 P.M. In order to serve the 350 covers on Saturday, it is necessary to have 3 cooks and 2 pantry men in the kitchen during the peak time period. In effect, unless part-time personnel can be obtained for this period of time, scheduling of personnel is dictated by the fact that 5 cooks must be employed during the week (normally for a 40-hour week). The manager's job, therefore, is to schedule production, days off, breaks, vacations, etc., based on 200 man-hours per week. Scheduling for the other days is again dictated by customer count. Since the peak period is from 6:30 to 10 P.M., the full staff for any day must be working during that time slot, but employees may be staggered either before or after these hours.

Although the menu governs what preparation must be done, the schedule of production must be made by the manager (or chef) so that a continuous production line may be maintained and all employees can be involved in some type of preparation during the entire working day. Convenience or ready foods should not be used unless an employee can be eliminated. If an additional employee is required to keep up with production (not, however, needed during the peak serving periods), then serious thought should be given to a revision either in the amount of food prepared on the premises or the state of the product when purchased.

Unlike other industries, in which production schedules are decided upon by management, the staffing requirements of the food service establishment are determined by customers—normally, the maximum consumption (number of covers) at any one time. Consumption is also highly irregular (peak lunch or dinner periods, peak days of week). Only by carefully making out production schedules can labor be effectively utilized.

The chef or manager must also consider the highly involved psychology of the food service worker. If lunch is served at 12:00, then somehow, with last-minute rushing and effort, the meal just manages to get out on time. However, if lunch hour begins at 12:30, the same situation exists, and lunch just manages to be ready at 12:30.

ASSIGNMENT OF TASKS

Work schedules should be made up well in advance of each day's production. Thus, management can fairly and efficiently balance out work loads as well as insure that production recipes and schedules are followed. Too often, the supervisor assigns one task at a time to each worker, with the admonishment, "When you finish this report back to me, as I have some other things that have to be done." If the workers are familiar with the total amount of work that has to be accomplished, a much steadier work pace can be achieved and maintained.

LABOR CONTRACTS OR LAWS

Often, limiting factors are governed by union contracts or state regulations, which may prohibit achieving the lowest possible payroll. In some states, if a worker is called in he must work for a minimum period of three hours. Should he be needed only to serve a banquet or just for a two-hour lunch period, the extra hour may be wasted, or if possible, additional tasks may be assigned to him. Although a banquet may be served within one hour, set-up time and clean-up time may fill out the balance of the waiter's work period. If, however, the minimum call-in period is 6 hours (as required in some union contracts), there may not be a sufficient number of additional tasks, and the worker may be paid for non-productive periods.

If union contracts prevent the use of service personnel in the performance of preparation items (coffee, salads, etc.), then extreme care must be taken in the scheduling of service staff. It may be necessary to attempt to arrange other types of service. Buffets may be one solution that reduces the number of service personnel required. In some cases, the service itself may be changed (Russian versus American).

Some contracts, however, even include the maximum number of covers that a waiter or waitress may serve. In cases of this nature, obviously the additional cost of payroll must be included in the selling price.

FIGURE 14-5 *Schedule of Waiters*

Waiters   *Time*

	9	10	11	12	1	2	3	4	5
A	X	X	L/X	X	X	X			
B		X	X/L	X	X	X	X		
C		X	X/L	X	X	X	X		
D		/X	X	X	X	X	L/X	X/	
E			X	X	X	X	L/X	X	
F				X	X	X	X/L	X	X

Code: X = On Duty
       L = Lunch Break
       / = Half-hour period

Figure 14-5 demonstrates a schedule that may be used for a restaurant in which six waiters are required to serve the lunch period. Labor laws (or contract) require a minimum work period or call-in time of six hours, with a half-hour break for lunch. By staggering the schedule, all waiters are working during the peak periods yet all have time to set up their own areas. At the same time, enough time is allowed for major set up (and preparation) by those arriving early. Final clean-up is performed by the waiters arriving on the later shift.

It would be desirable if the waiters were allowed to perform some extra side jobs, such as the cutting of pies, the dishing up of desserts (gelatin, puddings, cake, etc.), the making of coffee, and of course, the normal duties of filling waters, setting tables, changing cloths, etc., which would be performed prior to or after the main service period. Often, minor but important tasks such as the changing of menus or the setting up of dessert displays are assigned to service personnel if they are available.

Should it be permissible and should skilled service employees be available who wish to work shorter shifts, some of these tasks may be transferred to other personnel (cashier, hostess, or even kitchen personnel) in order to fully utilize their time.

OVERTIME

Overtime is difficult to prevent in many establishments, since in some cases the closing of an establishment is dictated by the amount of business rather than by set hours. In most case, however, the scheduling of personnel actually allows extra time for clean-up. In many instances, personnel are able to leave prior to the allotted time, if business is down or if the customers have left early, allowing personnel to finish their tasks more quickly. Overtime occurs when customers decide to linger over their dinners or in some cases (in banquets and functions) when the group falls behind schedule.

The best policy to follow is not to pay overtime unless authorized by a supervisor. Time cards and overtime slips must be initialed, and a careful record of overtime for each employee should be maintained.

By federal law and by some states laws, overtime must be paid at 1 1/2 times the normal rate of pay. Certainly, should overtime become a normal occurrence, a rescheduling of personnel may be required, or more personnel may be hired, since the additional time required may be worked by an extra employee at regular rates.

Some tasks may be postponed until the next day if possible. For example, dishes from the last customers in an establishment may be soaked overnight rather than waiting until the last minute to run the few remaining dishes through the dishwasher and then spending another hour cleaning up the machine. By closing the machine at an earlier hour, the clean-up can be performed without overtime and the few dishes can be washed early the following day.

TRAINING, MOTIVATION, INCENTIVES

Innumerable books have been written and will continue to be written regarding methods of motivating employees, providing incentives, and methods of training. Unfortunately, the food service industry generally has chosen to ignore these writings and practices. It is still far behind other industries in adopting modern methods that encourage worker productivity.

Statistics indicate that the industry has the lowest dollar output per employee of all industries. Wages are low in comparison to other types of employment, and working conditions as a whole still are considered undesirable. Workers are often required to work long and irregular hours (including supervisors, who may average 60 hours or more per week).

Vacations and paid holidays lag behind other industries, and insurance plans and retirement programs are minimal or non-existent.

Expenditures for actual training, amounts budgeted for labor relations and personnel practices in relation to hiring procedures, record keeping, etc., are still twenty years behind the times. Work standards and job descriptions are changing, but the industry still has not attempted to reevaluate positions nor to adjust wages and salaries in view of technological changes.

Students and graduates of programs in food service education (whether at the secondary or collegiate level) are most often still required to take entry level positions in industry. Little financial differentiation is made between the graduate who has been trained and the applicant off the street. Only a few members of the industry encourage workers financially or by scholastic grants to further their education. And few, if any, actively participate in educational programs.

In short, labor cost analysis for the food service industry can be accomplished, but the basic philosophy and fundamental concepts of management must first be changed before real progress toward improving productivity can be made.

Chapter 14

1. Discuss the advantages of using a labor cost analysis based on covers per man-hour.

2. What are the advantages of using a labor cost analysis based on a percent of sales by department?

3. Why can't payroll percentages or sales per employee be compared from one operation to another?

4. Perform a payroll analysis using a productivity factor analysis system (figure 14-4) on a food department.

5. Discuss scheduling and staffing based on peak production formulas.

Glossary

American service A method of service in which food is portioned on individual plates in the kitchen and served to the customer by the waiter. No additional cooking or portioning is required.

"As they fall" The term used in referring to meats in which the basic primal or wholesale cut is purchased.

Back order When merchandise is not available from the purveyor, generally he will place on the invoice the symbols "BO," standing for *back order,* indicating that as soon as he receives the merchandise he will ship it to the buyer, or merchandise will be shipped on the next order.

Bin card A written record, usually on a 5 x 8 or comparable size card, indicating the type of merchandise, the amounts on hand, and issues and receipts of this merchandise. Bin cards are placed at the storage location where the merchandise is kept.

Call liquors The name brands that are referred to or requested by the customers (e.g., a customer who specifically requests J & B Scotch or Beefeaters Gin).

Cash bar See no-host bar.

Cover One customer or one seat. A waiter who is able to serve ten covers is therefore serving ten people.

Cyclical menu A menu that rotates on a scheduled basis.

Dupe A short term or abbreviation for *duplicate.* This is the copy of a check used by the waiter or waitress to order merchandise and later as a verification to determine the quantities of food that have been ordered and served by a waiter or waitress.

Entrée A term used today to denote the main course. It may consist of any type or variety of item, such as fish, poultry, meat, or even a main dish salad.

Entrepreneur A person who owns and operates his own business.

Extended invoice   Each individual item on an invoice is priced by the unit of sale. In turn, this figure is multiplied by the quantity purchased. The resulting answer is the "extended" price.

Finish   The amount of exterior and interior fat of an animal, an indicator of quality.

French service   A method of service in which the food is received from the kitchen in a semi-finished state and the final cooking, preparation, portioning, and service is done at the table.

Gourmand   A person who eats in quantity. A glutton.

Gourmet   A person who is able to distinguish—and prefers—fine foods, properly presented and cooked. Generally, an individual who dines rather than eats.

Hard liquor   A term generally used to refer to alcoholic beverages with a proof content of at least 80 proof.

Haute cuisine   A term signifying the finest food (usually both in cooking procedures and style of service).

Host bar   In private parties or functions, a bar at which the host has previously arranged to pay for all the drinks that may be consumed.

Irradiation   A method of preservation in which some source of radiation is used to eliminate bacterial contamination and sterilize or pasteurize the food.

Last price   The latest price quoted (to an establishment) for products sold by a purveyor.

Liqueurs   Often called *cordials*, a sweet alcoholic drink normally served after a meal (e.g., creme de menthe).

Lug   A unit of measurement normally refers to certain produce items (e.g., tomatoes), weighing 30-32 pounds.

Maître d'hotel; Maître d'   In earlier times, the individual who was in complete charge of the food operation. Today, the term is normally applied to the headwaiter or person in charge of the dining room.

Mix of sales   The amount of each particular menu item that is sold. Mix of sales is important since some items may be of high dollar value and others relatively inexpensive. For example, steak may sell for $8.00, hamburger for $2.00. The mix of sales indicates an average check should equal amounts sold of $5.00. However, if two steaks are sold and only one hamburger is sold the average check for these three orders now becomes $6.00.

Open bar   Comparable to *host bar*, but usually there is no individual who is actually the host. Guests normally purchase tickets to attend the function and the price includes all the beverages that they wish to consume.

No-host or cash bar   In a private function, bar service where each drink must be paid for by the guest himself.

Par stock   The minimum and/or maximum amount of any merchandise that is normally kept on hand.

Peeled tenderloin   The state in which a whole tenderloin is received. Usually, peeled tenderloin means that all of the excess fat has been removed as well as the sheath or connective tissue that surrounds the tenderloin.

Post-checking   A term used when, after the waitress or waiter has picked up an order, an individual assigned by management (food checker) will verify that the merchandise picked up has been placed on the check. This is a visual and/or physical examination of the order.

Post-mix   A system in which water, carbon dioxide, and syrups are purchased separately and blended together in the establishment by the use of a mechanical device (carbonator). A post-mix system is normally less expensive to operate than either premix or bottles.

Pre-checking   Under this type of system, a waiter or waitress will use a specific register (cash register or other mechanical equipment) to print out the order and place the order on a check. In turn, the check or another slip printed by the register may be used for ordering purposes.

Premix   This refers to (carbonated) soft drink beverages that have been blended prior to being received by a particular establishment. The carbonated water and syrup are mixed in pressurized containers (usually 5-gallon) and than served out of these containers.

Primal cut   The wholesale cut of a particular animal from which retail cuts are then obtained.

Russian service   A method of service in which the waiter receives the food from the kitchen on a large platter and portions it to the customer at the table.

Straight up   A cocktail normally served in stemware—usually martinis, whiskey sours, etc. The customer has the option of requesting the same drink "on the rocks," which would mean over ice.

Stock-out   A term used when particular merchandise is no longer available in the establishment. Running out of merchandise.

Short slip   A memo indicating that merchandise that has been ordered was not received by the establishment and a credit memo is therefore issued.

Till   Same as *lug*. The size however, is slightly smaller (about 5-6 qts.).

Validation   A term used in verifying the information on checks and dupes to compare the totals of both.

Well-stock   The cheaper kinds and brands of liquor used for regular drinks when a customer does not specify a call brand.

Bibliography

"A Demonstration of Beef Carcass Yields and Cut-Out Values," G.H. Wellington and J.R. Stouffer, Cornell Miscellaneous Bulletin 73. Ithaca, New York: New York State College of Agriculture, 1966.

"Career Ladders In The Foodservice Industry," National Restaurant Association, 1971.

"Consumer Panel Reports on Dining Out Habits and Attitudes," Standard Brands Inc., © 1950.

"The Cutability Story." American Sheep Producers Council, Inc. Denver, Colorado, 1973.

"The Foodservice Industry, Type Quantity, and Value of Foods Used." Statistical Bulletin # 476, Marketing Economics Division Economic Research Service, U.S.D.A., 1971.

"How To Invest In People, A Handbook on Career Ladders." National Restaurant Association, © 1971.

Hughes, Osee, and Marion Bennion, *Introductory Foods* 5th ed. New York: The MacMillan Co., 1970.

Keiser, James, and Elmer Kallio. *Controlling and Analyzing Costs in Food Service Operations.* New York: John Wiley & Sons, Inc., 1974.

Kotschevar, Lendal H. *Management By Menu,* National Institute for Food Service. Chicago, Ill., 1975.

Kotschevar, Lendal H. *Quantity Food Production,* 3rd ed. Boston: Cahners Books, 1974.

Kotschevar, Lendal H. *Quantity Food Purchasing.* New York: John Wiley & Sons, Inc., 1961.

Kreck, Lother A. *Menus: Analysis and Planning.* Boston: Cahners Publishing Co., Inc., 1975.

"Lessons On Meat." National Live Stock and Meat Board. Chicago, Ill., 1972 (Revised)

"Meat Buyer's Guide to Portion Control Meats." National Association of Meat Purveyors. Chicago, Ill., 1967.

"Meat Buyer's Guide to Standardized Meat Cuts." National Association of Hotel and Restaurant Meat Purveyors. Chicago, Ill., 1961.

"Merchandising Beef Loins" and "Merchandising Beef Ribs." National Live Stock and Meat Board. Chicago, Ill., 1968.

Stokes, John W. *Food Service in Industry and Institutions,* 2nd ed. Dubuque, Iowa: Wm. C. Brown Co., 1973.

"The Study of the Different Handling Methods for Frozen Roasts in Institutional Service." B.E. Shoemaker, B.C. Breidenstein, and D.S. Garrigan. National Live Stock and Meat Board. Chicago, Ill., 1969.

"Turkey Handbook." National Turkey Federation. Mt. Morris, Illinois, 61054.

West, Bessie Brooks, Levelle Wood, and Virginia F. Harger. *Food Service in Institutions.* New York: John Wiley & Sons, Inc., 1967.

"Wine Growing and Wine Types." Wine Advisory Board, San Francisco, California, © 1960.

Index

A

Accounting, 19
  external, 20
  internal, 19
Addition, 97
Aging, 149, 159
  yield, 158-59
Amount to buy, 134, 137-38, 141
As purchased weight, 133, 139
Automated systems, 59, 66
  counters, 65

B

Bars:
  host, 79-80
  no-host, 79-81
  open, 79-80
Bartender:
  error, 99
  fraud, 99
Beers, 26, 81-83
Beverage costs, 68
Bin cards, 41, 46
Bottle-code, 31
  count, 80-81
Bottle sales, 74
Bottle stamping, 54-55, 67, 76
Buying:
  bids, 125
  contract, 125
  fixed price, 128
  futures, 128
  (*see also* Purchasing)

C

Canned vegetables, 166, 168

Career, 231
Cash-receipts, 18, 86
  addition, 97
  collection, 19, 81, 86-87, 101-8, 225
  control, 79
  counterfeit, 93
  handling, 93
  registers, 86-92
Checking, 9, 17
  Bar, 82, 84
Checking:
  dupes, 188, 190-92
  food checker, 188, 191
  high average check, 195
  low average check, 192-94
  position control, 188-89
  reducing check losses, 194
Checks:
  customer, 93
  guest, 94
  numbering, 94-95
Complimentary drinks, 78
Control:
  definition, 1
  purposes, 2-3
  reduction, 3
  system costs, 4-5
Cost control, definition, 1
Coupon sales, 81
Credit cards, 19, 86, 93
Credit memos, 35-36

D

Data:
  fixed, 136
  variable, 136
Date of purchase, 116
Dilution of liquor, 77
Discounts, 114-15, 139
Distilled spirits, 25-26

Drink-control, 59
  count, 80
Dupes, 17

E

Eating patterns, 232
  (*see also* Menu planning)
Edible portion, 134, 156-57
  prices, 162-65
Electronic controls, 59
Employee (*see* Labor)
Errors:
  bartender, 99
  cashier, 99-100
  waiter, 98-99

F

Fish and seafood, 166
Forecasts, 4, 140
Fraud:
  customer, 87, 90, 93
  waiter, 94-95, 97
Frozen products, 166
Function areas:
  ancillary, 10
  primary, 7, 11-19
  solar system, 7-8
  supporting, 10

G

Gratuities, 79, 84, 97

H

Head counts, 90, 93, 95

I

Inventory control, 13, 173
  ABC analysis, 174-75
  amounts on hand, 130, 171
  bartenders, 79
  batch, 172
  bin cards, 41, 46, 473
  dual bin, 173
  high value items, 185
  in-process, 171, 183-84
  issuing, 180-81
  liquor, 41

Inventory control (*cont.*)
  master record, 41
  open storerooms, 173
  par stock, 182
  perpetual, 174
  portion control, 188
  re-issuing, 182-83
  spoilage, 170, 172, 181, 183
  storage, 180
  turnover, 171, 185
Invoices, 34-35, 177
Issuing, 14
  liquor, 47-49, 65
  redistribution, 15
  (*see also* Inventory control)

K

Keys, 52
  emergency, 52
  reserve storeroom, 53
Kickbacks, 115

L

Labor:
  career, 231
  cost control, 230, 240
  equipment, 232
  laws, 231, 233, 244, 246
  minimum staffing, 234-38
  overtime, 246
  plant facilities, 231
  productivity, 230-31, 239-42
  scheduling, 243-45
  training, 246-47
  turnover, 233
  union contracts, 231, 233, 244-45
Laws:
  labor, 231, 244-46
  liquor, 25
Liquor:
  distilled spirits, 25
  inventory control, 41-48
  laws, 25
  mixers, fruits, and supplies, 28
  purchasing, 23
  quality, 24
  receiving, 39
  storage, 40-41, 52, 59, 65

M

Maintenance, 22
Malt beverages, 25

Master record, 41, 46, 55
Meats, 148
  beef, 153
  lamb, 154
  pork, 152, 155
  steaks, 151-52, 154
Menu planning, 15
  classification of markets, 196-98
    types of service, 199
  classification of menus, 205-11
  hours of service, 212, 232-33
  personnel, 211-12
  physical equipment, 211
Menu pricing, 204, 215-16
  atmosphere, 220
  cash collection, 225
  competition, 219
  high-low items, 222-24
  location, 221
  other costs, 221
  percentages, 216-18
  portion size, 221, 225-27
  quality, 220
  service, 219
  taste, 220
  wage rates, 221
  waste, 220
  weighted sales value, 218
Menus:
  formats, 15, 200-203
  (*see also* Menu planning)
Methods of buying
  (*see* Buying, contract)
Minimum recorder amounts, 41-47

O

Ordering, frequency, 130
Ounce control, 59, 67-68
Overcharges, 95

P

Par stock, 59, 68-69, 75-76
Percentages:
  food lost, 133, 216-18
  waste, 134
  yield (*see* Yield)
Perishable items (*see* Inventory control)
Personnel, 20
Pick-up slips, 36
Portion control, liquor, 70
Portion size, 134, 136-37, 140, 143, 160, 221,
  225-27
  control, 188
  cost, 134-35, 138, 141-42
  divider, 139-41, 143-44

Portion size (*cont.*)
  factor, 139-40, 144
Postchecking, 17
Poultry, 160
  yield, 160
Pourers, 59, 66
Pouring:
  over, 59
  short or under, 59, 76
  substitutions, 76, 97
Prechecking, 17, 188-90
Premixing, 70
Preparation, 16
Prepreparation, 16
Previous balance fraud, 100-101
Prices:
  edible portion, 162-65
  market, 136
  menu (*see* Menu planning)
Produce, 166-67
Purchasing, 11
  liquor, 23-28
  orders, 31-33
  purposes, 11
  reordering, 41-47
  requisitions, 29, 39, 46
Purchasing:
  food, 111-13, 170
  most economical, 135, 142, 144, 155-56
  timing of orders, 116

Q

Quality, 112, 220
Quotations, 118
  sheets, 128-30

R

Rebates, 115
Receiving, 12, 48, 50
  blind, 40
  liquor, 39
  purpose, 12
Receiving food:
  date stamping, 179
  food, 176-77
  receiving sheet, 177-78
  weighing, 179
Requisitions:
  purchase, 27, 30
  slips, 46, 52-53
Returns:
  credit memos, 35-36
  issues, 78-79
  merchandise, 12
  pick-up slips, 36

S

Sales:
  bottle, 74
  department, 9, 21
  potential, 72-74
Salesman, 113-14
Sanitation, 21, 235
Security, 52-53
Service, 18, 189, 191-93, 195, 199, 219
Shrinkage, 13-14
Solar system, 8
Specifications, 117, 125-27
  sources, 117-18
Standard sales, 69
  costs, 72-74
Standardized glassware, 70-72
Standardized recipes, liquor, 70
Storage, 13, 48, 50
  length of storage, 13
  physical facilities, 52, 130-31
  reserve, 53
  storeroom design, 52
  (*see also* Inventory control)

T

Theft:
  cash, 77
  cashier, 97-100
  merchandise, 77-78, 171
  waiter, 94-95, 97
Trim tests, 149
Turnover:
  customer, 236-37

Turnover (*cont.*)
  labor, 233

U

Unit size, 2

V

Validation, 17

W

Walkouts, 40, 87, 90, 93
Waste, 134, 220
Well stock, 23, 25
Wine, 25, 27, 81-82
  cooking, 27
  imported, 27

Y

Yield, 134, 136-38, 140, 148-49, 151-57
  aging, 158-59
  boning, 150, 158
  cooking, 157-58
  dressed carcass, 150-51
  live weights, 150-51
  serving, 151, 158-59
  trim tests, 149